Frost on My Moustache

Frost on My Moustache

The Arctic Exploits of a Lord and a Loafer

Tim Moore

ST. MARTIN'S PRESS
NEW YORK

ISBN 0-312-25319-2

First published in Great Britain by Abacus,
a division of Little, Brown and Company (UK)

First U.S. Edition: January 2000

10 9 8 7 6 5 4 3 2 1

To Martin, my grandfather

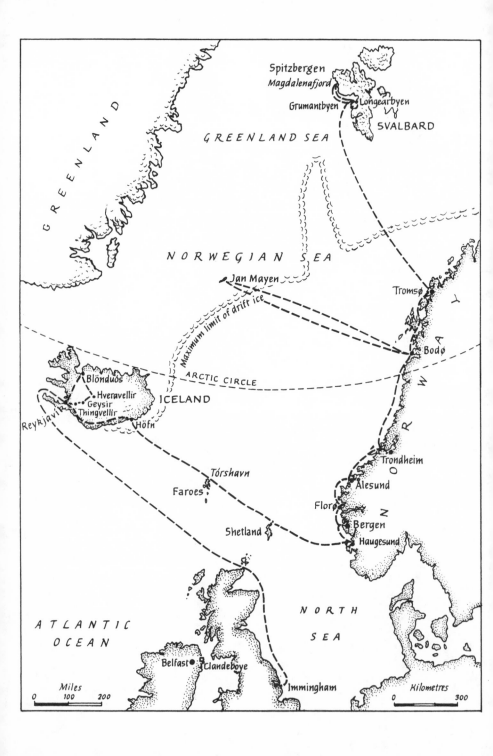

Acknowledgements

Thanks to: Birna, Kristján, Lilja and Valdís; my family; Sarah Leigh; Dilli; Lindy Dufferin; Lola Armstrong; Andrew Gailey; Tim Knox; everyone at *Esquire*, especially Clare Gogerty; Sverre, Sissel and Per; Hilde, Marte, Eline and Christian; Agnar Guðmundsson; Helgi and Guðrún; the crew of the *Dettifoss*; Richard Beswick and Antonia Hodgson; Eleanor Garland; Philip Gwyn Jones; Rosemary Cantor; Solla Friðríksdóttir; Paul Rose; Jessica Learmond-Criqui; Thor Jakobsson.

Photograph and illustrations (with original captions) by permission of the Marchioness of Dufferin and Ava and the photographic archive at Clandeboye.

Extra special thanks to Teletext, most particularly Tamara Bowles – an important Australian – and David Staveley: a big man, a brave man, and very much his own man. Oh, and Budget car rental.

PROLOGUE

It was when I saw the peacock picking about the bins that I knew I was in trouble. You get a better class of stray round this part of town, I thought, as I wandered down a broad and empty Holland Park thoroughfare spotted by early June rain. Two nine-year-old boys passed; one squeaked plummily that I was a bloody bugger; both cackled.

Ten minutes earlier, on the top deck of a 237 at Shepherd's Bush, I'd been reading the two pertinent entries in a volume I'd been slightly embarrassed to find on our shelves the night before. *Who's Really Who* is gossip columnist Compton Miller's 'wickedly funny' guide to the '450 people in Britain who *really* matter', or at least who did when it was published in 1983.

One began with pictograms denoting 'waspish', 'old money' and 'party-loving', and continued as follows:

Dufferin and Ava, Marquess of, 46, millionaire art patron and descendant of a Viceroy of India, an exotic example of the axiom that 'money begets money'. His mother Maureen is a Guinness *stout* heiress and his wife, Lindy, is a Guinness *banking* heiress. Bespectacled, whimsical, slightly fey, he loves giving parties for artistic friends at his Holland Park house – and the more outrageous and democratic the better. At a Sixties ball attended by Princess Margaret and Lord Snowdon, his shirtmaker Michael Fish wore a gold and mauve lamé jacket teamed with a gold miniskirt.

The marquess succeeded his father who was killed in

action in Burma in 1945. He inherited a useful £192,000 on his 21st birthday and his mother gave him Clandeboye, a beautiful Co Down estate, on his marriage. Sheridan Dufferin has no heir. Lindy, an enthusiastic artist, goes on painting expeditions without him to the Himalayas and the Amazon. Funnily enough you never see him drinking Guinness, only champagne.

The following entry kicked off with 'stylish', 'old money' and 'party-loving':

Dufferin and Ava, Maureen, Marchioness of, 76, sprightly dowager. With her blonde hair, Edna Everage specs and impish humour she is considered an international party asset. She is a great practical joker. Disguised as a slatternly housemaid, she once harangued dinner guests at her stately home in Clandeboye, Northern Ireland. Nicknamed Tea-pot, she used to drink gin out of baby's bottles during the Charleston era.

None of this did anything to bolster self-confidence as I prepared for my imminent debut at West London's premier venue for democratic outrage. It was not easy to picture the only Michael Fish I knew in a gold miniskirt. Nor would being harangued by slatternly housemaids constitute a suitable inauguration of my career as an international party asset.

Down in the subway under the roundabout the looming social ordeal started to weigh down on me, and the slightly sullen magazine sub-editor who descended the ramp at one end bore little relation to the flinching, bullied teenage apprentice who emerged at the other. By the time I pressed a huge and over-polished brass bell I'd devolved into a shifty-eyed, cinder-cheeked Dickensian urchin, and when the door opened I half expected to see Mrs Bridges throw up her fat, floury hands and scream for the cook's boy, who'd see me off down the drive with a tattoo of clouts from a large pair of bellows.

And in fact a uniformed tweeny did open the door, albeit an Eastern European one with a shy smile who ushered me down a hall lined with towering ancestral portraits. A second maid glided up to my shoulder and led me seamlessly upstairs and into a study filled with old furniture, vaguely familiar-looking paintings and a mantelpiece buried under copperplate invitations.

Now content that I'd hopelessly exceeded my bite/chew ratio, I looked around and saw a trim, brisk fifty-ish figure sorting through a mountain of correspondence at a table by the window. The Marchioness of Dufferin and Ava. Her first sentence included two instances of the word 'frightfully'. Her second was the offer of a glass of champagne. Her third:

'I'm sorry we're cooped up here. I don't really use downstairs these days – the rooms are just so formal and *large*.'

I had come – or so a tiny part of my brain distantly supposed – to talk about her ancestor-in-law, the First Marquess Dufferin, Frederick Temple Hamilton Temple Blackwood, KP, GCB, GCMG, born Florence, Italy, 1826, died Clandeboye, Ireland, 1902, Governor-General of Canada, Viceroy of India, Her Majesty's Ambassador in Rome and Paris.

'I've read your . . . narrative thing,' she said straight into my face with forthright jollity. 'Wonderfully *jazzy*.'

She was referring to the brief outline of my proposal to recreate a voyage the young lord had made in 1856, sailing his yacht, the *Foam*, from Scotland to Iceland to Norway to the Arctic archipelago of Spitzbergen and back.

Her description of this document was accurate in that it diplomatically touched upon the dearth of scholarship revealed within. 'Jazzy', in so far as I could guess from a word I had never heard seriously used in this context, was a synonym for 'idiotic'. All I knew of Dufferin was what I'd learned from the merry travelogue he'd written of his trip, *Letters From High Latitudes*, namely:

(1) He was a lord.
(2) He knew almost everything.
(3) He was indefatigable.

(4) He seemed like a nice bloke.

(5) He loved his mummy.

When the Marchioness ('Lindy, my dear, Lindy') announced that we should shortly be joined by Dr Andrew Gailey, Prince William's housemaster at Eton, whom she'd commissioned to write a biography of Dufferin, both of us realised that an unsightly mismatch of intellects would soon take place. Never again would my stupidity be so triumphantly exposed on such a grand stage. I loved my mummy, too, I thought, and with difficulty held back a sudden urge to summon her loudly.

'So – why?' demanded Lindy, cannily reading the very word imprinted in huge, bold capitals on my cortex. 'Is it the Dufferin bit, or the Arctic bit?'

There was a pause as I took in her pronunciation of the family name. Somehow, I really have no idea why, I'd got it into my head that 'Dufferin' was aristocratically contracted to 'Duffin'. Now I heard that it was not. Trying to avoid thinking how many times I might have treated her to this choice imbecility, I began to tackle her question, jabbering as my powers of speech leached away. First to go would be adjectives; later, and more debilitatingly, it was nouns.

I told her that my wife, Birna, was Icelandic. When she chanced upon a 1924 reprint of *Letters From High Latitudes* in a second-hand bookshop in York, she'd recognised it as an account by one of the few foreigners to write about her homeland and snapped it up at once.

I didn't tell her that the drab-looking volume had lain unread on a shelf outside the bathroom for a year, its hymn-book typography and heavily titled author promising only a procession of weary pomposity. Once, in a fit of desperate boredom brought on while pretending to put up a towel rail, I opened it at random to be greeted by this sentence:

'I am not well, but I will not out,' I soliloquized, with Lepidus – 'δος μοι το πτερου,' I would have added, had I dared.

But then one Saturday morning Birna ran eagerly into the bathroom and breathlessly addressed my Badedas-smothered form with a lengthy extract of Dufferin's account of a banquet at Government House in Reykjavík:

I knew well that to refuse a toast, or to half empty your glass, was considered churlish. I had come determined to accept my host's hospitality as cordially as it was offered. I was willing, at a pinch, to *payer de ma personne*; should he not be content with seeing me at his table, I was ready, if need were, to remain *under* it; but at the rate we were then going it seemed probable this consummation would take place before the second course: so, after having exchanged a dozen rounds of sherry and champagne with my two neighbours, I pretended not to observe that my glass had been refilled; and, like a sea-captain slipping from between his two opponents, left them to blaze away at each other the long night through. But it would not do; with untasted bumpers, and dejected faces, they politely waited until I should give the signal for a renewal of *host*ilities, as they well deserved to be called.

Then there came over me a horrid, wicked feeling. What if I should endeavour to floor the Governor, and so literally turn the tables on him? It is true I had lived for five-and-twenty years without touching wine – but was not I my great-grandfather's great-grandson, and an Irish peer to boot? Were there not traditions, too, on the other side of the house, of casks of claret brought up into the dining room, the door locked, and the key thrown out of the window? With such antecedents to sustain me, I ought to be able to hold my own against the staunchest toper in Iceland. So, with a devil glittering in my left eye, I winked defiance right and left, and away we went at it again for another five-and-forty minutes. At last their fire slackened: I had partially quelled both the Governor and the Rector, and still survived . . . could we hold out perhaps a quarter of an hour longer, our reputation was established; guess then my horror, when the Icelandic Doctor, shouting his favourite dogma . . . gave the signal for an unexpected onslaught, and the twenty guests poured down on me in succession. I really thought I should have run away from the house; but the true family blood, I suppose, began to show itself, and with a calmness almost frightful, I received them one by one.

After this began the public toasts . . .

There was something instantly appealing about this unexpected passage. Partly because it reminded me of the pagan excess that I know from my dozen or so visits lurks behind the Icelanders' educated stoicism (Dufferin's hosts were the country's most eminent citizens), but mainly because it somehow combined aristocratic understatement with Hunter S. Thompson hyperbole. Elsewhere Dufferin tots up what he claims to have drunk: three bottles of claret; four of champagne; two of hock; half of sherry and eight glasses of schnapps. It's just so obviously ridiculous, and the fact that as an intelligent man he must have known this somehow made it funnier. The revelation that he clearly suffered none of the priggish arrogance associated with wing-collared statesmen made his astonishing CV all the more unlikely.

I read the entire book that weekend, and more and more questions presented themselves. Why had he gone to Iceland? Where exactly was Spitzbergen? What of Jan Mayen, an active volcano marooned in the Arctic which sounded like something from a 'Here Be Beasties' map made up by bored medieval monks? How, if at all, had these places changed? Didn't people now live on Spitzbergen? And why had I never heard of Dufferin? I felt I ought to have come across the name during my A-level history course, which seemed at the time to have covered Victorian politics on an hour-by-hour basis. As the effective ruler of first Canada and then India, he would, after all, have had a reasonably impressive proportion of the globe's total land area and population under his aegis.

The discovery that Dufferin had, at 31, been two years

younger than me when he set off turned curiosity into an unknown emotion that I could only assume was determination. Victorian Empire-builders, I had always thought, were as old and cold and stiff as the civic statues raised in their honour; it had never occurred to me to regard them with empathy or to view their achievements with envy rather than incredulity. Struggle as I might (although in fact I had until then never bothered), it was impossible to find any residual spark of pioneering grit in the shrugging sneer that besmirched my bathroom mirror, and had done so ever since I first recognised that bunking off games in order to damage property was preferable to spearheading the quest for sporting excellence. Pre-war Britons had dropped the baton handed them at the turn of the century; my generation had gone back, found it, and thrown it into a lake. Our forefathers had done it all before and, as there was clearly no point doing it again, we'd made virtues out of under-achievement and torpor.

But the banquet episode made it difficult to dismiss Dufferin along with his dull and self-righteous peers. He was, I decided, different, contemporary, sympathetic; and, having accepted this, I started looking at his Arctic voyage as not just another inexplicably worthy, Queen-and-country trek, but as a challenge. The Dr Livingstone crowd was a different species, driven by forces I could never hope to understand. But Dufferin, as lordly and erudite as he was, also possessed a blithe flippancy I could cheerfully relate to. If he could do it, so could I. If he could conquer the icebergs, I could conquer my inertia. By the time I finished *High Latitudes*, the could had become a would.

I didn't, of course, say any of this as I stood before Lady Dufferin, toying blankly with the stem of my champagne flute. Addressing myself to the glass, I said: 'So I read the book and I enjoyed the book, and then I decided to go and follow him and write a book.' Sensing this was in some indefinable way inadequate, I tried to amend it with some of my favourite motifs from the banquet scene. 'It was a funny book. It had staunch topers in it and after this began the public toasts.'

Unseen hands opened the door and my sister's friend Tim Knox walked in. It was he who had arranged this meeting, following a stupendous coincidence I was now wishing hadn't happened. My sister had mentioned my fledgling Dufferin project, and he'd said, oh, well that was funny, because he'd just spent New Year's Eve with the current Lady Dufferin at some fantastic mansion called Clandeboye near Belfast.

'She's the last of the line,' he told me when I phoned him. 'Her husband died about ten years ago and they haven't any children. I think she's a Guinness by birth.'

It was poignant to think of her as the end of the dynasty, but the discovery added a certain impetus to my quest. At that point, I didn't even know if there were any Dufferins, let alone if they still lived at Clandeboye. At that point I was amazed, delighted, triumphant. But at this point, I was beginning to wish I'd never blithely promised my publisher I'd visit their baronial residence.

I'd done so safe in the knowledge that it couldn't possibly still be standing. All that would remain, after the leisure centre or superstore developers had done their worst, would be some small forgotten folly, maybe an ivy-wreathed sundial hidden in the woods. 'This is all the Asda people left behind, so it is,' the old dear who'd led me there would whisper. Then, with a brave smile, 'I remember as a wee girl playing in the ballroom with the Third Marquess. Once he showed me his how's-your-father and all, the cheeky pup.'

In his capacity as an architectural adviser for the National Trust, Tim is often required to mix in exalted company. I have yet to see him ruffled; he is, indeed, someone I imagine feeling restless if things are going too predictably. Something of a social subversive, he spent much of his early adulthood dressed as a cardinal, or posing as the high-born descendant of eminent Continentals. Once he was chased around a gallery by an over-excited guide shouting, 'Vicomte de Talleyrand! Please address us! Your Eminence!' I have fond memories of a visit to the church adjoining Jane Seymour's house near Bath, whose visitors' book Tim adorned with an open invitation in her name exhorting all visitors to repair to the conservatory for complimentary refreshments and a signed bottle of Le Jardin de Max Factor.

So he ambled into the study, helped himself to a glass of champagne and immediately embarked on an outrageous story incorporating the use of half a dozen accents.

Lindy loved it. The *Who's Really Who* entry on her late husband Sheridan had already led me to suspect a fondness for colourful characters and outré behaviour, an impression enhanced when she whipped out a pouch of Golden Virginia and began assembling the first of many roll-ups. Now, she listened to Tim with eyes wide and eyebrows arched, her mouth open in a down-turned kidney shape that said, 'Oooh, you are awful – but I like you!'

By the time Andrew Gailey and his wife turned up, I had shrivelled into 'should' mode – the odd kind of stilted, deferential subjunctive I invariably find myself using in conversation with elders and betters. I listened in helpless horror at the succession of 'Yes, that should be very pleasing's and 'Might I offer you some more's that dribbled from my mouth amidst the hilarious banter.

'Andrew, this is Tim Moore – he's doing a book about the First Marquess, and the lovely thing is he knows absolutely nothing about him!'

The Gaileys greeted me with a politeness that shielded any hint of the considerable irritation most people would have felt on learning that a 50-mile round trip had just been exposed as a complete waste of time. Lindy had obviously organised this event before reading my 'jazz', envisaging it as an academic forum for heavyweight analysis of Dufferin's pivotal role in the Syrian crisis of 1860.

We walked through to a room where a table wheezed beneath a dazzling festival of damask, silver and crystal. The wines, breathing almost audibly on the table, had four-inch corks and venerable, mould-spotted labels. It was now self-evident that the Dufferin clan remained a prosperous one, but the extent of this prosperity only sank in gradually as the maids brought through a succession of gourmet fancies.

'Tim – what do you think these are?'

I had been agonising over which pair of the dozen pieces of cutlery before me I should currently be holding, and raised my head from the table to see Lindy standing by a sideboard and holding aloft a couple of bronze ballerinas.

I'd managed to say nothing for half an hour, but now, as silence fell, there was no escape. As I weighed up whether pretending to swallow my tongue would be a better answer than 'shiny dancers', Tim said, 'Degas?'

Of course. She hadn't been asking me. But he was wrong, anyway. 'Rodins. I've just been given them,' she breathed carelessly, half tossing one to Tim. 'Don't you think they look rather good by this Hockney?'

There were other hints, usually involving bald statements of large cash sums. 'Sheridan and I had a frightfully difficult decision to make twenty years ago – if we didn't spend £350,000 on the roof, Clandeboye would be essentially uninhabitable.'

Courses came and went. It was odd to see our hostess sharing our surprise and delight as the covers were removed from each salver. How funny not to know what you're going to eat, what's going to be cooked for you, even in your own house. I supposed it was like this for her every night.

Now rather drunk, I was beginning to warm to Lindy. She was the sort of person who could – and did – say things like, 'You see, I simply don't *know* any black people,' in such a disarmingly open way that you couldn't bring yourself to mind. 'If many people saw this, they'd be appalled, and probably quite angry – us five sitting here, with all these crystal glasses and silver,' she announced, looking round the faces at the table. 'There's you two with the Eton thing, you and the National Trust, me of course, you . . . well, you'd probably be all right.'

I didn't mind. It was probably meant as a compliment. In many ways she reminded me of some of my mother's madder friends – the arty background, the Seventies heyday, the blurted vulgarities. Discussing the conservation courses she helped run at Clandeboye, she said, 'Well, you know what these students are like, out in the woods leaving sperm trails around the trees.' Then the raised eyebrows and down-turned kidney mouth again.

The Gaileys left at midnight, having diplomatically not mentioned Dufferin once. Lindy kept Tim and I there until 2 a.m., smoking roll-ups, drinking absurdly flash wine, being outrageous. Then, rather abruptly, she turfed us out into the rain, obviously unaccustomed to entertaining people who either have to get up for work the next day or don't have chauffeurs. Tim buzzed waywardly into the night on his Vespa; in the absence of cabs, I ended up having to walk four miles home.

Barely five hours later, before I had yet begun to decode the evening's many points of interest, the phone rang. It was Lindy, inviting me to Clandeboye the following weekend. 'Do you have an intelligent travel agent?' she demanded, opening a beguiling vista upon a world where people not only 'had' travel agents, but where they might dispense with their services on grounds of stupidity.

Having glossed over this issue, I suddenly realised something very important. Under no circumstances could I survive this mission alone.

'Could . . . would it be all right if my wife came along too?'

'Oh. Is she frightfully keen? One, two . . . seven . . . Well, that'll make us twelve. In that case you'll *definitely* have to leave on Sunday. Mrs Armstrong will meet you at Belfast International. Do try and see Andrew Gailey before you come. Wonderful. Now I can forget all about you.'

Somehow no offence was taken by this brusque riposte. She already had me in her thrall. I supposed this was how the British aristocracy had managed to stave off a bourgeois revolution.

A brief trawl through the newspaper cuttings libraries revealed that Lindy had married Sheridan, the Fifth Marquess, in 1964. There was ample confirmation of their status as leading lights in the jewellery-rattling sphere of Swinging London, hosting great parties at Clandeboye attended by the likes of Mick Jagger and

David Hockney. Sheridan ran a painfully trendy gallery; Lindy was a photographer and artist of some distinction.

I also read that Lindy had inherited a reported £10 million from her father, and another £15 million when Sheridan died in 1988, tragically young, at forty-nine. And it transpired that, at 90, her mother-in-law, Maureen, was still 'going strong' (though not that strong, as she's since died), having recently emerged victorious from a legal battle with her two daughters and Lindy over the allocation of her own enormous legacy.

There were other indications of Maureen's fearsome passion for confrontation. At the 1994 launch party for a biography of the recently deceased Duchess of Argyll, the dowager Marchioness told a reporter: 'She was an absolutely dreadful woman. Everyone I knew hated her and we called her "the Devil". She was spiteful, malicious and awful. Thank God she's not here.'

By contrast, a tabloid described Lindy as 'the Howard Hughes of Northern Ireland'. Though hard to equate with the irrepressible figure I'd met, this at least promised a reasonably subdued weekend.

But Dufferin, my Dufferin, was still proving an enigma. An obituary of Sheridan's sister, the novelist Caroline Blackwood, referred to Sheridan as 'the kind of man whose charm, generosity and modesty give aristocrats a good name', which struck a chord with what I knew of the First Marquess. It was hard to imagine a career diplomat being taken to court by his own children or calling dead old ladies the Devil. But I needed to find out what he was rather than what he wasn't.

Heeding Lindy's decree, I'd visited Andrew Gailey at Eton a couple of days later. Having no doubt satisfied himself that my flippant cobblers posed no threat to his erudite biography, he graciously laid before me his accumulated Dufferinalia: the notes for his book, an astonishingly dull thesis someone had done in the Seventies and copies of the two contemporary biographies mentioned in the introduction to my edition of *High Latitudes*: Sir Alfred Lyall's *Life of Lord Dufferin* and CED Black's *The Marquess of Dufferin & Ava*.

'He invented the amusing narrative of genuine travel,' says Lyall, 'never flinching before the deep potations of hospitable Norsemen or the fogs and icefields that barred his access to Spitzbergen.' *High Latitudes*, confirms Black, 'delighted a host of readers and ran through five editions, besides being translated into French and Dutch'.

I hadn't realised it had been such a hit. Readers, says Lyall, apparently enjoyed Dufferin's 'habit of taking mishaps and hardships with humorous philosophy, of dealing sympathetically with men of the rough, unvarnished world and of giving a comical turn to petty incidents or vexations . . . and taking an earnest interest in primitive folk.'

I was now starting to worry. The Arctic voyage was clearly one of Dufferin's less notable achievements, but already it was becoming clear that to retrace it even with modern conveniences would tax my spiritual resources to their limits. Beyond a rough approximation in age, the similarities came to a shamefully abrupt end. Taking hardships with humorous philosophy and dealing with unvarnished men are not my strongest suits. Dufferin seemed the personification of Kipling's 'If'. I'm more of a 'But . . .' man myself. My idea of tackling one of the world's most appalling maritime challenges is being able to stand up on a lilo. I somehow couldn't imagine Dufferin's parents reading an equivalent to this school report entry: 'Timothy has lost his fear of the water and is now swimming happily with a float.'

In two hours of rudderless research, I cobbled together a biography.

Born in Florence in 1826 as Frederick Temple Hamilton Temple Blackwood (savour that second Temple), he became Lord Dufferin at fifteen following his father's faintly ludicrous death, of an overdose of erroneously prescribed morphine (a Liverpool chemist apparently got 'flustered' by the clanging of a ship's bell). The great-great-grandson of dramatist Richard Sheridan (hence the Fifth Marquess's name), he was educated at Eton and Oxford (where he was elected President of the Union, but also scraped a Pass) before embarking on the inevitable Grand Tour to Italy.

A keen and acclaimed poet (he was a pall-bearer at Tennyson's funeral) and artist of some talent (the two dozen etchings in *High Latitudes* – the *Foam* accompanying Prince Napoleon's steamer *Reine Hortense* through an angry Arctic; a cross-section through a geyser – were all his), he abandoned any bohemian calling for a career as a Liberal politician. He rose to prominence as a diplomat who filled all the highest overseas posts in the Foreign Office with 'unfailing success and everywhere with astonishing popularity'. Successful stints as Governor-General of Canada (1872–8) and Viceroy of India (1884–9) earned him glamorous sinecures as Ambassador in Rome and Paris. When, in 1896, he retired to his Irish estate (having already made a reputation there as 'an enlightened land reformer') he would have been entitled to settle down and reflect on one of history's more fulfilled lives.

Except that, right at the end, his charmed and charming story takes a miserable turn. In 1901, I read, his eldest son was killed in the Boer War, and over the next two years the family fortunes rapidly dwindled away in the aftermath of the collapse of a finance corporation of which he was chairman. He died, apparently a broken man, in 1902. It was a sad and inappropriate conclusion that engendered an unexpectedly deep gulp of sympathy.

The night before we flew to Belfast, I hooked up to the Internet and searched for 'DUFFERIN'. I got eight results. Seven were Canadian institutions with addresses in one of the many Dufferin Streets that recalled his clearly successful period as Governor-General. The eighth, scrolling down with the information super-highway's usual painful sloth, was a crayon drawing.

This was quite a moment. Nowhere had I found a graphical representation of him. The picture showed Dufferin at twenty-four, a porcelain-skinned, pouting creature with what would be described as fine features. Placing my left hand on the screen to obscure his high collar and cravat, and my right over his fine, collar-length locks (whose high-forehead side-parting was clearly the opening gambit in a baldy cover-up campaign), I saw the elegant eyebrows and sculptured lips of a well-kempt society beauty. Above the lingering, watery-irised gaze drooped a pair of heavy lids that at the expense of imparting a slightly bug-eyed aspect, hinted at a come-to-bed sultriness. I had found my man – and all in all I quite fancied him.

1

We were met at Belfast International Airport by Lady Dufferin's archivist, Lola Armstrong. Tiny, cheerful and ruddy, she looked like she'd stepped out of a Brueghel. She was about the least Lola-like person I'd ever encountered. It certainly wasn't easy to picture her in a Soho club doing any of the stuff that the Kinks sang about.

The three of us squeezed into her son's Nissan Micra, and as we queued at an RUC checkpoint she told us she was a maths teacher by training, but had given it up to work on the estate. The Marchioness, noting her keen interest in the history of Clandeboye, had entrusted her with what we would soon see was the considerable task of putting in order the family's eclectic assortment of colonial ephemera.

'It'll be a life's work, so it will,' she said cheerfully in what I supposed to be a broad County Down accent, 'but Lady Dufferin is ever so understanding.'

It was slightly embarrassing that she referred to our hostess using this form of address, whereas we – now on the other side of the feudal divide – were expected to call her Lindy. It was no less jarring to find that Clandeboye's huge grounds lay so close to Belfast's rundown docks. Only ten minutes after passing the grim and deserted Harland & Woolf shipbuilding yard, we turned into an unmarked road which took us through the outskirts of what was clearly a substantial and well-tended estate.

Thousands of new trees sprung from protective plastic sheaths and, even before we could see the house, there were flower beds tended more carefully than a floral clock. On the horizon swayed the lofty greenery of what I later discovered was the largest broad-leafed forest in Northern Ireland. It was astonishing that this prominent outpost of British colonialism and its cumbersomely titled inhabitants had survived unscathed through thirty years of destruction on its doorstep.

We rounded a stable block and stopped in a small courtyard. 'This is really the side entrance,' said Lola, indicating an unassuming porch. The door within it opened and a large, red-faced butler – stripy trousers, tailcoat, the works – greeted us with a tilted nod. 'You're up in Simla, I believe,' he said in a Lurch rumble before leading us into a hall.

I say a hall. In fact it was like an annexe of the Museum of Mankind. The First Marquess's globetrotting CV was here in full, dangling from the beams, bolted to the brickwork, fixed to the floor. There were totem poles and tomahawks, a scale model of Mandalay, a pair of stuffed bears from Russia (Dufferin had shot the mother, Lola later told us, then found an orphaned cub which in a fit of guilt he took back to Clandeboye where it lived in a courtyard for several years), pikes, helmets, snowshoes, chain mail, daggers, hieroglyphic bas-reliefs and mummy cases, curling stones, bells and pistols. And there were countless items whose origin and purpose I could not even begin to guess at: long sticks with holes in, big round things with funny ethnic symbols painted on the side, triangular boxes with shaft-like handles.

Birna and I were speechless. Then I looked into a corner, and saw the original figurehead from the *Foam*, or at least the wooden dummy for it, beside a beautiful scale model of the boat itself. And beneath it, most arrestingly of all, a rug made from the flattened form of the polar bear the crew had shot at Spitzbergen, an event Dufferin describes in gloating detail.

Rubber-necking with open mouths, we wandered slowly after the butler, who, seeing our interest, flicked a finger at a framed photo fixed to a column. Dated 1902, the year the First Marquess died, it depicted the hall we were traversing, and confirmed what I had suspected. Nothing had changed. Here was

Dufferin, here was I, here was the *Foam*. Things were coming together.

Our butler-following adventure assumed the epic proportions of a Terry Gilliam animation. On we tramped, along a landing dominated by the swinging length of driftwood Dufferin had brought back from Spitzbergen, past a dolls' house with what we later learned (at the pawnbroker's) was real silver crockery on its tables, beneath huge family portraits, back down stairs I was sure we'd already climbed.

We passed endless doors labelled with what I recognised were Dufferin's diplomatic postings: Rome, Paris and so on. Simla, I realised (in so far as looking something up in an encyclopaedia a week later can be described as 'realising'), was India's summer capital during his . . . viceroyalty? Viceregality? Viceroyalship?

Lola had already told us that Clandeboye's current incarnation had been largely built to the First Marquess's own design during his retirement. As we trooped up hidden spiral staircases and crouched through low, semi-abandoned corridors, the touch of an enthusiastic but muddled amateur made itself apparent. He'd had a passion for natural light, and glazed ceilings and skylights looked down on every hall. No wonder the roof had cost £350,000 to fix.

On the half-landing of a forgotten staircase lined with Dufferin's architectural sketches, the butler stopped and dropped our bags. 'I think I'm lost,' he quietly boomed, before looking round with a wink. Just as our journey was reaching refugee-exodus status, we ducked down a low annexe and arrived outside a room marked 'Simla'. Our luggage was deposited and the butler withdrew.

'Should we have tipped him?'

'No!' squeaked Birna. 'Not *now*. We're supposed to give a collective tip to the staff at the end of our stay.'

The phrase 'collective tip' has the same resonance for me as 'The dam has broken!' does for valley-dwellers. 'What? Are you sure? How much?'

'I don't know . . . £20?' (After Birna revealed her source for this practice as a Georgette Heyer novel, I ultimately insisted we left nothing.)

The far wall of our otherwise mercifully unstately room was dominated by a peculiar hemispherical fanlight, which we later saw was the genuine part of a false window at the left edge of the house's splendid, chalky grey Georgian facade. On a dressing table beneath it was an old guidebook to the house, presumably published for house guests as Clandeboye is not open to scum like you. It kicked off with an introduction by Lindy's Sheridan. 'To most guests, Clandeboye would appear to be an extremely large house,' it began. Appearing to be extremely small people, we went down for tea.

'I'll tell you what,' piped Lola, interrupting my meek facsimile of a proprietorial hands-behind-back stroll by the main library's blazing fire. 'While we're waiting for Lady Dufferin, I'll show you around.' If I had imagined our trek to the lost kingdom of Simla had included an exhaustive tour of the house, I was now to be proven wrong.

'. . . and this is the third library,' she wheezed, half an hour later. Some parts of Lola's sprawling archival domain, like the 'third library' were well ordered; others she had barely begun to tackle. My crash course in Dufferin Studies was bewildering but, as in the hall, there was a time-warp, shoved-up-in-the-attic-last-Christmas quality to the haphazard archives that brought the First Marquess closer. Piled up in her cellar den was an endearingly shambolic heap of pith helmets, puppets, trays of Victorian printing type and, of course, correspondence in all its forms: household ledgers, letters, poems. My favourite object was a beautifully made octagonal box. Neatly chalked on it in ancient copperplate was the single word 'Empty'.

I'd also found a little handbound book of crayon caricatures. 'They're by the First Marquess's mother,' said Lola. 'As you might have discovered she was the real love of his life, so she was.' I had. The letters in *High Latitudes* are nominally addressed to Dufferin's mother, Helen Selina, Lady Dufferin. Married at seventeen to Price Blackwood, the Fourth Baron, she'd given birth to her only child a year later. After the baron died, Lady Dufferin, still only thirty-three, developed an almost claustrophobically close relationship with her son.

In some ways they were more brother and sister. 'Not every son can remember his mother's twenty-first birthday,' Dufferin said later, going on to record 'her loving, radiant face, which was my childhood Heaven, as indeed it never ceased to be'. They painted together and laughed together and doubtless strolled hand in hand together through the largest broad-leafed forest in Northern Ireland.

From her Dufferin acquired his artistic abilities and wit. In 1859, following the probably unexpected success of his book, she wrote a spoof account of a Mediterranean cruise with her son entitled *Lispings from Low Latitudes*. Lady Helen also bequeathed him a sense of studious self-deprecation. Speaking of her sisters to Disraeli (with whom she was once linked), she said, 'Georgy's the beauty, and Carry's the wit, and I ought to be the good one, but I am not.'

But in fact she was. All I could find in her son's writings were more and more non-specific glorifications of her goodness – 'one of the most loving and lovable human beings that ever walked upon the earth'; 'her passionate ecstasy of affection' (steady); 'the gift of self-sacrifice which enabled her to surrender everything to those she loved'. Before setting off for the Arctic he wrote in his diary that 'no one will love me like her', which must have been a bit of a kick in the teeth for the eighteen-year-old bride (sound familiar?) he married when he was thirty-six.

Dufferin turned Clandeboye into a maternal shrine. He built a nearby railway station on the line from Belfast and gave it the name it still bears today, Helen's Bay. The four-floor Gothic folly he erected in the woods a couple of miles from the house was called Helen's Tower; on each wall of its octagonal top storey hung golden tablets bearing poems dedicated to her. As well as one she wrote to him when he came of age ('My love – a thing not rare or strange/But yet – eternal, measureless – Knowing no shadow and no change') there are others he commissioned specially from Robert Browning and Tennyson: 'Son's love built me, and I hold/Mother's love in lettered gold.'

What's especially odd about the tower dedicated to her memory was that it was completed six years *before* her death. Maybe his mother's line about her love being 'a thing not rare or strange' masked a slight worry that it actually was, particularly in the light of all that 'passionate ecstasy'.

After she died, the slavish personality cult gathered in intensity. I later read that her death in 1868 'wrenched from his living body with forceps of steel his whole youth and childhood', and that even thirty years later her name could only be uttered 'with a lowering of the voice'. Certainly, when he buried his mother he also buried the aimless adventuring of his early adulthood. Five years before she died he'd been a workshy fop; five years after he was Governor-General of Canada.

Lola led us back to the main library via the kitchens, where introductions to the staff were effected. The cook and sundry junior female domestics lined up to nod shyly. I wasn't sure whether to respond with supercilious disdain or by saying, 'Very good . . . er, as you were, carry on,' so in the end I got them all pregnant then pushed them out into the snow to face the shaming wrath of the villagers.

'How marvellous!'

It was Lindy. She sat us down by the fire in the library, where an immense tea awaited. 'If you don't like it, don't eat it — that's the way here,' said Lindy briskly as she shovelled sandwiches into a waiting spaniel's mouth.

Other guests began to arrive, flopping louchely into squat leather armchairs, making me aware of the ridiculous buttock-clenched uprightness of my posture. Soon we had an earl and a countess, a property millionaire, and four other possibly titled, certainly wealthy intellectuals. After a few sentences of learned banter, it was clear that if any of them had more money than sense, it was a close-run thing.

I tried to rationalise the situation with my grandfather's advice on meeting anyone eminent: 'Just imagine them crapping on the bog.' When this produced only dangerously comic imagery, I willed myself into Tim Knox mode, preparing an outrageous anecdote about the *Foam*'s nubile figurehead. I didn't get far before a small inner voice warned me that the phrase 'Get your tits out for the lords' might strike a false note.

In any case, the game was up already. The guests' initial probings had left me hopelessly exposed. The property millionaire, on hearing our claim to live on Strand-on-the-Green ('off' rather than 'on' would have been a wiser choice), instantly brightened. 'Oh! Which house? Zoffany?' Zoffany House, a huge mansion on the river, was until recently the home of sitcom queen Carla Lane and her vast menagerie of stray animals. I spoke to her once through her intercom after we lost a cat. She sold it for a million (the house, that is). 'God, no!' I said, far too contemptuously. 'No,' said Birna, more thoughtfully, 'but not far from there.'

'Spitzbergen?' said another guest after somehow understanding a mumbled account of my itinerary. 'Well, you'll know of Evelyn Waugh's visit there.' This was accurate in that it placed my acquisition of this knowledge in the future. 'As I recall, it was the only journey Waugh made in the Thirties that he didn't find stimulating enough to make a book of.' Cheers for that.

Lindy did her best to shield us. I welcomed her repetition of the 'lovely young man who knows nothing' speech. But even so, our failure to sparkle was conspicuous. Over the next two days a seemingly endless parade of society wits arrived to pay homage to Lindy, and their politeness almost succeeded in masking a confusion as to the purpose of our presence. Some treated us like winners of a 'Be A Lord For A Weekend' competition. 'Oh, I *see*!' they'd announce with relief after she bustled over to explain my quest. ('Oh, I *see*! You're social and academic irrelevances invited here as charity cases by Lindy because she's so kindhearted.')

Feeling fat and stupid, we retired to our room, having been ordered to dress for dinner. A surprise lay within. 'Did *you* do this?' was Birna's blurt; 'My pants!' was mine. While we had been downstairs, our overnight bags had been disembowelled and their contents laid out with scientific rigour. My liver-spotted desert boots had shoehorns in; my Fred Perry hung from a heavy wooden hanger in the wardrobe. My electric razor had disintegrated in transit; all the scurf-incrusted components were arranged in descending order of size on the dresser beneath the fanlight.

It was deeply unsettling. I suppose a true aristocrat would think nothing of a peasant wench staring into their skidmarks, but from then on we felt compelled to tidy away our shaming chattels every time we left.

Clad in my funeral suit and fortified by a pair of ill-advisedly generous Bloody Marys from the help-yourself aperitif trolley, I plunged into the dinner-table silverware and conversation with staunch toper gusto. Lindy had kindly seated me next to Birna, but feeling possessed by the spirit of Dufferin's uproarious Reykjavík bacchanal I ignored the refuge of her company. I loudly butted into a whispered cricket debate on the opposite side of the table, and said 'Cheers!' to the uniformed staff busily occupied in replenishing my brace of wine glasses. The property millionaire was on my left, and I asked him where he was from. Lytham, he replied evenly.

'Nice one! We went to a wedding there a couple of years ago.'

'Oh, whose?'

I chose to interpret this innocent enquiry as symptomatic of the tiny, closed world of wealth and privilege in which he resided. *Whose wedding?* Honestly.

'Well, he's one of the Lancashire McGhees.' A blank face. 'You know – Lord Pete of Maine Road!' My lonely laugh waned, then died.

'No . . . you really wouldn't know them,' said Birna quickly. She had just realised that conversation was being marshalled in strict rotation. During the first course you were to speak to the person on one side of you, during the second to the one on the other. Talking across the table, a practice I had warmly championed, was right out. She managed to whisper as much to me.

'Don't be stupid,' I hissed too loudly. 'How does everyone know which side to start with?'

'I think the hostess starts off on one side and everyone else takes their lead from that.'

'Cobblers.'

But of course it wasn't, and my drunkenness proceeded directly to the contrite remorse stage. I had gone for a Dufferin-style deep potation and blown it. My breeding had failed me.

We filed past the candelabra out of the dining room. As I stumbled cravenly through a long hall, Birna reminded me that at one point I had tried to get the property millionaire's attention by tapping his shoulder with a spoon. Almost in tears of shame, I looked up and was met by the soft, heavy-lidded gaze of the twenty-four-year-old Lord Dufferin. It was the original of the drawing I'd found on the Internet.

The young lord's feminine face beamed out a gentle forgiveness, a kindly beatitude that seemed to say, 'Okay, son, you messed up. But stick with me and I'll see you all right.' Of course! None of this mattered, not in terms of my journey. Come on, Duffers, we've got a sea to sail! Rejuvenated, I gave him a discreet wink. And a less discreet belch.

There was a book by my bedside. The next morning, in a bid to dislodge some of the pickled gravel I had carelessly allowed to be rubbed into my pupils during the night, I began to read it. It was called *Helen's Tower*, and was the work of Harold Nicolson, aesthete, diplomat and my Dufferin's nephew. The year of publication was 1937. Flicking through it I came across an arresting statement, which I read out to Birna. 'It is the tradition at Clandeboye that one's porridge at breakfast should be consumed standing up.'

'Well, we won't have to worry about that,' she assured me. 'No one will be up yet. I heard people going to bed after two.' Indeed. And when I'd got up even later than that to ingest a dozen glasses of water, I'd seen Lindy out in the grounds walking her spaniel.

After wrestling with the bath – a terrifying beast the size of a skip with great brass faucets and a handle marked 'WASTE' which let the water out through a Titanic-bilge-style grating – I eventually found the breakfast room. In fact, at 9.15, everyone had already been and eaten and gone. The stamina of these people was phenomenal.

Andrew Gailey had warned me that Dufferin's journals had been bowdlerised by whoever typed them up, probably after his death, and what I read from them after Lola let me loose in the chilly 'second library' cast little light on his character. There was no reference as to why he'd chosen to go to the Arctic, although I did find a letter from Fanny Russell (wife of the former Prime Minister Lord John Russell) asking where Reykjavík was and finishing, 'I dare say you will enjoy the North Pole,' an ignorance which confirmed the perceived extremity of his quest.

That, of course, would have been another of his aims. Iceland had yet to be demythologised. Perhaps with Fanny in mind, Dufferin commented that 'most educated English people firmly believe the Icelanders to be a blubber-eating, sealskin-clad race,' and 140 years on this image lingers. Before my first visit there, my mother enquired with a disturbing lack of irony whether Icelanders still lived in igloos.

The diaries' coverage of his Arctic voyage is sparse and some-times surreally bland. Two consecutive days' entries as he prepares to leave Scotland read: 'At 7 off Kyleakin, Capt Wood sent us off for some milk.' 'Capt Wood sent me some milk; told me Spain had declared war with Mexico.'

Things pick up briefly when he resumes his journal after return-ing. Before assuming his diplomatic duties, he spent some years as a lord-in-waiting at Windsor Castle, and I found an intriguing account of a game of consequences there in February 1857:

Omer Pasha and the Duchess of Wellington
Singing a Duet
Consequence: Drowned

Mr Wellesly and Miss Byng
Washing each other's faces
Consequence: Reconciliation

The Archbishop of Canterbury and the Duchess of Sutherland
Upside down
Consequence: They came to blows

Colonel Vyse and Miss Butteel
Flirting in a shower bath
Consequence: Not known yet

'Here come the young people!'

Lindy's ringing tones echoed down the hall. We had learned that half a dozen of Britain's more notable junior aristocrats would be visiting; in our trough of inferiority, mere mention of names like 'Ned' and 'Randall' had sufficed to build up a frenzy of paranoia. Birna honed a scenario of drunken, cowardly bullies in Flashman riding boots queuing up to thrash each other's servants. 'No, Ned!' a frail beauty would implore before being pushed roughly away with a ragged cry of 'Impudence!'

But of the six loafer-clad yuppies walking across the polar bear's back, only a couple betrayed the louche swagger that suggested an afternoon of knocking the heads off busts and braying around the grounds with a 12-bore for a crack at the Mick. Apart from one glance which had a whiff of the 'Lindy, who invited that ghastly spastic?' about it, the intimidation we feared limited itself to swearing a lot in funny accents and smoking an enormous quantity of Silk Cut Ultra.

Inevitably, the most outré behaviour emanated from our hostess. Unfazed by anything, she clearly took relish in showing them how it should be done, or at least how it was done in 1969.

As we repaired to a freezing conservatory where an epic luncheon was laid out on salvers, she embarked upon a tale centring around a visiting rock star's cherubically tiny penis. (Sadly not Mick Jagger.) Then, as we filed out into the wind for pavlova on the lawn, she barged a hapless noble to the turf and straddled him with a triumphant yelp of 'I am going to bounce the young Lord Durham!'

The young Lord Durham took the bouncing in good heart, smiling indulgently as Lindy and her spaniel flailed about on top of him in one of the more arresting spectacles of my adult years. I was very glad it wasn't me. I would rather remove contaminated sharps from a blocked hospital sink with my teeth than be on the wrong end of audience participation.

Afterwards she took us on a tour of the outbuildings, beginning with a stable-block newly converted into a corporate banqueting facility. Lindy seemed an unlikely entrepreneur, but her expensive hunches are apparently paying off handsomely. The estate now includes five golf courses and a Michelin-star restaurant, and a personal appearance is sold as part of the conference package. It was funny to think of her shaking hands with Mitsubishi UK's Sales Achiever of the Year (Light Commercials). 'Even I couldn't have afforded to maintain the house unless we sorted out some business,' she said. But no one was really listening. When someone is rolling up a cigarette with a full wine glass balanced on their head your attention is not focused on their verbal output.

We went through the environmental conservationists' greenhouse complex and ended up at a tunnel alongside Clandeboye's own church. This was the entrance to the recently rediscovered ice house. A nonchalant comparison of ice houses ensued.

'Ours is less ovoid. Yours?'

'Had to knock it down a couple of years back.'

By now they knew better than to ask us. A freezer in a cupboard under the stairs probably doesn't count.

Birna tried. As part of a conversation on the land of her fathers, I heard her telling the previously bounced young lordling that Magnus Magnusson's brother had been her gynaecologist. He laughed, then said, 'Well, I think I can trump that,' before relating how George Formby was once one of his grandfather's stable boys. I felt I should have taken him aside. 'Nice story, son.

But next time, try this: "Well, I think I can trump that – I am the Earl of Durham."'

We set off on a tour of Clandeboye's grounds, taking in two huge lakes excavated by Dufferin. During the 1846 Potato Famine he'd found 'dead bodies putrefying amidst the sick remnants of their families', a sight which moved him to spend £78,000 on bettering conditions on his farms. He instituted public works schemes on the estate in times of famine or unemployment, most notably the lakes and the building of Helen's Tower.

But as a keen supporter of the Union and the rights of land-owners who also believed in compassion for Irish farmworkers, his political position was awkward. Moreover, Andrew Gailey had told me, his romantic sensibilities made him ill suited for the cut and thrust of parliamentary debate.

As he approached thirty he appears to have accepted that his painting and poetry weren't quite good enough to pursue professionally. His cruises seem to have been devices to postpone a decision as to what to do with himself, an escape from social and political expectation which gave purpose to his dilettante lifestyle. Given that my own motivation in replicating his voyage encompassed a similarly vague desire to achieve something notable for once, this thought afforded a little pulse of empathy.

Two years before the Arctic voyage, aged twenty-eight, he'd taken the *Foam* (which, though run by a crew of twelve, was still a flimsy-hulled pleasure yacht) across the Baltic to check out the Crimean War. While there he almost died aboard a warship sent to 'draw the fire of the Russian forts'. He sailed home to Clandeboye with two enemy cannon and a young walrus stowed on the *Foam*'s deck.

On the Arctic trip, I supposed, icebergs and polar bears would have taken the place of Russian artillery as the challenges he aimed to pit himself against. Having somehow failed to damage his fragile craft in the Crimean War, he would cement his credentials as an enthusiastic amateur adventurer by piloting her through some of the most unforgiving seas on the planet. With Iceland only as far from the tip of Scotland as London, he could be an explorer almost on his own doorstep.

The youths yahed away in their BMW estates and we sat down to dinner. 'You're in at the deep end now,' said Lindy, motioning me away from Birna to a seat by her side.

But she let me sink to the bottom gently by doing all the talking. She'd once been a photojournalist for *Harpers* (but of course), and had worked with Don McCullin, giving it up after she got married. 'I was already quite grand, but when I became *very* grand, it was impossible to feel any pride in getting a story or a picture – people would just let one do anything because of one's grandness, not one's talent.'

It was only later that I did more research and discovered just what a worthy Dufferin she is. She's everything that he was: patron of umpteen charities and artistic foundations, a keen watercolourist and photographer, a firm believer in nurturing homegrown talent on the estate (as well as installing Lola as the estate's archivist, she'd put a local lad in charge of her multi-million-pound golf courses after forming a favourable opinion of him as he cooked her lunch at a roadside café). And she's the one thing that her ancestor wasn't – an astute business tactician.

My three-date tour of Clandeboye's libraries finished next morning. This one doubled as a billiard room. A table filled one end; the other was dominated by a print of the Dufferins presiding over a curling match in Canada in the 1870s.

I watched from a fat old Chesterfield as Lola's legs appeared beneath a stack of huge mounted photographs taken during the Arctic voyage, all of which I'd read somewhere were stored in a London museum and had been lost in the Blitz. Before laying them on the baize, she carefully peeled away the tissue that sandwiched each print. The vacuum-packed swish with which it reluctantly parted from the mount suggested the photographs hadn't been looked at for some years – probably, said Lola, not since Dufferin's time.

Willing myself to believe this was so, I expectantly examined the first, a portrait of a youngish chap, his face encircled by a black Quaker Oats beard. The watch chain looping from his plaid silk waistcoat marked him out. Here was Dufferin's skipper, Ebenezer Wyse.

Just a week before the *Foam* was to set sail for Iceland, her captain fell ill. Dufferin suddenly found himself in search of a replacement, and received Wyse's name with a glowing reference, a recommendation that rested on one notable achievement.

In the early 1850s, there had been a frenzied demand in Australia for river steamboats, which in the absence of local shipyards could only be sent over from Britain. A Scottish consortium agreed to finance one such venture, knowing that while it was almost suicidally impossible to sail what Dufferin calls 'these fragile tea-kettles' across three oceans and around the Cape, the huge returns justified the risk. Five boats were despatched; each foundered with all hands before reaching the equator.

Finding crews for the sixth and last steamer was in the circumstances a challenge. Two captains lost heart as they were setting off. Eventually, a Mr Ebenezer Wyse volunteered.

Initial progress was good, but when they were 1,000 miles south of the Cape a huge wave loosened the hull's iron plates. As water poured in, the crew readied the lifeboats. Wyse attempted to impress upon them the lunacy of setting out in a rowing boat a thousand miles from shore, but with the mood turning ugly, he feigned conversion to their cause and went into his cabin. They'd need his compass and chronometer, he said. When he reappeared, though, it was not with navigational aids, but a revolver in each hand, swearing he'd shoot any man who touched the boats.

With chains lashed around her hull, the boat limped to her destination, where she was sold for the unimaginable sum of £7,000. In recognition of his heroic role Wyse was presented with the gold watch and chain apparent in the photograph.

The fuzz-faced young man peering out at me from under his floppy cap looked far too silly to have resolved such a desperate scenario. I'd wondered how Dufferin had persuaded a crew of

TAKING A SIGHT.

twelve to accompany him on such a hazard-strewn voyage and, recalling the infinitely starker dangers of Wyse's earlier mission, now I understood. Life was cheap, people died young; as well as earning a fair wedge on this voyage, they'd also have the chance to return as pioneering heroes, or if not to be remembered as brave but doomed adventurers. It was better to live one day as a tiger than a lifetime as a whelk, or whatever it was.

The next photo showed the assembled deckhands. With their Age of Steam complexions and blanket-like clothing they looked shabby and disreputable, the original motley crew. I could see how Dufferin would have been glad of a captain with a proven track record of putting down mutinies single-handed.

Then there was Dufferin himself, a shot of him taking an on-deck sextant reading, one leg braced, hair blown back behind a nautical cap, eyeglass pressed to a familiar hooded lid. The most obvious facial departure from the crayon drawing of six years before is that the powder-puff softness has disappeared under a Peter Sutcliffe beard. It's probably the only photograph of him at this age which survives, but despite this significance I couldn't concentrate on the foreground. Behind Dufferin raged a grey sea whose anger had tilted the *Foam* away from the horizon at an interestingly oblique angle. As one of life's whelks, it was a prospect that did not appeal.

Nor did a print of the *Foam* gliding through the still chill of a thin fjord in Spitzbergen, a vast iceberg the size of a cathedral drifting ominously by. This had been shot from a hillside, and the miserable panorama – gravel, slush, greyness – bleated out a mournful desolation and inhospitability.

Cursing my rash pledge to authenticate the retracing of Dufferin's voyage by maximising its marine element, I read in deepening sobriety through the heavy household ledgers drawn up in his day. Filed under the heading 'Antiquities and Miscellaneous' was:

'Stuffed Alligator brought home alive by Capt J Hamilton' (with *'DESTROYED'* pencilled intriguingly next to it).

'Stuffed Walrus brought home by Fred. Lord Dufferin in the yacht Foam and the sauce [sic] of which is spoken of in Letters From High Latitudes.'

'The skin and stuffed head of a polar bear brought home by Fred. Lord Dufferin on the yacht Foam.'

Lola led Birna and me out to the Micra and we drove off into the heart of the estate. Gamekeepers and cowmen opened gates for us; the tracks receded from gravel to grass; at one point we got lost. After twenty minutes we corkscrewed up a small hill, and there was Helen's Tower.

Like much of the estate, the frail-looking tower had been rescued from delapidation by Lindy. Huge steel plates shielded the door from the attention of local youths, who had been forced instead to satisfy their antisocial urges in aerosol form on the dirty granite.

But though the tiny rooms – one per storey, three in all, and topped off with a roof terrace – had been restored to make the tower habitable, it still possessed an air of abandoned-shrine pathos. The ground-floor shower room and Hygena kitchen were dusty and carpeted evenly with dead flies like a caravan after a long winter; the smell was of mothballs and wet bricks.

The top-floor room, though, was set in Dufferinian aspic, free from sofabeds and telephone points. Here, if anywhere, said Lola, was his soul. Above the Gothic swoops and dark arches of the mahogany window seats were the mother-smothering poems he had commissioned, each etched into brass plaques spotted white with damp and age.

It was not difficult to imagine the bereaved young lord sitting here for hours drowning in his own melancholy; by building this place six years before her death he'd been practising for some time. In this sort of room the only appropriate noise would have been the slow ticking of a large clock.

The ear-burning wind up on the tiny roof terrace blew away

the curse of the mummy. On tiptoes, you could just see the house, and the church.

'The church!' yelped Lola. Lindy had requested our attendance at morning service in a tone suggesting that to opt out would be to confess allegiance to the Kraken. We bundled down four flights of stairs and into the Micra.

I wasn't looking forward to church. We slipped in through the toffs' door, a private entrance to a private pew at right angles to the massed congregation of serfs, almost as if they were paying homage to us as much as to God. As we took our place beside Lindy and Co., four dozen pairs of Ulster eyes bored into us, readily adopting the 'What are *you* doing here?' quizzicality that had been the weekend's leitmotif.

When the collection plate came round, the countesses wafted in tenners and twenties; our tinny cascade of pennies for heaven rang out shamingly. We trooped out at the rear, earls before swine, back through the crenellated hedges and almost seamlessly into a waiting minicab. Suddenly, jarringly, we were back in the world of Ford Sierra GLs and *Gary Lineker's Sunday Sport on 5 Live*.

Then at the airport we met one of Saturday's young lordlings, who stood up in deference (to our age) and said that he was frightfully sorry, but he couldn't give us a lift back from Heathrow. 'We *do* have a car,' I said, failing to suppress a note of shrillness. 'It's in the long-term car park. Actually.' This was supposed to sound nonchalant, and in failing to do so it betrayed the fact that the looming expense had been sticking in my craw all weekend. Long-term car parks at airports are stored alongside dry cleaning and fresh pasta in my lexicon of unwarrantable extravagance.

As indeed are hired cars, which failed to jolly my mood as I sluiced up a sodden M1 in a Budget Ford Mondeo two weeks later.

2

I'd been up since 4.30 a.m., an awful thing, so awful that it wasn't until I approached Grimsby that my higher brain functions kicked in and I decoded the shipping forecast I'd heard in the car park at Leicester Forest East services. 'Humber, Tyne, Dogger, Force 6, rising Gale Force 8, imminent.' That blurred, churned slather of brown on my left was the Humber, I realised. And swaying on top of it, somewhere down the road at Immingham Docks, was the Icelandic container ship on which I would shortly be embarking on the first leg of my voyage.

So extravagant had been my fatigue that at one point I'd considered protecting myself from lane-wandering collision by putting on my cycle helmet, only refraining from doing so when I estimated this would raise my chances of being arrested. I felt incongruous enough as it was: my red anorak looked all wrong in this shiny new repmobile, as did the rucksacks and bits of partially dismembered mountain bike filling the car's rear half. When I'd hired the car the night before, the bloke behind the counter had looked me up and down uncertainly before pressing a document firmly into my hands with the words, 'And this is what you show the police if they stop you.'

Now, feeling more torn than worn, I drove into the thwarted ugliness of Grimsby's outskirts and realised that I had no idea where the Budget office was. It was 9 a.m. and my ship left at 10. With the first stirrings of panic feathering my stomach, I pulled into a petrol station to ask directions, expecting the old 'Yes, chuck, over to the old scrattling plant, then second left where young

Albert Belt had his fall' routine. Instead, the woman at the till just pointed at a big sign about 40 feet away, reading: 'Budget Car Rentals, You Patronising Metropolitan Ponce.'

I reflected upon the pitifully narrow parameters of my life as it then stood. Waking at 4.30 was about the sixth worst event to have befallen me for a decade; finding the Budget office so painlessly was maybe the seventh best. But to make up for it Budget then billed me £200 for denting their car's bloody door, a monstrous fabrication for which I still despise them. And also, in about five hours' time, I would have new entries filling all the top places in my chart of bad things.

'The thing to do is to eat, like, twelve Mars Bars,' shouted the minicab driver as the gale that had been imminent announced its arrival by heaving us around the road. 'Fill your guts with something to chuck up.'

'Is that the thing?' I said, wondering which was worse: eating a dozen Mars Bars expressly to vomit them up, or just sitting it out for four days with your head in a bilge bucket. 'Isn't it supposed to be all right if you just keep your eye on the horizon?'

'Won't see the horizon in this,' he yelled with a cheery wink, thumbing at the dung-coloured, windswept drizzle.

The best I could say was that this was perfect Icelandic weather. Next time you watch the BBC weather forecast, check out the top left-hand corner of the map, and in particular the tight vortex of isobars that invariably blots out Iceland. It's astonishingly windy there. The winters, at least in the inhabited parts (namely the coastline), aren't actually as severe as the country's name implies. New York, for instance, is generally far colder. But the wind . . . Every Icelander visiting England for the first time is amazed by the umbrellas. No one in Iceland owns an umbrella. Open one up there and you'll be the hapless participant in a demonstration of why Mary Poppins never visited Reykjavík.

Birna's grandfather, a former whaler and trawler captain, had pulled the strings which had landed me a berth on the *Dettifoss*, a container ship with a capacity of 8,000 tons, ferrying frozen fish out of Iceland and a bit of everything back in. It was a brilliant coup – the *Dettifoss* was not supposed to take any passengers, and the only nautical alternative from Britain to Iceland was a very unDufferinian ferry from Scrabster, up near John O'Groats.

Probably because someone else had organised it, the Britain–Iceland leg was the only part of my Dufferin-trailing itinerary I'd been able to pencil in with any confidence. Afterwards, it petered away into doubt (would there really be a military plane to take me to Jan Mayen from Norway?), over-ambition (every time I told people I was mountain biking across Iceland, they'd repeat these last four words back with incredulous verbal italics) or, as in the unresolved voyages from Iceland to Norway and Norway to Spitzbergen, a simple blank.

So I was hugely grateful to Birna's grandfather. In theory.

I don't do boats. My previous record voyage was Cherbourg–Portsmouth; the only occasion on which I had spent any time on a boat smaller than a ferry I had been extravagantly unwell.

Additionally, I had been stupid enough the previous night to reacquaint myself with Dufferin's account of his crossing from Oban to Iceland. 'I had always heard the seas were heavier here than in any other part of the world,' he begins, and just as I awaited a 'but', he carries on with 'and certainly they did not belie their character.'

On this basis, the ship that we drove up to across the empty marshalling yards and stacks of rust-streaked containers was not nearly big enough. Nor, as I could see as the driver dumped me out on the wet dock in front of it, new enough.

My vague fantasies about acquiring full bicycling fitness by speeding up and down the *Dettifoss's* sprawling kilometre-long decks blew away, off across the estuary. The ship's containers were stacked four-high right up to the edge of its squat, rust-bubbled deck, squeezing the living quarters and bridge into an area at the rear about 15 feet long by six decks high. It gave the *Dettifoss* a ridiculous ark-like top-heaviness, and I found myself recalling the grotesque footage I'd seen on Icelandic TV the year before, of dented and listing containers bobbing about in the North Atlantic after the mysterious wrecking of a ship just like this.

As I reassembled my bicycle on the quayside, my fragile confidence took another blow when I saw the heart-sinking word 'LIMASSOL' painted beneath the ship's name. Why was this boat registered in Cyprus? Struggling to suppress the riveting premonition that I would be making a posthumous appearance in a documentary exposing the fatal shoddiness behind flags of convenience, I made my way to the gangplank.

In middle age, many Icelandic men evolve prematurely into gruff but kindly old coves, and I could see instantly that the Bergerac-style fellow bouncing sternly down the narrow walkway towards me was a definitive example.

'I am the CO,' he said. 'Welcome aboard.' He hoisted my bike with one hand and strode on deck; I hobbled behind with my ludicrous assemblage of rucksacks and plastic bags.

'We have barbecues here on a normal summer weekend,' he said as he lashed the bike with an expert couple of half-hitches to a railing beneath a plastic-roofed open landing.

'Yes,' I said.

'But this will not probably be a normal summer weekend.'

'No,' I said.

As we spiralled up the staircases, tightly coiled as a DNA helix and linking one identical deck to the next, he told me that the *Dettifoss* was fifteen years old and had originally been German. 'My cabin,' he said, pointing out a door labelled 'I Offizer'. CO: Chief Officer. Then, on the next deck up: 'Your cabin.'

The little sign on my door was interesting in that it happily identified me as the 'Funker'. Later I found out this meant telegraph operator, but at the time it sounded as if I might be called upon to teach the crew the LA Walk and the Mashed Potato.

I hadn't expected a cabin at all, let alone one with an ensuite shower. This was marvellously cosy, albeit in a slightly cold Eastern Bloc way. The oatmeal Formica and aggressive fluorescent lighting gave it the air of a junior party official's private ward in a Dresden healthcare centre.

It was while unpacking that the first subtle portents made themselves known. You had to lift the drawers two inches before they'd slide out; there were rubberised grip mats on every surface; the waist-high cot-bed was inset behind a sturdy anti-roll-off plank. And the bookshelf was inclined back at angle of 30 degrees, with straps across the front to restrain its contents should that prove insufficient.

It would.

Sombrely, I went down, down, down and out on to the deck. Britain was in the last week of its wettest June this century, and the weather was hilariously appalling. Here we were in Wimbledon fortnight, and I was begloved and buttoned up to the neck in a bloody anorak, having to lean into the wind to maintain balance, tears and rain whisking horizontally into my ears. (In the shop I'd boldly convinced myself that my red Goretex outer layer imparted a touch of Oasis-style glamour; now it was only too clear that in conjunction with my day-glo rucksack and purple cycling shoes, it confirmed me as the least appealing kind of soiled, friendless, ageing Interrailer.)

I went back in and nosed about. *Supermarket Sweep* was showing in a small cabin labelled 'Hobbyraum' lined with Wimpy Bar sofas and pictures of the north Icelandic waterfall after which the *Dettifoss* was named.

'It is most . . . big waterfall in Europe,' said an uncertain, high-pitched voice. I turned to see a jolly, Yeltsin-esque figure extending a chubby hand. 'Five hundred cubic metre of water in one second. I am the captain.'

I found it a slight shame that no one on board wore a uniform, but they made up for it by only ever referring to themselves and other crew members by formal rank. In four days, I never learned anyone's name.

I presented the captain with a bottle of single malt, which he accepted with an eagerness that Boris himself could scarcely have bettered. But alcohol wasn't the scourge, it seemed, judging by the plethora of recently affixed posters about the Hobbyraum saying (in English): 'The use or possession of drugs is strictly forbidden on board this vessel.' The boredom of on-board life in the age of automated navigation and the *Dettifoss*'s regular trips to Rotterdam, were, I supposed, the problems. Unsavoury images were conjured, along the lines of drugged-up GIs in 'Nam, ferry-trashing England fans on acid and other scenarios from the unmellow and non-groovy end of the narcotic abuse scale.

Illustrations of maritime disaster in all its forms drew my eye to an adjacent safety poster. But the text was Icelandic, and Icelandic is not one of the world's more forgiving languages. I have tried, really I have, to master the endless declensions – the word mirror, *spegill*, can be: *um spegil*, about the mirror; *fra spegli*, from the mirror; *til spegils*, to the mirror. Even names change. If you were labelling a present 'To Egill', you'd have to write 'Til Egils' – and if he sent you one in return you'd never know because it would be signed 'Frá Agli'. And I once saw a brilliant front-page headline which seemed to translate as 'I Married A Salmon!', only to be told it was in fact 'I Married For Salmon!' (Well, that's all right, then.)

It helps, apparently, if you speak Latin, which displays similar stupidities (hence its popularity as a foreign language at the time of Dufferin's visit). And luckily I have an O level in Latin, and am therefore easily able to draw a diagram of a Roman hill fort.

Then there are what linguists refer to as 'the funny letters': þ and ð. The former is a sibilant 'th' sound, as in 'I *th*ink I'm going to be sick'; the latter is the more nasal 'th' found in '*Th*ere goes another Mars Bar'.

The upshot is that I rarely attempt to speak Icelandic. For one thing, everyone speaks perfect Björk-style English, and for another, no one ever understands anything I say. During my mother-in-law's presidential campaign (caught you off guard there!), I volunteered to invite passers-by for coffee and waffles at her campaign office. So much did I enjoy this low-level vote-buying that I failed to distinguish joyful acceptance of the offer from incredulous hilarity until some kind old man explained I was actually advertising 'coffee and doggies'. No wonder she lost.

It doesn't help that there's little in the way of exported culture. A friend of mine managed to gain a reasonable degree of fluency in German just from watching war films (this does mean, however, that his conversation is liberally studded with sudden cries of rage or pain and phrases such as 'Put your hands above your head and move away from the kontroll panel').

My final excuse, and I'm quite proud to have racked up so many, is that Iceland makes strenuous efforts to preserve the purity of its language by expunging foreign influences. Beside this broadsword defence of the tongue of the Vikings, the more noted struggle against Franglais is exposed as a tinny rattling of Gallic sabres.

Whenever some new consumer phenomenon reaches Reykjavík (usually a year before we get it, incidentally, in line with their feverish technophilia), they hold a national competition to decide upon a native name. Computer is *tölva*, an amalgam of *tala*, number, and *völva*, a prophetess. Television is *sjónvarp*, 'throwing out of pictures' (an accurate description of most of the native output); CDs are *geisladiskar*, 'ray discs'. What is extraordinary is that despite a very strong Yankocentric youth culture, unlike in France the young natives all happily stick to these convoluted constructions, never being tempted by slack and hip Anglicisms.

And it gets worse (sorry, *better*). In most European countries, important words like police, doctor and passport tend to cross the language divide reasonably unscathed; in Iceland, they are, respectively, *lögreglan, læknir* and *vegabréf*. A recent book about Iceland by a couple of English poets makes a telling point, a chapter-ending point, out of the fact that the competition-winning Icelandic word for telephone, *sími*, derives from an old Viking word for 'threat'. Actually, it's 'thread'.

But then few Scandinavian tongues flatter the inept linguist. I remember interviewing the Australian Abba tribute band Björn Again and asking whether they had endeavoured to speak in the native tongue during a recent tour of Sweden. Indeed they had: at the start of every gig they joined at the front of the stage to bellow Benny's old rabble-rousing cry of 'We want to rock you!', carefully translated and rehearsed. The reason this always went down far better than they dared hope only became clear when, after their last appearance, a local journalist told them they had in fact been shouting 'We want to shave you!'

★

'Yes, we must show you how to wear the survival suits,' said the captain as I squinted stupidly at the safety poster, a comment I made the terrible error of thinking was a joke. As it transpired, I didn't even see a lifejacket, and even in my darkest hours I was too embarrassed to ask again about the survival suits. Shouting 'No, no! Come back! Please! Please show me how to live!' as the captain whistled away down the corridor wouldn't have sounded great, and might easily have cursed the voyage in line with some 'Scottish play'-type nautical superstition. All I could do was to try and recall from my Bronze Survival Medal course (failed) how you go about making a float by inflating a pair of pyjama bottoms. 'Excuse me, could you blow into my trousers to make them swell up?' was not a question I wanted to ask a sailor.

A last-minute delay to load up a container of steel had the crew wearily sticking their hardhats back on, and as the CO climbed into his overalls I quizzed him about the cargo on the *Dettifoss*'s regular Reykjavík–Rotterdam–Immingham route, known as the 'Golden Triangle' (by me). Leaving Iceland, he confirmed, the boat was always fuller; now, the top two layers of containers were empty 'reefers' – refrigerated containers – which had formerly been filled with frozen fish. I was delighted to have this snippet of container slang with which to impress the small boys who would inevitably mob me on the quaysides, but less so when the CO explained that, as a result, the boat was much lighter, stood further out of the water, and would therefore roll about like a Weeble with BSE.

So what was in the full containers . . . not the, you know, 'reefers'? 'Who knows? Some cars, maybe. And the steel.' I had an idea, though. One of the salient features of Icelandic culture is its incredible homogeneity. Consumer crazes arrive and are instantly taken up by almost the entire population.

A few years back there was a fashion for those idiotic 'big truck' affairs propped up on tyres the size of Ferris wheels. One winter, half of Reykjavík had one; the next, they'd all been replaced by twin-cab Toyota pick-ups. You can always tell the Keflavík flight is in at Heathrow when the arrivals lounge begins to fill with very tall men in moss-coloured raincoats and very tall women in tiny-framed, oval-lensed Obergruppenführer glasses. Christmases are times when the Icelandic nation gets together to give each other exactly the same present. That oddly shaped parcel under 100,000 Reykjavík Christmas trees in 1982 was an electric foot spa; 1989 was National Pictionary Exchange Year.

And every so often, some random phenomenon gets stuck in a consumer groove. To most West Europeans, the fashion for platform trainers was a mercifully brief rush of blood to the foot; only among Spice Girls and Icelanders has it somehow become a shaming perennial. When the kiwi fruit belatedly hit Reykjavík at the end of the Eighties, it was embraced with a '*Beaujolais Nouveau est arrivé*' hysteria which still persists today, years after the rest of us noticed that it tasted vaguely of sick. In Iceland it remains a symbol of cosmopolitan exotica, and you can buy 'kee-vee' flavour sweets and fizzy drinks, as well as recipe books (kiwi with halibut cheeks, anyone?).

The reefers swaying about from our twin cranes started up the first lateral motion. Wishing I hadn't thought of containers full of fizzy kiwis I retired to my cabin to medicate myself. I had bought eight packets each of two brands of seasick pills, Stugeron and Dramamine. As I prepared to drop a tab of the former, I suddenly looked at the packets and realised how unhappily named both varieties were. Stugeron was only a rattled Scrabble rack away from 'sturgeon', an appallingly evocative image. They might as well have gone for 'Rancid Vomity Fihs Fat'. And it was even easier to conjure unhappy nautical allusions from the alternative medication: placing a mental hyphen before the final syllable created 'drama-mine'. Only Anusol, I thought, could command a loftier place in the pharmaceutical brand-name pantheon of the absurd. And that tastes awful, too.

As a result of the delay while we steeled ourselves, we were still in port for lunch. I had been expecting ship's biscuits topped with slabs of pemmican (whatever that might be: a spam version of pelican, probably), but down in the spartan yet well-tended mess I was presented with a plate of fishcakes, potatoes, pasta and salad. As I shovelled this down (plus an extra helping of scurvy-forestalling salad), it seemed difficult to think that this would be my last food for thirty-six hours.

'We are eating at 8.00 hours, 12.00 hours, 18.00 hours,' said the bearded cook. 'And some coffee and cakes at 15.00 hours.' Preparing three meals a day for the crew of eleven and doing all the washing up afterwards, he had the toughest job on the ship. Even in the crew's time off, the poor bloke had to traipse around Dutch hypermarkets buying provisions while the rest were busy whoring themselves stupid and getting tattooed. As I was to find out, the work pattern for the crew proper was up to fourteen hours' non-stop whirlwind activity at ports interspersed with dog days of utter tedium. The boat sailed itself; there were no mainbraces to splice. The captain and the CO both urged me to come up on the bridge whenever I felt like it to break up the monotony of their lone watches.

The engines started as I finished, and at once the ominously bilious swells and rumbles kicked in. 'We will need two tugs to pull us out in such weather,' said the CO as he pressed upon me my fourth coffee since going aboard two hours earlier. Normally I can only permit myself one strong coffee a day without suffering side effects ranging from prickly heat to a sort of tunnel vision of a world without hope, but in Scandinavia (and Iceland in particular) one is socially obliged to overdose on caffeine. They serve complimentary coffee in shops and banks; on the boat, percolators expectorated in every cabin. If my body was a temple, I had just peed in its font. Penance lay in wait.

At 1.20 p.m., after a brief alarm when the gangplank was blown into the sea, tousled mariners clanged past the Hobbyraum to winch in the hawsers, and we were off. Our passage through oil storage tanks, cranes, chimneys, rain, fog, wind and the thick brown sea was all rather dismal, but – I was at this point able to convince myself – still fun in a kind of filthy, heavy-industrial way. There is something inherently awesome about truly large ships, probably because the only time most of us get to see them is when they're on the news in two pieces at the bottom of the Baltic or upside-down on a Shetland skerry.

Immingham Docks had the semi-abandoned air associated with ultra-mechanised container systems (though I later read that the port is now busier than Liverpool). Nevertheless, being towed out by tugs was pleasingly redolent of an old through-the-arched-window *PlaySchool* slot. Everything was monochrome, except for the pilot's greasy orange bib; the foghorns, the hawsers, the locks, the business-like waves exchanged between tug and crew as we eased out into the estuary . . . Then someone adjusted my vertical hold.

'May cause drowsiness. If affected do not drive or operate machinery,' read the caveat on the Stugeron packet. Ah, the cheery mantra from my youth! Especially when supplemented with the magical coda 'avoid alcohol', this was what to look for when examining over-the-counter medications for potential narcotic effects: 'Will make you feel a bit funny. If affected, drink two cans of Kestrel and do not operate mouth or limbs.'

I certainly was affected. I sank down into my cot bed and curtained myself in, suddenly bewitched by the voodoo throb of the engines.

> Few people can have any notion of the cosiness of a yacht's cabin under such circumstances. After having remained for several hours on deck, in the presence of the tempest – peering through the darkness at those black liquid walls of water, the wind roaring through the rigging – timbers creaking as if the ship would break its heart – the spray and rain beating in your face – everything around in tumult – suddenly to descend into the quiet of a snug, well-lighted little cabin, with the firelight dancing on the white rosebud chintz . . . the certainty of being a good three hundred miles from any troublesome shore – all combine to inspire a feeling of comfort and security difficult to describe.

When I first read this description of the 'challenging' first days of Dufferin's run up to Iceland, the only point of convergence I could find was to agree that yes, it would be difficult to describe a feeling of comfort and security. You're in a terrible storm in a tiny wooden boat, miles from anywhere, and there's a bloody fire in your cabin . . . Jesus. Now, though, I felt myself suffused with an empathetic sense of calm, albeit one already tempered by mild but uncontrollable hallucinations. I drifted off, my mind awash with cross-images of blazer-clad Victorians playing deck quoits and sou'westered men throwing armfuls of haddock into slimy bins.

Dufferin had set sail from Oban on 7 June 1856, making first for the Hebrides. It was at Stornoway that the weather had picked up, while the *Foam*'s carpenter (and cook) affixed the new bronze figurehead, still warm from the London furnace. As they lay in harbour, the gale 'increased to a perfect hurricane', and in the morning, the storm having abated, a Navy ship towed in a long line of wrecked and empty fishing boats.

It's hard to think of this sight raising the crew's spirits as they sailed away from the Isle of Lewis on 11 June. They now comprised six seamen, a ship's boy, two cooks, the first mate Leverett, the master Wyse and a steward. Dufferin also had along his friend Charles Fitzgerald (known throughout as Fitz), a surgeon; his valet, Wilson; and a mysteriously acquired Icelandic law student, Sigurður Jonasson, who would be his chess partner on board and guide around Iceland. Also on board was a cockerel, who would shortly die from seasickness.

When I awoke groggily at 3.30, it seemed it would be my turn next. Things had gone horribly awry; someone was peering at me while I slept, twitching the curtains around my cot. But as I sat up to accost them, realisation abruptly dawned: the swell was so violent that it was yanking the stiff drapes back and forth. I staggered comically to my porthole – tiny little steps, followed by dramatic extended lopes – expecting to see us bravely perched, à la *Foam*, atop 50-foot monsters and dwarfed by crashing walls of angry spume. In fact, from my lofty fifth-deck view, the sea looked strangely benign, despite the evidence of the swinging curtains and the fact that a book had fallen off the shelf, which together suggested the angle of pitch was in excess of 30 degrees. More confusingly, I felt fine. See? All along I'd been a natural reefer-talkin', foc's'le-climbin' mariner.

Over the coming weeks, I came to learn that there is a ten-minute non-nauseous grace period after you wake while fluid fills your ear canals or something. So it was just as I was preparing to go down for coffee and doggies that I started to get the sweating shakes – always my body's first symptom of impending unwellness, right back to when I was six and threw up all over Marta Patel's labrador in the back of her dad's Triumph 2000 TC.

Then, for the first time, I noticed the smell. Whoever discovered under the influence of nitrous oxide that the secret of the universe was that 'a smell of petroleum pervades throughout' can't have been on a large boat at the time, or he'd have written down 'diesel'.

I sipped water. The swell grew. Smell, swell, swell, smell. Resisting a powerful urge to surrender, to lie down and embrace the lavatory bowl, I retired to my bunk and lay flat, unable to read, drink or eat. The nausea could be contained, I found, if I closed my eyes and tried to imagine an alternative explanation for the motion. After some minutes, however, the Stugeron guaranteed that such explanations began to involve mythical beasts rending my body asunder.

Dufferin's jocular comment on the famously heavy Atlantic swells churned around my cabin. 'They certainly didn't belie their character.' Come on, seas, spoil yourself. Belie your character. Listen to me!

I thought it might take a month; in fact it had taken three hours. A tiny part of me had begun to question Dufferin's impregnable character. For a man in the grip of shamingly profound seasickness, all that jaw-jutting, spray-in-the-face defiance was too much. I was facing my predicament with a disappointing lack of indefatigable chutzpah, and the desperate idea that Dufferin was in some way to blame by being too perfect was my only source of comfort.

Dealing with adversity brings out the best in some people, the hysterical, doom-laden coward in others. Hours after leaving Stornoway, the *Foam* is crashing about in the black liquid walls of water previously described. 'Guessing we were in for it,' writes Dufferin, 'I sent down the topmasts, stowed the boats on board, handed the foresail, rove the ridge-ropes and reefed all down.'

For the next week without let-up the storm rages. Dufferin is confined to his cabin with the relapse of an undescribed malady he'd had for months; Fitz is struck down with epic seasickness.

It was while bravely rereading this account in a bid to rationalise my own physical distress that I realised something that comforted and disturbed in equal proportions.

As a doctor, Fitz resolutely sets about using his sorry condition as a chance to 'observe the phenomena of seasickness from a scientific point of view'. He doses himself with a quite outrageous spectrum of remedies – 'brandy, prussic acid, opium, ginger, mutton-chops' – without success. On the third day, his spirit almost broken, Fitz attempts to draw consolation from Dufferin's valet, Wilson, who as a one-time steward on an Australian steam packet had great experience of such suffering. Dufferin eavesdrops:

> I heard Fitz's voice, now very weak, say in a tone of coaxing cheerfulness, 'Well, Wilson, I suppose this kind of thing does not last long?'
> (The Voice, as of the tomb): 'I don't know, sir.'
> Fitz: 'But you must have often seen passengers sick.'
> The Voice: 'Often, sir: *very* sick.'
> Fitz: 'Well; and on an average, how soon did they recover?'
> The Voice: 'Some of them didn't recover, sir.'
> Fitz: 'Well, but those that did?'
> The Voice: 'I know'd a clergyman and his wife as were ill all the voyage; five months, Sir.'
> Fitz: (Quite silent)
> The Voice: 'They some times *dies*, sir.'

What a brilliantly miserable bastard. I read on as Dufferin described Wilson in more detail.

> Of all the men I ever met he is the most desponding. Whatever is to be done, he is sure to see a lion in the

path. Life in his eyes is a perpetual filling of leaky buckets and a rolling of stones uphill. He brushes my clothes, lays the cloth, opens the champagne, with the air of one advancing to his execution. I have never seen him smile but once, when he came to report to me that a sea had nearly swept his colleague, the steward, overboard.

Now I saw it. Now the hideous truth revealed itself. Of course I am not Dufferin − charming, scholarly, fearless. But it was worse than that. *I am Wilson.*

The serial pessimism, the misanthropy, the schadenfreude . . . even, as I read on, the upbringing in West London. 'The son of a gardener at Chiswick . . .' I live in Chiswick. This is ridiculous. People had no right to even live in Chiswick in 1850. They should have all been living in Whitechapel and Bolton and Barsetshire. Not Chiswick.

The more I read of Wilson, the more I saw of myself. Birna has even developed a verbal shorthand to save me the bother of

High Latitudes   WILSON.

dampening any jolly plan with my perpetually filled leaky bucket of cold water. We were in Prague on a glorious autumn morning: the golden city burnished by a hazy golden sun, its people still in a state of skittish excitement after their recent Velvet Revolution. If nothing else should have cheered me up, a one-day travel pass was about 3p and you could stuff your face and get blind drunk for considerably less than a fiver.

As we walked out of our hotel, Birna outlined a planned excursion up to the Hradcany Castle. We had both been keen to appreciate not just its Renaissance splendour, but the sweeping panorama its lofty station afforded. Yet I would not be denied a sullen grumble. 'It's miles up a huge hill,' I whined. We'll take a taxi, compromised Birna. 'He'll rip us off.' We'll take the tram. 'It'll be full of those bloody Spanish tourists,' I countered. Not if we go there at siesta time, she pointed out. This went on for some time, me conjuring ever more absurd gambits, she gamely correcting them. We'll miss the last tram back. Everything will be closed for repairs. Our mineral water will run out and the shops will be closed and we'll drink from a tap and get poisoned like we did in Minsk. A massive statue of Stalin will come to life and run about stamping on tourists.

Eventually, I was spent. My stock of Wilsonisms was exhausted. I could prophesy no more doom, no matter how obscure. As we headed off towards the tram stop, I hoisted the strained plastic carrier bag that had served as a dutiful holdall for water bottles, guidebooks, sandwiches and bits of Berlin Wall for the last month. 'Well, all right, but this bag will break,' I mumbled, thereby providing the catch-all rejoinder to muttered remonstrations from that day on.

Wilson, Wilson. However distressing it was to have my own shortcomings mirrored back, I was strangely reassured. Some, like Dufferin, are leaders; others, like Wilson and I, prefer to slope along behind, moaning wearily. Just as I was conspicuously failing to 'Dufferin' – to experience adversity with detached jocularity – here was a kindred spirit whose miserable, self-pitying mean-spiritedness could only flatter me by comparison.

Sadly, I had to extrapolate wildly from the occasional brief mention of Wilson in *High Latitudes*. I could find out nothing else about him. 'The son of a gardener, he first took to horticulture; then emigrated as a settler to the Cape, where he acquired his present complexion, which is of a grass green; and finally served as a steward on board an Australian steam-packet.' Biographically, that was it. Oh, except that in the 'dramatis personae' at the start, his first name is revealed as William. And there was also Dufferin's etched portrait of him, showing a suitably dour-looking middle-aged man in a high, wingless collar, bearing a remarkable likeness to the former boxer and, um, 'controversial' tycoon, George Walker.

There was no Wilson in the index of the copy of *Helen's Tower* Lindy had lent me for the trip; no mention of him I could remember in the diaries. Wasn't there something in the notes I'd made when I went to Eton? Maybe. But I'd left them behind.

This window of rational contemplation soon blew shut as the boat's increasingly dramatic movements blotted out all other sensations. First there was the awful, rollercoaster anticipation as we mounted a wave, the engines shuddering with the effort until they almost stalled and the ship seemed about to slide backwards . . . then we topped the crest and swept down the other side at Stuka velocity.

Somehow I fell into drugged stasis for a further hour and a half, being awoken in the most distressing fashion when, after a real curtain swinger, the light bulb next to my bed exploded impressively. Now the structure and design of the ship was called into question as a series of alarming shakes, thuds and jerks reverberated from the hold. The best I could hope was that these were the death throes of mangled consumer durables colliding in their containers. I imagined a forlorn stevedore at Reykjavík docks picking through a mass of kiwi pulp, sodden platform trainers and the shattered remains of little oval spectacles. 'Contents may settle during transit,' the cereal-packet small print says, and this was where all that settling happened.

Time sloughed on reluctantly. At 18.00 my Funkerphone buzzed aggressively; I struggled to my feet to answer it and was greeted by an unwelcomely strident chef.

'Dinner is now! We have special Icelandic salted lamb!'

Hearing this message was one of the worst of the many bad things I had recently endured. I was reminded of the time my Aunt Bobby, laid out during an Atlantic crossing with mal-de-mer and morning sickness, ordered the most insipid foodstuff she could think of – a grapefruit. Ten minutes later the Portuguese steward appeared by her sickbed with a covered salver. 'Madam,' he announced, removing the lid with a cocky flourish, 'here is your goat foot.'

But driven by some ridiculous determination to save face, I set off. Progress was difficult: the exuberant motions of the boat made the staircase helix a helterskelter, more so since I'd been obliged to remove my footwear after overhearing a couple of earlier rumblings about 'shoe' and 'outlander'. Wearing shoes indoors is a pan-Scandinavian taboo, one which in a spirit of charity I will ascribe to the long and slushy winters rather than some indeterminate mania. The crew all had very unsailory shower-shoe flip-flop things which they slipped into as they came in from the deck; I, of course, had only socks, and as a result spent much of the next four days sliding in and out of shot slapstick-style in the pitching seas.

I accepted the whole dining enterprise was doomed when, skating wanly down the mess corridor, I saw that the view through the porthole alternated neatly between an angry grey sky and an angry black sea. In such conditions, I expected to find the crew huddled round the table, holding hands, clutching crucifixes and Björk albums. The captain would rise unsteadily, place one shaking hand on my shoulder and announce in a brave but quavering voice, 'It is for us to stay with the ship. But you, outlander, you must save yourself.'

Instead the cook, one foot blithely braced against the fridge and the other against a door, ladled out my soup (I waved away the special salted lamb) as a trio of vast, sloshing tureens on the stove heaved towards him.

He half pushed me towards the captain's table, where the CO glared at me haughtily. His skipper, though, gamely attempted to engage me in nonchalant small talk. If I may draw an analogy from the performing arts, it recalled the scene in *Carry On Up the Khyber* where Sid James, Joan Sims and the rest of the Viceregal court continue with tiffin as the palace is destroyed about them by the mutineers' artillery. (With a start I now realise that Sid James's character could, historically speaking, have been based on Viceroy Lord Dufferin.)

As he blathered on to me about something – football, footwear, foot spas, I don't know – I felt a strong urge to grab him by the ears and shout: 'Look – are you all blind? Look out there! Man the lifeboats! Mayday! Mayday! Blow into my pyjamas!'

It was enough. After momentarily contemplating the waves on my soup, I mumbled that I had to get past.

'Please-pardon?'

'I've . . . just got to go. Away.'

'You have to go?'

In desperation I began to shove the captain, not caring that this meant easing his stomach into his soup.

'Please – please let me out,' I croaked.

'You want to get out?'

'Look . . . get out of the way before I make your salted lamb a bit less special.'

'Are you well?'

Eventually I squeezed through and rushed out to a chorus of exhortations to come up to the bridge and tell stories. 'It will help you to get better!' But it was many hours before I was able to even consider moving from my sick bunk. I came, I saw, I chundered.

I was already cutting down the recommended eight-hour interval between Stugerons, and my final tab of the day clearly constituted a dangerous overdose. Within minutes I had lapsed into a slack-jawed twelve-hour coma (meaning I had now slept almost fifteen hours in the past twenty-four), during which I experienced the first of many vividly surreal Stugeron experiences.

I was in deep conversation with some sort of grease-painted vaudeville character, with white face, black tailcoat and a Cockneyish Bertie Wooster manner of speech. The crux of the debate was my attempt to convince him he ought to have more of a social conscience; at the dream's climax, he abruptly announced his conversion to this way of thinking by leaping to his feet and marching purposefully to the door, saying he was 'going to buy some scruffy feller a vase'.

This experience was particularly unsettling for me as I never, ever have interesting dreams. My average dream involves something like me waiting for hours at a bus shelter, and then someone who looks like a dinner lady from school walks past, but it isn't her. If I've had a really big lump of cheese or something, I might find twenty quid at the bus shelter.

So the fate of the scruffy feller's vase was still a concern as I eased myself upright. During the night (the last darkness I'd encounter for two months) the swell had calmed, and peeking through the porthole I noted that the galloping herds of white horses had devolved to an occasional dun-coloured Shetland pony. But as soon as I got up, of course, the curtains were swinging again, and my shower (taken during the ten-minute grace period) was reduced to a drunken, staggering shambles by the comedy double act of Mr Gravity and Master Momentum.

At 6.10 a.m., shoeless and soapy, I made my way up to the bridge. The CO was there alone, staring idly out at a panorama that I was immediately gratified to note depicted conditions of blatant extremity.

'Nice day for it,' he said without looking up from his newspaper. Knowing how reluctant all Icelanders are to concede that the weather is bad ('*This?* You call *this* a *blizzard*? You have much to learn about our weathers'), here was further confirmation that things were indeed unusually lively.

'Isn't it . . . quite bad?' I asked before being hurled backwards, arms wheeling, towards the chart table.

'Well . . . yes,' he said, after some deliberation. 'For the price in Iceland of a Plymouth Voyager year 1993 I can buy a new one in Holland. But then there is of course the import tax.'

At length he looked up from the classified ads. After a decent pause, I tried again. 'How big are the waves?' He looked impassively out of the bridge windows. 'About 5, maybe 6 metres. This is a Force 7. We had 8 yesterday.'

Force 8? That sounded enough for me. The CO said it had to get to 11 before anyone got worried, but right on cue a mayday call came in from the coastguard, delivered in a bland monotone that somehow made it scarier. 'Mayday. Mayday. Mayday. Beacon signal picked up by civil aircraft. Signal weak. Vessels in area please report their positions.'

Could we help? 'It is over 40 nautical miles,' the CO mumbled wearily. 'And to me, I would say this was the beacon being washed overboard.' He returned to his paper. I was quietly appalled, until (a) I realised the detour would mean several more hours of nausea; and (b) a later coastguard announcement proved him right.

We had coffee. I asked him about his sailing career.

'On my last boat, I travelled 500,000 kilometres under the flag of Iceland. It was very difficult to lower that flag. So now I only fly it at home.'

Registering ships in Limassol was something to do with cheap insurance, he said, and to open the possibility of running non-Icelandic crews, though this hadn't yet happened. As a nation with a perhaps unrivalled seafaring tradition — fishing still provides three-quarters of Iceland's wealth — this would have been a betrayal too far.

'So what happened to your old ship?'

'Oh,' he said with a bored shrug, 'It sank by the south coast of England last year.'

I really wished he hadn't said that, especially not in that blithe 'These things happen' kind of way.

'But it . . . it wasn't a container ship,' I said unsteadily.

'No, no. Aluminium carrier.'

Then, a minute later, 'But one container ship has sunk between the Faroes and Iceland in March. The CO on this boat dies falling off the bridge as the boat goes down, and another man coughs on oil in the sea and dies from this.'

He was on a Wilsonian roll now, and failed to pick up on the faint whimpers from my distress beacon.

'And this year one more container ship went aground in the south coast of Iceland. One of the rescuers died. If the weather improves perhaps we will see the wreck later. It is on the beach still,' he said brightly. 'Come – I will show you something.'

I followed him in pale silence to the chart table. 'Here – on these charts . . . Do you see these X-marks?' He ran his finger over the tight shoal of tiny crosses through which ran the pencil line of our current course. There were *thousands*. I had a feeling they weren't disused triangulation stations or the sites of famous mollusc battles. 'Yes – they are . . .' and here his face suddenly arced up into mine with a crazy-eyed Peter Cushing leer, 'shipwrecks! All of them!'

The problem was the whisky, I now saw clearly.

In accepting my bottled offering the day before, the skipper had mumbled the very vaguest of 'Oh you shouldn't have's, to which I'd responded with a loud and oily, 'Well, of course – I mean, *you're* the captain.' Exiting the Hobbyraum after this fawning speech, I'd found the CO and half the crew loitering in the corridor. One had given me a pursed-lip, head-jiggling look which clearly said, 'Oooh, *you're* the captain, oooh, lovely captain big-boat.' My interpretation of this one look spawned a vast and complex conspiracy, whose final scene was all too easy to construct.

'Well, well, who is it we have here, Ragnar? Seems to me it is perhaps the captain's little visky boy, yes? I say old chap, perhaps a little cap-night before the bed? That's a good little visky-boy. Let us give you a drink.' And as large, oily hands pressed me back into the chair and the neck of the brimming whisky bottle was forced towards my trembling mouth, I would spy the craven figure of the captain, guarded in a dim corner behind by two smut-faced, folded-arm stokers, his eyes wide, head half-shaking in silent, impotent apology.

What use would Dufferin have been if things had turned nasty?
I remembered being surprised by a journal entry I'd read at
Clandeboye, one of the last he'd written before setting off from
Oban: 'Men singing and noisy; Leverett's hand too light; brought
them to order myself.' This briefly cast him as a closet brayer, a
butler-beating bully, but it wasn't easy to sustain an image of him
as a man who knew how to take care of himself when things went
pear-shaped. The flouncy-shirted crayon picture marked him out
as something of a big earl's blouse.

But then of course he was a diplomat, a defuser, a charmer.
He'd probably brought the men to order with a jolly game of
consequences:

Mr Leverett and Mr Wyse
Shaving a walrus
Consequence: Reconciliation

Anyway, on this particular morning, the CO was especially jovial.
'We call the captain "Smiler", as he is, you understand, always jolly
with a smile. Most smilers have not much brain, but this is not
the case with him. He is very good at organising the containers,
keeping the crew happy – and he is a good seaman. You can't
have more.' The captain had clearly paid the ultimate price for
accepting my tarnished offering, and this was his epitaph.

So merry was the CO, indeed, that having shown me the basics
of navigation (it's unbelievably automated – you tap in some
waypoints and the satellite-linked autopilot steers you there) he
popped out to the loo and left me in sole command for three long
minutes.

Drained by this responsibility and the effects of yet another
premature Stugeron, I was soon back in my cabin enduring two
more hours of deranged imagery. This was ridiculous. It was like
hibernating, only without all the eating beforehand. Worse, time
– or at least distance – seemed to be standing still. When I awoke,
I went back up to the bridge to be told we were passing Aberdeen.
Aberdeen? After twenty-four hours? The CO said we were doing

9 knots, which as a bare single digit sounded appallingly lethargic, though of course I had no idea what it actually meant. Maybe rockets go 13 knots. I don't know.

But at least the swell had briefly abated, to the extent where I braved a meal in the mess, raggedly consuming as many bits of fried fish as I could shovel in during the two minutes I managed to stave off nausea. As well as Stugeron, I now had a second vomit-forestalling addiction – staring at the horizon. As I tore blindly at my haddock, I found the essential porthole vista obstructed by the considerable form of the second engineer's elderly wife. (What was she doing on board? I never found out.) Undeterred, I gazed through her, not caring that in doing so I attracted first her attention, then her pity, then her trembling fear.

With its unrivalled views of the horizon, the bridge became my regular haunt, it being the only other place besides lying flat out on my bunk where I had any success in keeping my nausea at sort of chest level, a permanent tightness across the ribs, as if I was physically stopping it descending to my stomach. The bridge's sole occupant in these first days seemed to be the CO, and perhaps because I felt my survival in an alien, terrifying environment depended on this thoughtful and considerate fellow, I noticed something strange starting to happen. I was falling in love with him.

Perhaps it was what psychologists call 'Stockholm Syndrome', after the hostages in a Swedish hijack who became absurdly grateful to and in awe of the men who held their life in their hands; perhaps it was guilt about the captain's whisky. Or maybe I just genuinely wanted to leave my wife and children and spend the rest of my life with a lovely big man.

With his almost immaculate English, the CO was the arche-typal descendant of the Latin-spouting farmhands encountered by Dufferin. The only English phrase I heard him mispronounce was 'summer solstice', which half the UK population would probably define as a cocktail. As we passed some geographical feature near John O'Groats he asked whether it wasn't named in Macbeth. Shamefaced, I replied that unless it was Mount Outdamnedspot, I really wouldn't know, whereupon he launched into an impressive burst of plausible soliloquy. Then he started on the sagas.

Such was the vacuum in which Iceland existed until this century, its language remains almost unchanged from that used by its tabard-wearing Viking forefathers. Children of ten can (and do) read the original saga texts, despite their frank (and, to be honest, flippant) coverage of mass murder and detailed individual acts of debauchery.

Given this, it was perhaps not so surprising that the CO quickly turned from the Burning of Njáll to the Valkyrian splendour of Margaret Thatcher. Loathe her or loathe her, one cannot deny the awe in which large swathes of Europe still hold Thatcher.

There was some excitement when he went on to express grave dissatisfaction with Iceland's president, elected almost a year ago to the day. Excitement, because this at last gave me a chance to reveal nonchalantly that the candidate who finished a very close third was, actually, in fact, none other than my mother-in-law.

It would have been easy for the CO to have responded to this with a series of vague hums and nods loosely implying admiration and commiseration at the unjustness of her treatment, but to his credit, not being English, he spurned this path. 'I did not vote for her,' was all he said. (In fact, my own enthusiasm for her victory had rather diminished when, during the election build-up, Birna pointed out that as the spouse of the head of state's eldest child, I would be Iceland's Princess Di. If Elton John had sung at my funeral, the natives would have commissioned him to write 'Goodbye England's Ponce'.)

The CO went back to the classifieds. Before Björk and twenty-four-hour clubbing, Iceland's international image was one of sou'westered fisherman's friends whose idea of extravagant decadence was to splash some cod liver oil in the bath. As with most stereotypes this was cobblers, but I'm sure the lingering memory of it partly accounts for the orgy of early-adopting, Plymouth-Voyager-buying consumerism in which Iceland has been embroiled for the last couple of decades.

Icelanders visiting Britain spend more per capita than any other nationals. Their country has the world's highest percentage of Internet users. Iceland had electric rotating billboards, photo cheque cards (despite a negligible crime rate), plastic-sheathed hay-bales (those Swiss-roll bin-liners) bendy buses and step aerobics years before I saw them in England.

It's a touching post-war, pre-cynical, 'new is good' futurism. Girls in Britain stopped dreaming of being air hostesses about the same time that boys stopped dreaming of Lesley Judd. When Icelandair advertised for a handful of cabin staff a couple of years ago, over a quarter of the nation's eligible female population applied.

On the one hand, Icelanders are obsessed with what outsiders think of them, elevating silly competitions like Miss World or the Strongest Man in the Universe into supreme judgements of international worth. Tumbleweed blows through the streets of Reykjavík for the three long hours of the Eurovision Song Contest.

On the other, the innocence is tinged with a rather aggressive one-upmanship. The incredible, retina-fusing festival of incandescence that is the New Year's Eve fireworks' display marks the apogee of this conspicuous consumption. In half an hour, enough krónur go up in smoke to build a healthcare centre or a 300-foot brass Viking or something (there's some telling comparison made each year by the tiny anti-firework lobby). It is a time when Icelanders get together to say: 'Look, world – we spend twenty bucks a head on damn-fool fizzers and whizzers, and you know why? Because we can! That's right! We've just got it, baby! Bang! Bang! Gone!'

Culturally, politically and, I'm afraid, racially, Icelanders are possessed of a boundless sense of fierce independence bordering on the arrogant. The original Icelanders were Norwegian nobles who preferred to sail off into the unknown rather than pay homage to a king they did not recognise or respect, and that insanely stubborn pride persists today. Nearly all Icelanders are direct descendants of those haughty nobs, and if you're unlucky some will pull out the documentation to prove it.

Partly as a result of its fishing policies, but mainly as a result of a determination that Icelanders never, ever, ever shall be slaves, they'll never in a billion years join the EU – the president (boo) has gone on record comparing the EU's policies to those of the Soviet Union. Iceland is left in the decaying rump of EFTA, the European Free Trade Association. Now that Britain, Austria and most of the other original members have left, this currently comprises Iceland, Norway, Switzerland and Liechtenstein, which makes it about as much of an association as the Beazer Homes League.

Every night – and at regular times during the day, it seems – the state TV channel broadcasts a thumpingly orchestral version of the national anthem, overlaying it with thundering seas, lava wildernesses and other images of their land's powerful majesty. And foreigners raising children in Iceland are now obliged by law to employ the patronymic naming system, whereby a child's surname is comprised of the father's first name appended by 'son' or 'dóttir' depending on the gender. This works out fine if your name is Richard or David or Mandel or whatever, but Timothyson lacks a certain something, and how could you not bully a Garysdóttir?

Of course much of this, as with the uncomprising defence of their language, results from a tiny nation's need to protect its identity in an ever shrinking world and so on. In this light, I was especially wary of mentioning the Cod War, the 1972 territorial fishing dispute between Britain and Iceland which we lost because our armed forces decided that taking out plucky Reykjavík coast-guard patrols with Polaris missiles might be misunderstood on the world stage.

Something of a joke in Britain, the Cod War is a very serious matter indeed in fish-dependent Iceland. It certainly wasn't a topic I'd be raising with the CO. He was clearly a deep patriot, whose recurring summer holiday involved dragging his wife on a 300-kilometre yomp across the glaciers, cliffs and freezing estuaries of his homeland's almost uninhabited northwest. Earlier, he'd delivered a brusque lecture when I suggested that Icelanders were a very proud people, so proud that perhaps they couldn't take a joke about themselves, that perhaps they found criticism difficult. 'If the facts are correct, there is not a problem. But many people do not write the correct facts.'

I'd cringed inwardly. My very first visit to the country had provided me with a lesson on the lengths Icelanders will go to in order to expose and denounce foreign ignorance and flippancy.

In 1988, my journalistic income was solely culled from a review of the week's television in the slowly dying *Record Mirror*. It was a tiny column, on a subject of at best peripheral interest to the dwindling number of club DJs who formed the magazine's core readership. As I was spending Christmas for the first time with Birna's family in Reykjavík, I pondered fancifully that my minuscule audience might appreciate a change from the fatuous critiques of easy-target minority-interest programmes on Channel 4 that they devoured so feverishly each week.

By compiling a review of Icelandic television, I could instead conduct a fatuous critique of an easy-target minority-interest national broadcasting network.

Over the course of three rollercoaster paragraphs they would cry with disbelief as I mercilessly savaged a broadcasting regime so brutally authoritarian that, until the mid-Eighties, it blacked out the nation's screens every Thursday and throughout June and July as a bulwark against decadence and commercialism. The tears of anger still hot and wet on their cheeks would quickly be joined by those of helpless mirth as I described the inexplicable national obsession with *Taggart* and the appalling Jim Davidson vehicle *Home James*, and lampooned the cack-handed amateurism of the biro-waving weathermen.

Two weeks after the review appeared, Birna received a large, Reykjavík-postmarked Jiffy bag. In it, along with a rather terse-looking note from her mother in Icelandic, was a copy of one of the country's biggest-selling daily papers. And within, filling a generous portion of page 3, was an article liberally sprinkled with three words I recognised at once. Not because my Icelandic was coming along nicely, but because the words were 'Record', 'Mirror' and 'Moore'.

Let us be clear about this. *Record Mirror* then sold about 15,000 copies in England, and was deemed such an irrelevance that within a year it would be closed down. It is unlikely that more than a few hundred were despatched abroad; of these perhaps twenty were destined for Scandinavia.

Yet some rogue Icelandic DJ with mysteriously strong journalistic connections had skipped through the accounts of the Manchester club scene and adverts for strobe lights, and homed in on a 200-word TV review tucked away near the back.

As Birna translated, the full horror slowly became clear. The headline ran along the lines of 'Cod-Thieving Foreign Bastard In Conspiracy To Undermine Icelandic Culture'. After patiently detailing the fifteen or so basic factual errors I had somehow contrived in my three paragraphs, the writer slowly worked himself up to the sort of indignant Doomsday paranoia associated with the more maverick Eurosceptics.

I was genuinely concerned when, six months later, I once more presented myself at Keflavík immigration control. Even today, the affair is never mentioned. Well, not to me, anyway. Thank Christ Birna's mother didn't win the presidential election. I wouldn't have been Princess Di. I would have been Mark Thatcher. Or Terry Major-Ball.

I thought I might have better luck debating the Cod War with the second mate, an earringed Pepsi Max youth. But memories are long in a land where most of the interesting history happened 1,000 years ago.

'I think you will find it is the only war your British Navy have lost. Do you know, if you move about the letters in "cod war", you can make a new word?'

It was clear I had made a mistake. But now it was too late.

'Yes – coward! Ha-huh-ha-ha! I was once in Ireland on vacation, in a pub, and when the barman discovered I had been an Icelandic coastguard, he gave me free drinks all the night for beating the English.'

Sounds eerily like when I go to France and get free drinks all the night for beating the Germans, I thought.

'But now we have new cod war – with Norway.'

I'd heard about this. An Icelandic trawler had been allegedly fishing without permission in disputed waters. The Norwegian Navy's heavy-handed response was to board the vessel, forcibly attach tow ropes and drag it 400 miles to a Norwegian port, refusing to release it without payment of some vast fine. A major diplomatic feud was brewing.

'But the Icelanders had a revenge – oh yes!' His voice was now slightly too loud. 'When they are on the dockside in Norway, they put down lines and start fishing, and every fish they get, they take a big pen and write "ICELAND" on the fish and throw it back in the sea alive!'

I didn't ask about the Cod War again.

I had become more or less resigned to the prospect of another three days of debilitating nausea, and so was somewhat confused the next morning when my porthole depicted a pair of mathematically perfect, constantly horizontal hemispheres, one azure, one aquamarine. Late the night before, as we passed through the Pentland Firth, the gloom had lifted to afford pleasing views of John O'Groats and his mate the Old Man of Hoy. The waves abated and a current pushed us up to the apparently almost terminal velocity of 20 knots. The wind had temporarily resumed its work back out in open water, but now the sea was eerily, utterly flat.

Having essentially fasted for thirty-six hours, I embarrassed myself at breakfast, eagerly devouring a shamelessly vast plate of foods that only brief hours ago would have been star performers in the circus of nausea inducement: pickled herring, thick porridge, pressed tongue.

Suddenly my whole sphere of existence expanded, and I set off happily to explore the ship. But its stupid layout – each of the seven tiny decks was almost identical – did not make this easy. After a trial run down to the Hobbyraum and back, I twisted up the unending spiral stairs to my cabin. The door was open. And there, reading a paper on a chair in my little entrance hall, was the old sailor whose large wife I had stared out in the mess.

Well, fine, I thought. No secrets among sailors and all that. We exchanged brief looks of slight alarm, when for some reason I decided that the best thing to do was to continue past him into my bathroom. This was a disappointing choice, because as I threw open the bathroom door I was presented with the striking image of his ample spouse lowering herself on to the lavatory. In maybe less than three seconds, I had reversed rapidly out of the bathroom, past the old man, up the stairs to my cabin on the next floor and into it, mumbling idiotic apologies all the way.

This rather curtailed my wanderlust, with the result that I didn't discover the ship's gym, complete with an exercise bicycle which I could have at least pretended to use, until about two hours after we docked at Reykjavík. But still, the reduced level of pitch and yaw improved my quality of life no end. I was able to sit happily at my desk and winch containers through the huge gaps in my laughably threadbare itinerary. I could bend over to put my shoes on.

I even felt well enough to resume my shy flirting with the CO. Adopting my now habitual seat opposite him – on 'our' table – I blurted, 'You're a really fast eater – I mean, I think you eat faster than anyone else I've ever . . . eaten . . . near.' If this carried on, I'd soon be blushing and saying 'Gosh!'

We sighted Iceland, in the form of the seemingly hovering form of the Myrdalsjökull Glacier, at 1.15 p.m. the next day. It was an arresting spectacle, as the Icelandic coastline invariably is. Pink on the horizon, white in the middle distance, brown from a mile and blue close up, glaciers are an endless source of awe. Dufferin's first sight was of Vatnajökull, Europe's largest glacier dominating the southeastern corner of the country, about whose 'pale aureolae' he got rather over-excited. It had taken the *Foam*, sailing into that awful gale, ten days; the *Dettifoss* required just four.

'So, there is Iceland,' said the second mate.

He'd been busy on the night shift for once, painstakingly composing the pixellated initials of his Icelandic football team, KR, on the radar monitor (the captain later affected outrage at this flippant and possibly hazardous act, before briefly attempting to add additional characters to form the name of his team, Akranes).

'You will of course be happy there tonight.' He sounded strangely bitter. 'You know they call Reykjavík "the Bangkok of the North"?'

Well, no. I'd heard a lot of – let's be honest – farcical media puff about Reykjavík being the new London. And let's be more honest, Birna and I had ourselves played cameo roles in this farce with an article we wrote for the *Evening Standard* on how (1) Damon from Blur going to Reykjavík twice to have it off and get drunk and (2) Scary Spice being engaged to an Icelandic bloke sufficed to constitute a phenomenon. But these things are as ephemeral as the media fad for such comparisons is idiotic, and as such the whole thing soon disappeared up its own arse. A week later I read: 'Stockholm is the new Reykjavík.' Nice, friendly place that it is, to describe Reykjavík as the new London is like describing Lego as the new sex.

'Bangkok?'

'Yes,' he continued sourly, 'the girls here like to go with foreign men. You can get laid for free in Reykjavík – as long as you don't speak Icelandic.' I pondered that this had certainly proven the case for me, although I would have been puzzled and rather disappointed had my wife presented me with a bill.

This was the poisoned harvest it was my just punishment to reap. I had, after all, helped create the myth of supercilious outlanders poncing across the North Atlantic for an easy shag. There also appeared to have been some sort of defining incident involving the second mate's best friend's girlfriend and a Canadian fellow.

Fortunately, just as I noted that the mattress of the bed I had made and was now being forced to lie in was a little firmer than I prefer, the first mate spotted a killer whale. Having managed a hurried snapshot of a fin and part of a large, smooth black-and-white flank disappearing into the water, I remarked how friendly it had been to come so close to our ship.

'It was not being friendly. There was something wrong. In fact, I think we maybe hit it.' As I imagined what would have happened if we'd been on a whale-watching cruise, two further amazements occurred. First, the incredible silhouettes of the Westmann Islands hoved into view. Then the sun came out.

In the low, clear evening rays, the islands cut into the horizon like broken-off bits of green-iced chocolate cake. Like everything about Iceland's landscape, there seemed a peculiar sharp freshness to their jagged outlines and smooth, grassed surfaces. Time has not softened Iceland's edges. The whole country is fresh out of the earth's core. Especially so in the Westmann Islands, all thirteen of which are estimated to be younger than 10,000 years of age. The area has seen two notable eruptions since the Sixties, the first creating the island of Surtsey; the second, in 1973, almost rendering the largest island, Heimæy, uninhabitable.

For five months the crater of Eldfell disgorged ash and lava (the ground is still hand-hot in many places), almost cutting off the town's livelihood, its harbour. As it was, the flow stopped just short, so providing much enhanced protection from the sea (at the price of making the passage of larger ships like ours dangerously awkward).

'They were very lucky,' I remarked to the CO as we watched the Heimæy harbour pilot leap from a speeding and wayward tug into a hatch just above the *Dettifoss*'s waterline, a manoeuvre I would guess carries about a 10 per cent chance of death.

'If you say losing half your town is lucky.'

'But no one died?'

'There was one death – a thief who went back to a house which had been left to the lava and was killed by breathing volcano gas,' he said with grim satisfaction.

With the background glaciers on the mainland now reflecting pink sun from their hazy peaks, the scene was almost too beautiful. I shot off a roll of film, partly in acknowledgement of the visual splendour, but mainly as a heartfelt tribute to the dimly recalled concept of dry land. Manoeuvring gingerly between a cliff full of sleeping puffins and the low, evil lava banks, we saw the docks lined with waving, fish-fed schoolboys, who'd descended on the Westmanns for a national schools' football tournament.

Their bright smiles and red cheeks; the neat, gay wooden houses with blue or red roofs and almost astroturf-green lawns; the happy little rowboats bobbing in our wake in the Bekonscot-perfect harbour . . . And yet something was wrong. Look ever so slightly up and to the left and there loomed the ominous black lava-field shards and garish, poisoned yellow-and-orange craters. It was an absurd juxtaposition, like *Camberwick Green* set on Uranus.

Negotiating the gangplank in unconvincing homage to a sailor keen for some R&R after a nine-month voyage around the Horn, I trod purposefully on to the rather ugly container quay, hoping to feel a portentous affinity with Lord Dufferin's words on reaching Reykjavík: 'We have landed in Thule!' But instead a shout from the deck chivvied me back on board. 'Please! Passport! Customs!' As a rare non-Icelander, and one arriving in such unorthodox fashion, I was summoned by two eager uniformed officials and made to fill in a landing card whose geriatric design lent it the air of a ration card. 'To be held in passport. Return when leaving Scandinavia.' I wasn't required to account for myself at any subsequent border, and the card still sits guiltily in my passport. The Icelandic immigration hit squads are probably roaming the glaciers to this day.

I downed the gangplank again with diminished portent, more of a Buzz Aldrin now than a Neil Armstrong, on to the deserted quay.

The local youths, I quickly saw, had far better things to do than wave at ships. Or rather one better thing, which was driving their parents' brand new Mitsubishis for hours on end up and down the main drag (which, in a town of 5,300, is more of a gentle tug). One other spin-off from the eruption was the provision of a vast supply of carriageway-quality ground lava, which the fish-rich islanders have eagerly used to build lovely new roads that go nowhere in order to buy lovely new cars they don't need.

Down they drove to the dead-end harbour, back through town, up to the dead-end crater, back through town. Not for the last time on the trip I was reminded of the computer game *Sim City*, and the obedient little cybercommuters who will drive 400 miles to a cul-de-sac in the desert as long as you build a road there. It all seemed rather mechanical and joyless. In Dufferin's time they would have been at a Latin-conjugating carnival.

The prosperity has provided this tiny island community with other modern conveniences, such as the world's most advanced cashpoint (the world being defined as all Barclays cashpoints in West London). Automatically recognising my card as British, it treated me to a dazzling colour image of a Union Jack, then, with further graphics of astounding resolution – an animated hand, a set of shiny whirring cogs enmeshed in an Escheresque helix – it triumphantly climaxed our interface by displaying: 'Unable to communicate with credit card company!' I particularly enjoyed the exclamation mark.

Suddenly worried that I might be left behind, I aborted a trip up to the crater and settled instead for the CO's recommendation, a jaunt up one of the steep hills facing the harbour. 'I go up to the TV antenna – it is maybe twenty minutes.'

In a belated attempt to push-start my cardiovascular training regime, I elected to run up the hill. When this caused me to terminate my assault in some distress with the TV mast still a distant, lofty needle, I remembered it would of course be sheer folly to neglect the second plank of my trans-Icelandic cycle preparation – the determined laying down of fat and calorie reserves. The chef had promised steak and chips before we set sail.

Limbs still trembling and booming lungs interestingly relocated in a kind of gill-like position just below the ears, I tottered down to the container docks through a rusting graveyard of British-built mobile cranes. The *Dettifoss* boys were still busy winching ashore empty reefers, shouting above the cranks and clanks and whirring fork-lifts, and the mess was empty. But there, lying in wait, was a splendid plate of steak and chips, complemented, I was charmed to find, by a welcome glass of red wine.

Savouring this feast ruminatively, I began to ponder in detail – for the first time – my post-*Dettifoss* travel plans. It was now 9 p.m., which suggested that we'd be docking at Reykjavík at some horrible dawn-type hour, especially unwelcome as Dilli, the youngest of Birna's four brothers and the one who'd been press-ganged into cycling with me across his homeland, had said we'd have to set off that same day.

One of the engineers came into the galley as I dropped my soiled crockery into the sink with a lusty belch. 'Ah yes . . . could I ask you what time we're docking at Reykjavík?'

'It is maybe 4 hours of the morning. Now I ask you a question.'

'Sure,' I said, heartily knocking back the dregs in my glass.

'Have you seen my dish of meat and some red wine?'

3

Everything was different when I woke up the next morning. There was stillness and silence; there was laser-bright sunshine. (Plenty of the former lay ahead, but I'd have appreciated the latter more had I known it would be the last I'd see of it for weeks.) We'd docked, obviously hours ago, and after roaming the *Marie Celeste* at length I eventually rediscovered my bike. Having laboriously liberated it from the CO's proud, firm knots, I wheeled it down the gangplank, celebrating my arrival in Iceland proper by spectacularly upending myself on the mercifully deserted quayside.

Pain fizzed up my right leg. I had twisted my ankle. I remounted, half hoping to feel a cataclysmic wrench as I undertook my first pedal revolution, a debilitating agony which would rule out my cycling trek. But there was almost nothing. I shrugged a farewell to the abandoned *Dettifoss*, and set off through the deep, cold shadows of stacked banks of containers.

'The town consists of a collection of wooden sheds, one storey high . . . built along the lava beach, and flanked at either end by a suburb of turf huts . . . no tree or bush relieves the dreariness of the landscape,' wrote Dufferin after landing in Reykjavík. It's an uncharacteristically frank appraisal of a shanty town that probably looked as much a mess as the blighted homesteads he'd visited during the Potato Famine.

Still, it must also have seemed a poor-but-honest haven from the choking squalor of the Industrial Revolution, a place where old money and noble birth had yet to be squeezed out by pushy commercial philistines. And a place which respected knowledge above all else, and continues to do so. More books per capita are read and written in Iceland than anywhere else on earth.

The blend of racial and cultural purity in a nation of poor-but-honest autodidacts was irresistible to Victorians, notwithstanding the Icelandic preference for the deep-potation school of relaxation (with the literary equivalent of an embarrassed cough, Dufferin's biographer Black glosses over the banquet incident, quickly pointing out that later in life Dufferin drank almost nothing).

Though he leaves the place before page 100, Iceland was clearly the book's focal point for Dufferin's fanbase. Extrapolating from his experience of mud-caked crofters emerging from turf-roofed huts to address him in Latin, Black notes that 'recent statistics show that *all* Icelandic children of ten can read, and peasants, besides being well versed in Icelandic literature, read foreign languages fluently . . . [they are] the most decent, innocent, pure-hearted people in the world'.

Dufferin and other first-generation eco-tourists – most obviously the fanatical cottage industrialist William Morris, who translated a couple of sagas and visited twice in the 1870s – were seeking in Iceland an antidote to the confusing filth, bustle and cynicism of the Railway Age, just as all the Germans and French snow-scootering across the Icelandic glaciers today have come to escape the smog and melanoma of their usual teeming Mediterranean holiday hangouts. Like them, but somehow less irritatingly, Dufferin had come to Iceland on a nostalgic, 'experiential' personal quest.

My own motivation for this particular leg of the journey was more basic. I've touched on the often (but not always) unspoken assumption that Icelandic Man is the embodiment of the human ideal. Physically imposing, he combines his pure-bred might with an intellectual sensitivity towards art and language – he is, in short, soft, strong and very, very long. It is clearly regrettable to see such a vintage bloodstock diluted by mutated gene-plonk from More Than One Country of the EEC, and it has on occasion been obvious that my sedentary lack of vigour, inadequate physique and fondness for lowbrow pursuits are all attributed to cross-bred genetic malfunction. When Birna's family and friends discovered she was pregnant by an outlander, there was a discreet but persistent socio-medical investigation that stopped just short of skull measurement.

For some years I'd been resigned to my fate as a sickly, feeble, cretin-spermed foreigner, conceding that nothing I would ever feasibly achieve could improve my standing. But now I was presented with a chance to silence the whispering campaign. Ever since I'd first announced I was planning to cycle across the unforgiving Icelandic interior, Birna's relatives had begun to appraise me in a new light. This would be a genuine feat, the making of a man of any creed or colour. If I could conquer the worst their unforgiving country could throw at me, I'd almost be an honorary Icelander. (But seeing as I'd obviously fail, they'd better send my kid brother-in-law along to drag me home.)

Despite being Britain's nearest Nordic neighbour, Iceland is the furthest outcrop of Europe, and Reykjavík the world's most northerly capital. And as a barren volcanic moonscape, it's barely changed since Lord Dufferin's day. The roads are still laughably inadequate, making many villages and towns inaccessible without four-wheel drive. A microscopic population density means you can drive for hours without seeing anything more animate than the lichen streaked on a scree slope. Drive for hours . . . cycle for days.

But Reykjavík is an exception. Few European capitals can have grown and changed to such an extent in such a short space of time. In the 1801 census, its population was just 307; a year before Dufferin's visit it was 1,354. Now it's 110,000, very nearly half the country's population.

Dufferin occupied his few days in town buying ponies, speaking Latin and being introduced to local society by Sigurður. With the young lawyer as interpreter he flirts with an eighteen-year-old local lass and visits Bessastaðir, described by him as 'inexpressibly desolate . . . an old-fashioned farmhouse' and which is now the presidential residence (boo).

In most houses the bare blocks of lava, pointed with moss, are left in their natural ruggedness [he'd have made a great estate agent]. Instead of wood, the rafters are made of the ribs of whales. The same room but too often serves as the dining, sitting and sleeping place for the whole family; a hole in the roof is the only chimney, and a horse's skull the most luxurious *fauteuil* into which it is possible for them to induct a stranger . . . the beds are merely boxes filled with feathers and sea-weed.

Horses' skulls as chairs? Are you sure? But if that's improbable, it's soon forgotten by the far taller story of the notorious Governor's banquet.

Dufferin, Fitz and Sigurður arrive at Government House at 3.30, to be greeted by the Governor, the Bishop, the Chief Justice '&c &c, some of them in uniform, and all of them with holiday faces'. Over the next eight hours, each guest is apparently required to consume over ten bottles of wine; despite this, Dufferin is able to round off the event with an endless oration in Latin.

There followed a great chinking of glasses – a Babel of conversation – a kind of dance round the table – a hearty embrace from the Governor – and finally – silence, daylight and fresh air as we stumbled forth into the street. To go to bed was impossible. It was eleven o'clock by our watches, and as bright as noon. There were neither knockers to steal nor watchmen to bonnet. What was to be done?

Not much, really. They somehow persuade an apothecary's wife (a despicable euphemism if ever I heard one) to let them into her house, pinch her knockers and dance reels around her parlour in the company of a number of French officers from Prince Napoleon's steamer *Reine Hortense*, which had docked a couple of days after Dufferin. Then the *Foam* contingent sail out in a dinghy, run aground on an island in the harbour and blunder about mistaking puffins for rabbits. Incredibly, within hours they're off on their trans-Icelandic pony trek.

The sliproad segued into an enormous freeway flanked by squat Seventies blocks and slightly messy trading estates. Inevitably, in the midst of what distressed Icelandic ruralites refer to as the 'concrete lava fields', I got lost.

I'm going to get in trouble for saying this, but Reykjavík is not lovely. Yes, the old centre, with its cheery duck pond and Victorian verandahs, is trim and cosy (though the current mayor has managed to spoil even that with a hideous Nissen hut town hall). But a hundred yards in any direction and you're in an off-the-peg Legoland suburb, traipsing forlornly through colourful but soulless tenements or having your holiday face blown off in a wind-tunnel underpass.

And it's so *big*. From the size and number of the featureless, multi-lane thoroughfares and gyratory systems, you'd imagine you were entering the outskirts of Chicago, not a place whose population is dwarfed by that of Norwich. (Another handy glib statistic is that Ealing has more residents than Iceland.)

Standing on Birna's parents' balcony at the far eastern edge of town, you see Reykjavík sprawling into an infinity of suburbs and dockyards, like some sort of Nordic São Paolo. Walking from one side of town to the other would take a good four hours, and here I was, lost in a place where over the years I've spent perhaps six months.

All this makes Reykjavík's perceived status as a popstar's playground all the more confusing. I can without qualification recommend Iceland as a holiday venue for those in search of unsullied wilderness, the humbling might of nature and so forth. And yes, despite its treeless, wind-blasted featurelessness, the warmth of the people does give Reykjavík a villagey communality. The patronymic system means the phone book lists people by their first names, like a primary school register, which always cheers me. Children play alone in the streets at midnight without a care; if you go out with an Icelander they'll meet and greet about seven people they know every hundred yards (which would personally drive me spare, but still). And whenever an Icelandair flight lands in Keflavík the stewardess says 'Velkomin heim', which I shouldn't have to say means 'Welcome home'.

I suppose all this interdependent chumminess is probably essential if you've been cooped up together for a millennium. Certainly it was the same in Dufferin's day. As well as being devout, pure-hearted and so on, he finds the Icelanders almost embarrassingly hospitable, lavishing coffee and rusks upon him whenever he slows down in the street.

But international party assets don't care about cheery waves and homely banter in the queue at the foot spa repair shop. All they want is an exciting new stage on which to parade their vibrant decadence, and on this basis they will not feel at home in Reykjavík. I'm sorry. It's too parochial, and too bloody windy. Yes, the people are slender and tall and beautiful, but they wear stupid shoes and glasses. And the beer is a fiver a pint. Drugs would appear to be surprisingly plentiful, but if you bliss out in a park you'll die of cold by mistake. Norwich might have fewer nightclubs, but in terms of their cutting-edge trendiness it would be a close-run thing.

That said, as spectator rather than participant, a Friday night out in Reykjavík is essential entertainment, in the usual watching-underage-kids-get-drunk-and-fight sort of way. Whatever the season, whatever the weather, they're all there, thousands of them, drinking homebrew from Coke bottles, not wearing nearly enough clothes, shouting 'Ferck you' in high-pitched voices, splashing through puke in their platform trainers. It doesn't start until midnight and doesn't end until four. But, you know, change the homebrew to Diamond White, the kick-off time to 8 p.m. and lose the platform off trainers and you could be in Rotherham, or – as I was to discover – any other town in Scandinavia.

Nordic drinking etiquette is a worry to outsiders. To a Scandinavian, drink is a collective noun with a mean value of eight. Suggest going for a drink on a Wednesday night and people will hum and ha and explain that they'd love to, but they've got to work on Thursday. There's little social drinking, but plenty of antisocial drinking. People abstain all week, then down enough on Friday to ensure their Saturday morning bed-guests are two black eyes, a set of traffic lights and at least one person of the opposite sex. (I was going to say 'not necessarily of the opposite sex', but, at variance with the image of tolerant Scandinavians, Icelanders adopt a highly 'traditional' stance to life choices such as vegetarianism and homosexuality.) Dufferin's experience suggests that the deep potation has been a way of life in Iceland for well over a century. Why? Opinion is divided into two schools of thought:

(1) Work Hard/Play Hard: Most Icelanders hold down two jobs; I read somewhere that, as a teenager, Björk worked simultaneously in a fish factory, a record shop and an underground squeaking club. This theory is backed up by the incredible leisure facilities in Reykjavík: two full-time theatre companies, an opera house, a concert hall, six multi-screen cinemas, two covered shopping malls, a dozen museums and galleries, half a dozen swimming pools.

(2) Viking Berserker Mad Bastards: This theory is backed up by a survey which found that 53 per cent of Icelanders believe in elves.

In the end it took me an hour and a bit to pedal the 8 kilometres (including stupidity detour) to my in-laws' place. Their large suburban home presented a reassuring but not especially intrepid goal. 'We have landed in Thule!' has derring-do; 'I have bicycled to Birna's parents' house!' has derring-don't. No one was in but Dilli, my guide, pacemaker and paramedic for the cycling leg of the trip.

'All right?' he mumbled as he let me in. 'Good, you know, journey?'

Dilli and I always seem to converse in the manner of self-conscious teenagers.

'Yeah, well, sort of a nightmare at first, but then kind of a bit better. Look – I got some beer.'

The origins of Dilli's name lie in a birthmark on his stomach – it really does mean 'Spotty', which should be enough to consign anyone to a more than usually trying adolescence, as well as low self-esteem and chronic career underachievement in later life. His real name, obviously, is Kristján, but just in case he entertains any fantasies of wanting to be called that, we also gave the name to our eldest son.

Anyway, overcoming this handicap, old Spotty had just finished his medical finals and was about to start as a hospital house doctor. Speechlessly grateful for his offer to accompany me, I realised I'd be in admirable hands if, or rather when, my saddle-battered bottom burst. We were well set: he was Dr Fitz and Sigurður; I was Wilson. Now all we needed was a Dufferin.

Despite Dilli's undoubted medical savvy, I don't think it is too insulting to suggest that in most other ways his capacity for practical thought is barely less retarded than my own. I recall with particular fondness the shopping list he once gave me as he and two friends prepared to supply themselves for the three days of the Reading Festival. The second and third items on the succinct list were 'gin' and 'crisps'; the first and last were both 'Fanta'.

Of no less concern was our shared ignorance of the art of bicycle maintenance. I'd been splendidly well advised by the bike shop on what components would be most at risk on the lava ruts of the Icelandic interior, but neither Dilli nor I had the slightest idea how to use the great jangling sack of tools they'd provided to affix the great jangling sack of spare parts. Dilli thought the spoke key was a chain-link cutter. I thought the chain-link cutter was a bottle opener. Rather than problem-solvers, we were problem-makers.

Birna had already dubbed our expedition *Beavis and Butt-head Do Iceland*, and our shambolic preparation lent a further Laurel and Hardy gloss to the proceedings. I had a sudden image of us crossing Iceland not on bikes but one of those push-me-pull-you railway trolleys, dressed only in barrels suspended by ropes over our shoulders.

In one day, and presumably with an epic hangover, Dufferin had contrived to organise a cavalcade of eighteen horses, each loaded with 140 pounds of equipment and provisions: '. . . at last everything was pretty well arranged – guns, powder, shot, tea-kettles, rice, tents, beds, portable soups & c'. Not to mention running around Reykjavík exchanging farewell souvenirs with the notables – a drawing of a dead soldier in the Crimea for the Governor ('Oh, you *shouldn't* have'); an Arctic fox from the French Consul. In the same time, Dilli and I managed to buy five packets of dried fruit, two bars of chocolate and a pair of cycling shorts. And we ate the chocolate outside the shop.

So, at 8.30 p.m., with the morning's glorious sun having naturally given way to a steady drab drizzle, we stuffed everything into our panniers in a blithely hopeless way, and wobbled away from suburbia. Birna's parents saw us off, their expressions reflecting encouragement, sympathy and amusement in roughly the proportions Eddie 'The Eagle' Edwards would expect as he pushes off at the top of the ski jump. 'Enjoy to endure!' shouted my father-in-law Helgi.

There was a lot of outstanding work to be done on the first half of this aphorism by the time we arrived at Thingvellir in dull – but certainly not dark – dampness at 12.30 a.m. I'd cycled unburdened from the *Dettifoss* – my belongings being picked up later by car – and now, with everything piled on, it was immediately obvious that our mounts were ludicrously overloaded. With my shiny Karrimor panniers front and rear additionally burdened with a sleeping bag and a tent respectively, it felt like cycling to market with a fair-sized piglet on the handlebars and its prize-winning father on the back mudguard. Manoeuvring had to be undertaken in oil-tanker fashion – a U-turn could not safely be achieved with fewer than five points – as any attempt to redirect the handlebars by more than about 2 degrees resulted in the bicycle's centre of gravity shifting to a point somewhere in Malaysia, sending you into an unstoppable collapse. Following such incidents, I also noted that I could not lift the bike unaided.

My concentration was also being hampered by a nagging doubt, a conviction that I had forgotten something important. At length I realised what it was: I had forgotten to do any preparation. Every time I glanced down at the multifunction LCD odometer on the handlebars, I was confronted by guilty digits reflecting the extent of my pre-departure fitness training and bicycle awareness scheme. As we wound towards route 1, the ring road, it read 1:15 (hours); 20.2 (kilometres). Of these, 8 kilometres had been clocked up en route from the *Dettifoss* to the in-laws. The rest had involved cycling to Richmond and back twice and going to Ealing to pick the hire car up.

As a result, Dilli's thoughtfully planned scheme to break me in gently (he, a decade younger and a millennium fitter, was at this stage sublimely untroubled) had after less than an hour been amended to replace 'gently' with 'half'. We had planned to reach our first day's target, Thingvellir, less than 50 kilometres away, in maybe slightly over two hours; it was now clear it would take double that. (The original plan had been to go over twice as far – to Geysir, where Dufferin turned back – on the first evening, a journey which eventually occupied us for two and a half days.)

But whatever happened, it could only get progressively worse. Dilli had to be back to start work at the hospital on Sunday; it was now Tuesday, or in fact almost Wednesday, and there was nearly 300 kilometres to go. Neither of us was honest or brave enough to point out the abject hopelessness of this itinerary – the sort of deluded and desperate folly, I was now thinking, that did for Scott and Oates.

I tried to focus instead on my surroundings, which was not easy in the persistent, claustrophobic mist. Intending to describe the fickleness of the climate, the CO had told me, 'We have no weather in Iceland, only examples.' If so, this was setting a very bad example. 'It's not actually raining,' shouted Dilli in a futile attempt to unflag my spirits. 'We're just wet because we're in a cloud.'

As a result, I couldn't see a thing – not the glorious majesty described at length by Dufferin as he approached Thingvellir, not Dilli's rapidly disappearing rear wheel, not even the farmer helpfully trying to rub the mud off the side of my helmet with his overtaking tractor's rear tyres.

Perhaps this is the time to explain that Icelandic driving patterns are affected by a series of compulsory government studies. The longest-running of these is research into the effects of centrifugal force at roundabouts: those drivers able to provide the exceptional data associated with heavy acceleration throughout approach, entry, rotation and exit are, as a mark of civic respect, permitted to remove the indicator stalks from their steering columns. Other eagerly adopted trials cover varying designs of take-off ramps (or, as we know them, speed bumps) and a national pilot scheme to deduce the precise angle which maximises the useful area that may be occupied by one vehicle in a supermarket car park. Model performers in all experiments compete for the ultimate accolade – a chance to cruise Iceland's ring road in a large pick-up truck, aiming its specially extended wingmirrors at the elbows of foreign cyclists.

Birna's brother Aggi – which ought to be a cruel nickname meaning Smelly or Fatso, but is actually a harmless diminution of Agnar (meaning Fat-Bottomed Lady-Boy) – is an anthropologist, and never short of a theory about a nation's behavioural traits. His theory on Icelandic driving is that it is an expression of independence. Having for centuries been under the colonial yoke of first Norway and then Denmark, a particular aggravation for such a proud people, they now eagerly grab any opportunity to assert their free will. To indicate is to surrender to an authoritarian diktat to keep others informed of your movements. *I* know where I'm going, thinks the Icelandic driver as he scythes in front of you, but what's it to *you*, Stalin? Then you both slide into a fjord.

It's the same with other public safety pronouncements. I've seen bobble-hatted toddlers strafe their cowering grandparents with improvised sparkler bazookas; returning to lit fireworks is a widely enjoyed New Year's Eve tradition.

But, that aside, part of the special antipathy towards one-wheel-drive vehicles is that the majority of their riders are Germans. This oughtn't to be quite enough to damn them so, but the truism in Iceland – which I saw little evidence to dispel – is that German tourists like to take their holidays seriously. Going to Iceland means going on a wilderness endurance and self-sufficiency test, so they come prepared with all their own food, clothing, lavatory paper, kontroll panels, and so on. Off-road vehicles even bring their own petrol, strapped to the roof in jerry cans. This has the net effect of bringing no wealth into the country whatsoever, thereby embedding a deep-seated national grievance.

The CO on the *Dettifoss* had told me a story about some German campers who asked one of his farming friends if they could dry their boots in his outhouse. He agreed, but when he returned they had also hung up their damp bedding. The point of this isn't the story itself – such was its innocuousness I kept waiting for the punchline, that they'd then crapped in the milk churns or gelded the bull with a tent-peg mallet or whatever – but the vehemence with which the normally mild-mannered CO told it. As he said 'wet sleeping sacks', his face twisted into the spiteful grimace Mexican bandits normally produce shortly before spitting on to the cantina floor.

Because this was an Icelandic summer, things brightened up slightly as the night wore on. Occasionally through the thinning cumulonimbus I could make out the smudged silhouette of a farmer rounding up animals, children playing, workmen asphalting a pavement. None of this activity seemed odd, until I accidentally punched my multifunction odometer while narrowly avoiding a sheep and caused it to flash up the time: 11.02 p.m.

The permanent daylight of an Icelandic summer does strange things. On my three previous summer visits I've found myself staying up until 3 a.m. and getting by on five hours sleep. Conversely, in winter, where the three hours of desultory dawn between around 11 a.m. and 2 p.m. bridge twenty-one hours of total blackness, I essentially hibernate: going to bed at 10 p.m. and waking up, still tired, thirteen hours later. But it was odd to think that even the locals obviously did the same.

There are advantages to this ridiculous situation. During my trip, I was able to – or more usually, obliged to, given an inability to get organised before midday – ignore usual travelling hours, leaving in the afternoon and arriving at 1 a.m. The usual twenty-four hours could be shifted around at will. This was especially so on the *Dettifoss* – the crewmembers taking shifts on the bridge were expected to grab a couple of hours sleep at any time, which may explain why they thought it acceptable to burst into my cabin at 2 a.m. to tell me to come and look at a particularly gnarled bit of driftwood they'd spotted in their binoculars.

But I never quite got accustomed to this disjointed pattern. During the nights we spent in the tent I would wake repeatedly in the constant light, and seek to reacclimatise myself by looking at my watch. 'Oh, it's all right, it's 4.10 a.m.' 'Oh, it's all right, it's 4.20 a.m.' 'Oh, it's . . . oh. It's lunchtime.'

Midnight approached. I began to drop back. On the rare occasions that I stayed close enough to Dilli's wheel to maintain breathless verbal contact (and to have my face Jackson Pollocked by the muddy spray from his rear wheel), we devised a morale-boosting game that neatly exploited the few objects visible in our cloud. As most people will have remarked, it is impossible to move slowly past a herd of cows or sheep without eventually succumbing to the irresistible urge to submit the animals to an inane Old Macdonald interpretation of their call. This we began to do, but after one loud bleat triggered off a full-scale ovine withdrawal, exciting possibilities suddenly suggested themselves. The quality of impersonation forgotten, we now competed to elicit stampedes by the miracle of the shriek. One point for an unimpressed single sheep slowly reversing into the misty tussocks; ten for a domino-effect multi-species hoof-over-udder retreat.

When our already overworked lungs began to boycott this pastime, we started taking regular stops 'to plot our progress'. This we agreed to do every 10 kilometres, which is to say every 8 kilometres, then every 6 kilometres. I was now becoming critically weak, a condition my physiology heralded by presenting my subconscious with Stugeron-flashback images of huge plates of fat chips.

Learning from Dilli that, after almost three hours, we were approaching the Thingvellir Plain, I dimly supposed that it would have been about here that Dufferin briefly lost half his party.

They'd set off from Reykjavík at midday, with the thermometer reading an improbably tropical 81 degrees Fahrenheit. The plan was to ride out to Geysir and return, a two-day trip each way, before resupplying and setting off across the interior to meet up with the *Foam* on the north coast. In consequence most of the crew stayed on board in Reykjavík; they would set sail when their lord returned from Geysir.

The procession clattered through the wooden streets gingerly. Dufferin was amazed to find that those of his urban-bred crew who were to accompany them on this excursion had little riding experience. Wilson gravely informed his master that the cook, who had never once sat on a horse, was so petrified that 'I fear very much he will die of the ride.'

But despite this dramatic prediction, it is not the cook who brings up the rear of the eighteen-strong party. The night before Wilson, drunk I imagine, had slept on deck on top of a chicken coop and awoken with a crick in his neck, his face 'immovably fixed over his left shoulder'. Now, riding a distance behind the rest, 'plunged in profound melancholy', he wore 'by way of protection, I suppose, a huge sealskin helmet, seaman's trousers, a bright scarlet jersey and jackboots fringed with cat-skin'. Oh, what a hopeless buffoon, we all titter. But then: 'He proceeded along in his usual state of chronic consternation, with my rifle slung at his back and a couple of telescopes slung over his shoulder.'

Despite my empathy with Wilson, I had up until then felt only pity for Dufferin as he struggled to jolly along the often demoralised crew in the face of his valet's miserable prognostications. But now, for the first time, I questioned Dufferin's Wilson-baiting. The poor guy's more or less sitting backwards on a horse because his neck's gone, and you make him carry your rifle and 'a couple of telescopes'. Fine, decide you simply have to take loads of telescopes, and fine, you're the boss, make your crippled valet lug them about if you must. But don't then have a good old laugh at him for looking stupid because he's carrying them.

I supposed Dufferin's famed paternalism meant that even while poking fun at his staff, he would also be paying them over the odds, but looking at Wilson's spartan presentation in Dufferin's etching, that might not have been such a comfort. It had been easy to imagine Wilson, at least nominally a Scotsman, sharing my 'careful' lifestyle. Indeed it was difficult to see where whatever money Dufferin paid him went, though the hen-coop incident encouraged a suspicion that porter and grog accounted for most. The puffy, dour man that gazed flatly across page 34 of *High Latitudes* looked the product of lost evenings of solo debauchery; his was a pub face. But Dufferin's occasional ribbing could not alone have stripped him of mirth and joy. Most of the cracks in that face were old and deep, and picturing it again I suddenly knew everything about William Wilson's pre-Dufferin history. The truth, I now decided, was a tragedy of thwarted achievement and spurned affection, of bitter blows and last straws.

1815: Born in Chiswick. His father, a gardener, dampens the exuberant William with a daily mantra. 'The heavy rains come, and strike off the young buds,' he hisses every evening, 'and then comes the sun, to wither the leaves. Fear the rain, my boy, and fear the sun, also.' 'And seek solace only in drink,' mutters his crippled mother, a retired wet nurse.

1826: William wins a scholarship to Middlesex County School. Running gaily home, he composes a poem with which to impart the news to his parents, but gets no further than 'apprentice to the wise Minerva' before his mother, cackling bitterly into a mug of gin, chokes to death on her own phlegm. He is forthwith enrolled by his father as a gardener's boy at Chiswick House.

1832: A natural horticulturist, William creates a hybrid tulip of astonishing beauty, rewarded with a beating from his father for 'meddling in God's work'. Only when he falls hopelessly in love with the mistress of his master's kitchens does he vow to make his discovery public, planting a display bed with his new bulbs to read 'I WORSHIP THE DUKE'S COOK'. But two bulbs in the penultimate letter fail to germinate; the O becomes a C; there is an investigation; William emigrates to the Cape.

1840: A hero amongst the tribesmen of the veldt after his sensitive teachings bring sustainable farming and the end of generations of famine and suffering, Wilson takes a sabbatical, emerging after two years with a blueprint for a revolutionary power-sharing structure that his covert enquiries tell him will prove satisfactory for Boer, Briton and Zulu alike. The Cape's leading intellectuals assemble at his model farm near Durban for the first public reading of his proposed constitution, but as he clears his throat a phalanx of whooping natives rush through the orchard. Their celebrations are misinterpreted, new and old racial wounds are opened and the fledgling nation is plunged into a century and a half of war and oppression. Wilson, found guilty of sedition, is deported to Australia and his unread constitution publicly burned.

1848: During five years as a steam-packet steward, Wilson's groundbreaking compendium of opening chess gambits is eaten by an albatross; his prototype internal combustion engine, stowed on deck, is melted by ball lightning; a shadowy passenger with a goatee makes off with Wilson's manuscript of *David Caperfield*. Despite these setbacks, he finds happiness again with an infirm widow sailing in first class. She abruptly proposes marriage; the captain performs the ceremony. Rejuvenated with love and champagne, that night his new wife challenges him to a race along the top-deck handrail. He attempts to stop her; the captain appears as she slips into the sea and is lost. A distraught Wilson tries to explain the situation, but after the size of her fortune comes to light he is placed under arrest and locked in his cabin. When the ship docks at Perth, the cabin is empty, the porthole open. It is presumed that Wilson has done the decent thing.

1851: After a two-year lost weekend, a filthy and drunken Wilson is found retching in a gutter behind the House of Lords. In a typically philanthropic gesture, Lord Dufferin stops to help; within half an hour he has offered Wilson a position. 'Thanking you, my Lordship,' he groans, 'but could you promise me one thing?' Dufferin smiles kindly. 'Could you promise me so as I'll never have to work on no ships ever more?'

But Wilson is not a character it is easy to sustain sympathy for. When Dufferin, Fitz, Sigurður and Wilson separated from the others and failed to meet up at their agreed camp location, Wilson's eager hypothesis was that the cook had met his predicted end – the delay was the result of his colleagues stopping to bury him by the roadside. As the wet tarmac before me faded in and out of focus, it was an uncomfortable parallel.

Some time later, I really couldn't say how long, we reached the dim edge of Lake Thingvellir, which in my calorie-starved, cramp-ravaged condition looked to me like the sea, complete with jagged islands and cliffs running down to it. I became briefly but vividly convinced that Dilli had made a navigational error of the crassest stupidity, until he gently brought me round with reason and dried apricots. The 47.3 kilometres had almost ruined me, and I did my best to cast away the chilling realisation that there was almost no tarmac left, and that we would soon need to average almost 100 kilometres between stopovers or freeze to death in a glaciated desert. That would mean twelve hours' cycling a day. On that first day we had pushed the bikes up hills when the speedo dropped to 9 kilometres an hour. The next day we'd be lucky to hit 6 on the flat.

Two incompetents pitching a tent in the rain is never going to be a brief or noiseless procedure. The light made us forget that it was 1.00 a.m., until incoherent protests to this effect issuing from a neighbouring tent reminded us that all the prim nylon peaks around us contained people, or at least campers. These protests grew as I failed to disrobe in appropriate silence within our tiny, sagging dome.

I had initially been concerned that my all-in-one Karrimor cycling undergarment – a black skin-tight Lycra bib with integral leggings – might make it look as if I knew what I was doing. Prostrate and arch-backed in the tent trying to peel it down below my pelvis I saw this was indeed true, but only in so far as knowing what I was doing if I had been in a beach hut with a like-minded party of sado-masochistic Edwardian bathers. Roadside relief stops were to prove memorable – city street or arctic desert, the only way to guarantee a modicum of hygiene was to take almost all my clothes off.

This situation also helped me to reason to postpone showering, a decision assisted by the discovery that there were no showers.

Nor even hot water, which is surprising when it's essentially free in Iceland. The land's geological youth means an abundance of super-heated geothermal springs close to the surface. The near-boiling product is sent around Reykjavík in pipes, so that houses have hot running water, often routing it under the drive to melt the ice in winter. One of the municipal swimming pools gets through 1.3 million tons a day.

But it has to be said that this water has a distinctive odour, which one may categorise as invigoratingly elemental if one works for the Icelandic tourist board, or as horrid eggy-smelly smell-smell if one doesn't.

One's first Icelandic shower invites a terror that the sewers have blown back, and it takes some time to come to terms with bathing in a fluid that blackens your jewellery. On the other hand, I reflected as I flopped like an effigy on to my sleeping bag, it does mean that you can fart with impunity while doing the washing-up.

Still sour and damp, we were awoken rather earlier than hoped by a slap on our collapsed awning. The campsite caretaker had come to demand payment, antagonising Dilli by assuming we were German and me by assuming that we were on honeymoon. It was still rather fetid, but with the clouds now at least back above us I could at last appreciate some of the awesome scenic might that had so inspired Dufferin. 'I could scarcely speak for pleasure and surprise; Fitz was equally taken aback, and as for Wilson, he looked as if he thought we had arrived at the end of the world.'

Just up behind our campsite was the terrifying Almannagjá, 'everyman's chasm', a savage, shredded tear in the lava field which screams silently through the plain for miles. Treading gingerly over little rips in the ground which disappeared into distant blackness, we almost fell into the utterly sheer 150-foot gorge. Even from 3 yards it's impossible to detect, so perfectly aligned is the ground on the other side, sometimes 20 feet away, sometimes 100. Here, if anywhere, was the country's navel, the tectonic wound separating European Iceland from American Iceland.

The sharp freshness of the jagged outlines lends the impression that the unimaginably disruptions that tore the land asunder only occurred a couple of years ago. (In fact, just seventy years before Dufferin's visit a vast earthquake had dropped the entire plain by a metre.) This illusion is partly down to the wind and climate reducing the softening effects of vegetation, and partly down to the landscape's youth – in a geological time-scale, Iceland didn't exist this morning.

What heightened the senses was the complete absence of warning signs, fences or barriers. In Iceland, a healthy respect for the nation's geological and climactic extremes is taken for granted. If they went around trying to signpost every danger the nation would be bankrupted. 'Warning – enormous hidden hole in ground', 'Danger – no shops or petrol or any living thing for miles and miles – oh yeah, and you just fell into a geyser'. That's what Iceland is about – confronting the elements, and man's puniness beside them. Don't look where you're going in the English countryside and you tread in a cowpat; here you disappear into a glacial crevasse. Get lost in the English countryside and you miss last orders: here you freeze to death up an unknown mountain and have the trolls pick at your bleached bones for a millennium until an earthquake affords you a proper burial.

Almannagjá rendered Dufferin for once speechless, or anyway wordless. Succumbing to a typically Victorian urge to explain and describe, he resorts to a painful series of Geography O-level style annotated diagrams and phrases such as 'when the pith or marrow of the lava was still in a fluid state'.

To my mind, you can only really understand Thingvellir's significance to Icelanders by preserving a sense of mystery about the unimaginably angry forces that created it. In AD 930, the first Viking settlers chose this dumbfounding place as the site for their parliament, which Icelanders will tell you is the oldest democratically elected body in the world.

If you want to really annoy an Icelander, ask him whether it isn't the case that because of a brief hiatus when the ruling Danes suspended the Icelandic parliament, the Manx Tynwald is in fact

THINGVALLA.

High Latitudes

the oldest *continuous* democratically elected body. You could also perhaps demand elaboration on the fearful massacres that regularly interrupted the livelier debates, or on the Pool of Execution, a nearby waterfall over which unfaithful wives were flung. But anyway, the main point is that the Icelandic for parliament is '*thing*', which is simply the best ever name. And in Norway, the parliament is the Storting – the Big Thing. Houses of Big Thing. Member of Big Thing. We should give it a go.

With the rain now into its stride we stuffed our soaking tent and growing stock of undryable clothes into binliners and set off for breakfast at the nearby roadside shop. Reminded for the first time of the hideous cost of Icelandic provisions – two quid for a packet of biscuits – we managed to sound so pathetically impoverished ('How much is this chocolate? Oh. That one? Can we have some more coffee sort of without paying for it?') that they let us off twenty krónur. Inadequately nourished, we set off towards Laugarvatn and our first real test: an introduction to the pleasures of cycling on a rutted, muddy lava track.

Most of us will be aware that wind and hills are rude words to a cyclist, but Dilli and I had recourse to supplement these with a terrible variety of more traditional compound curses during the following three hours. Forty minutes of attrition up some relentless incline was rewarded with a swooping hairpin descent requiring permanent braking and consequently much disturbing lateral movement on the shiny clay. Hit even a tiny pumice pebble and the bike jerked sideways as if you'd just cycled over a bar of wet soap; I could almost feel Oðin's icy embrace every time I somehow avoided a large one.

The regular, unsettling sounds of stones pinging into the frame, and, less resonantly, my calves and face, took some getting used to. It always sounded as if some vital part of the bike had been scythed off, and indeed usually it was. The bolts attaching my front pannier rack were rattled loose, leading to an exciting 'air-bag' moment involving the binlinered luggage it bore. After an untraceable but deeply worrying whiplash twang, as of an oil tanker breaking free from its steel mooring hawsers, my rear brake pads started rubbing against the wheel rim, a demoralising energy sap that I was too stupid to know how to correct. Then some vital component of the front gear cog adjustment was staved in, depriving me of access to what the man in the shop had dismissively referred to as the 'granny ring' – the lowest set of gears, which only an invalid planning to cycle up the side of a tall building would ever use, he said. Man in the shop, you are a bad man.

Dilli, though later plagued by an errant bed-roll, had fewer mechanical woes, but despite this I was determined not to let him escape as he had so often the day before. For some reason I have yet to determine, in recent years I have developed a mild fascination with the Tour de France, and using its vocabulary I talked myself up to the task: Dilli was the young star on a breakaway; I was the 'policeman' assigned by my rival team to wear him down by sitting in his slipstream. Ageing, slightly overweight, I was still at the end of the day a pro who knew that team orders were all, and doggedly held his rear wheel despite the appalling terrain and his fearsome pace.

Other aspects of this fantasy were that it allowed me to justify letting him take the wind, rain and flies in the teeth, and to test his urine for stimulants.

Arriving at Laugarvatn, now so drenched that despite my best efforts to shield myself behind Dilli my gloves had doubled in weight, we pondered the options. The campsite at Geysir lay in some accursed Flanders field 30 kilometres away. The family summerhouse, with its shower and beds and electricity, set within an enclave of similar edifices serviced by a shop, a swimming pool and a bar, was half that distance off. Dilli's knees were starting to click audibly, adding a backbeat to my orchestra of incoherent curses and low groans. I would dearly love to be able to say it was a difficult decision.

Was it against the ethos of my voyage? Was it cheating? In some ways, yes, and also in all other ways. But Dufferin started it. He had servants and porters and eighteen horses. The only advantages I had over him were Goretex clothing and relief against the misery of trapped wind in four refreshing fruit flavours.

And in any case the summerhouse itself had been built in the north and, being refused transit on Iceland's ring road as a dangerously wide load, precariously transported on a lorry across the fearsome Kjölur Pass that was to be our ultimate challenge. So . . . we had to sleep in it . . . to see what kind of house could . . . oh, you know.

We toasted our inadequacy with hot dogs – *pylsur* – bought from the petrol station shop. Scandinavians would probably like to convince you that their individual national dishes are smorgasbord-type marine delicacies with intricate little garnishes. But go into almost any shop – not even food shops, but things like newsagents and chandleries – and you'll see on the counter a little rippled steel unit like an unfinished toast rack, and behind the counter a garish array of three-gallon, rack-mounted bins with condom-like dispensing udders, like feeding drips for diseased aliens. These are respectively the temporary home for completed *pylsur* awaiting customer collection, and the sauce containers used in their convoluted assembly.

At not much more than a quid a throw – and gloriously, sometimes less – *pylsur, pølse*, whichever national variant of the word the locals would fail to understand me saying, would become a staple for me in countries where a loaf of bread costs anything up to £2.50. The Norwegians, I was to learn, like to top theirs off with pickled cabbage; the Danes go for lurid, dog's-cock-red sausages. The Icelandic model is a comparatively restrained variant: raw onion, fried onion, ketchup, mustard and remoulade.

Remoulade, for those unfamiliar, is a miracle mayonnaise-like condiment containing more saturated fat per gramme than any other substance known to man. We would have taken some along as the perfect chain lubricant cum calorific energy fluid, but this would have meant boring out the intake-straws on our drinking bottles as well as suffering restricted vision when the resultant sebum excretions slid easily down our lustrous faces.

Dining noisily on the first of the ensuing nine weeks' hundred or so *pylsur*, not even the sight of a nine-year-old boy crushing dozens of flies on the shop window with his bare palms, not even the sight of him then holding up his currant-splattered flesh for his parents' head-patting approval, could dampen my suddenly buoyant spirits. Just as well, as it turned out, because the following 15 kilometres before the summerhouse were the worst we were to face. The road was being prepared for asphalting, which for some reason involved huge tankers neatly dribbling a thin solution of mud over a bed of skull-sized rocks.

The opportunities for scenic appreciation were still limited by the mist. I knew from previous visits to the summerhouse that the views around Laugarvatn were majestic – the distant silver-snowy back of the still-active Hekla, the perfect Fuji-like cone of Skjaldbreiður, the plunging gorge of Bruaráskört. All this was inked out, my view restricted to the smudged lower reaches of the surrounding hills – black rock with the odd irregular oval of unmelted snow, like the flanks of a killer whale – and the plunging gorge of Dilli's taut cycling shorts.

I have always marvelled at the way football players condition themselves perfectly to run about for exactly ninety minutes. Get into even ten minutes of injury time and they're collapsing with agonised cramps and bending each other's toes back. So it was pleasing to note that, with rather less in the way of conditioning, from the first day I somehow managed to ration my limited physical resources exactly to the point where our day's ride was to end. Every evening I could literally cycle not a foot further. Consequently, when we took a wrong turning in the summerhouse enclave requiring 200 yards of backtracking, I had only the energy to fire off a quick Dilli-directed epithet before collapsing out of the saddle and pushing my burden unsteadily up the angry orange mudtrack.

But when we finally arrived, I almost cried with relief. It sounds pathetic now, and didn't sound particularly great even then, but the unimpressive statistics of our journey to date – ten hours in the saddle over two days to cover 96 kilometres, about the same distance that drunk students in nightdresses cycling backwards on tandems manage in the annual London–Brighton charity event – could not equate with the almost delirious fatigue and acute pain it had earned me.

Aside from the usual calf and knee soreness, the sensations in my back and shoulders suggested I'd been absent-mindedly wearing a tractor chassis inside my stupid leotard. My bottom hurt – of course my bottom hurt. But in fact the expected buttock pains had been so constant that I had managed to sublimate them, occupying my mind by picturing the changing shape and consistency of the saddle as suggested by the raw data passed on by my ravaged arse-neurones. By the end of the first day the saddle retained the marginal elasticity of a Tupperware lunchbox; on the final approaches to the summerhouse it was a brick – not a friendly, smoothed London stock, but a stark, heavy, geometrically precise engineering brick, a harsh, earth-red solid with three cylindrical holes through the centre.

We clumsily inspected the house's treasures like the apes at the start of *2001*, prodding its cosy pine bunks in disbelief and struggling to establish the functions of dimly recalled conveniences like the radiators, oven, telly and shower. It took an hour in the outdoor hotpot – heated by geothermal water up to 42°C – accompanied by our entire stock of alcohol (two cans of beer and a miniature of cognac each) to restore our self-awareness. So much so that we ruthlessly flung open the neatly demarcated kitchen cupboards and assembled an effective pasta/biscuit concoction from the combined provisions intended to see the next family guests through a long weekend.

Dizzily replete, we slumped slack-jawed on the L-shaped sofa, Dilli watching *I, Claudius*, me idly studying a map on one of our plastic bags, originating from a state-run liquor store. Suddenly, I sat up, appalled: the map revealed that none of Iceland's booze outlets graced our route. Then I counted: there were only twenty-four in the entire country. My fatigue forgotten, a righteous anger blazed within me. How could this outrage be permitted? A country almost the size of England with twenty-four off-licences? No wonder I'd seen tramps arriving at them in taxis.

Having slept too long on comfy beds and spent an eternity gathering together our still damp clothes and camping materials from the radiators, we didn't set off until 1.20 the next afternoon. But on downhill tarmac and with the wind behind us, which, mercifully, it was almost the whole way – once we had to cycle into it and found ourselves pedalling hard to descend a hill – we soon arrived within sight of Geysir's vapour plumes. The skies cleared slightly, exposing the grand approach I recall from my first visit ten years ago. The road crosses a vast, friendly green plain, endlessly flanked by stern, forbidding Tolkienesque grey peaks without a scrap of vegetation on their brutal flanks.

I remembered the same vista had impelled Dufferin to imagine the place as a suitable home for mythical beasts and golden-haired princesses. Of course, in the azure clarity he enjoyed, he was then able to spy the 'three snowy peaks of Mount Hecla', leading him into a *Now That's What I Call Lava* whistle-stop anthology of the nation's best-loved eruptions. Hekla's entry, at number 2, is its 1766 smash hit 'I Pitched A Six-Foot Boulder (20 Miles Away)'. (In the same eruption, so much ash was spewed out that Dufferin notes that 'at a place one hundred and forty miles off, white paper held up at a little distance could not be distinguished from black', which strikes me as a very strange thing to do.)

But we couldn't see it at all, so the fact that it's well over-due for a full-on festival of boulder-pitching (it seeped a bit of lava a few years back) seemed distant and irrelevant. What was striking, as the road wove slightly towards the mountains, was the purple frill incongruously lined along the otherwise bald mountains' lower reaches, like Thor in a tutu. And then I realised what it was.

Every nation has its taboos. You don't say 'Vietnam' to an American; you don't say 'Jonathan King' to a Briton; you don't say 'Vichy régime' to a Frenchman (too often). In Iceland, though, the gauche foreigner must be even more on his guard. It is one of the few places on earth where one must resist the admittedly faint temptation to make jokes about erosion.

During a typically determined and sustained quest for winter fuel a thousand years ago, Iceland's tiny band of settlers conspired to incinerate almost the entire arboreal wealth of a land three-quarters the size of England. Shorn of roots to bind the earth, the ever-raging North Atlantic gales dispersed the topsoil. Now, Iceland's Gothic grey peaks and treeless valleys are being etched away before they've even entered geological adolescence.

In an attempt to purge the guilt brought on by the fiery excesses of their pagan forefathers, Icelanders have embarked on an almost hysterical anti-erosion programme, and here, swaying happily in a sinuous ribbon beside us, was the main plank of this programme. The lupin.

Dilli had mentioned these bizarre plantations, but I hadn't believed they were a serious proposition. Having miraculously avoided cracking any careless one-liners about topsoil removal ('Help the loam-less', perhaps, or, more brutally, 'Sod off'), I made the almost as heinous error of referring to the lupin with insufficient gravity. Sternly, Dilli informed me that national studies had revealed the lupin as a fast-spreading plant able to flourish on the desolate slag-heap foothills, an obsessive binder of thin soil and fiendish nitrogen-fixer. After languishing alongside hostess trolleys and Peak Frean's Abbey Crunch in Victoria Wood's lexicon of suburban mediocrity, here was the lupin's revenge. From Highly Commended at the Stevenage Horticultural Festival to Saviour of the Land of the Vikings.

Subsequent research revealed that the lupin had in fact been waiting since just after the last helmet laid up its horns in Scandinavia to right a great historical wrong. The plant was apparently named after the Latin adjective for wolf-like because of 'a belief that the plant ravenously exhausted the soil'. The plucky underdog, burdened for years by a great injustice, had at last been given the chance to redeem itself by revitalising just what its medieval detractors said it depleted. It seemed a very Icelandic solution.

We freewheeled down to Geysir. Our approach had shared much with Dufferin's experience, but that brief period of harmony ended with a silly discordant clash as soon as we arrived. Geysir itself has almost changed more since my first visit in 1988 than it had in the century and a bit following Dufferin's visit. When I first went, there was just a petrol station selling over-coloured

Fifties postcards and a hardy clutch of pioneering tourists getting steam burns from the barrier-less ejaculations. Now there's a large chalet-style hotel, a big cafeteria and souvenir superstore and an incredible, unending parade of Germans on whistle-stop coach tours of the 'Golden Circle' – Geysir, the Gullfoss waterfall and Reykjavík.

To be brutally honest, Geysir isn't terribly exciting. Even Dufferin couldn't get that enthused. Yes, it was fun to watch as the cook 'turned an idle babbling little geyser into a camp kettle, dug a bake-house in the hot soft clay, and improvised a kitchen-range on a neighbouring vent', and to sit down and eat the results in sunlight at 1 a.m. But then it was just chess, blowing away the local fauna and photographing 'the encampment, the guides, the ponies and one or two astonished natives' while waiting for the Great Geyser to go off.

The sulphur-streaked earth gives the whole place a poisoned, barren aspect, and the eponymous phenomena are rather small-scale. There are two spouting geysers, the smaller of which, Strokkur, shoots off about 50 feet in the air once every five minutes or so, which didn't stop Dufferin chucking a load of turf sods down its calcified orifice to persuade it to hurry up. The Great Geyser, a 200-foot performer in its day, has been rendered so impotent by a couple of centuries' worth of turf sods, gravel and miserable valets that by the late Eighties it was taking 50 kilos of soap powder to get a half-hearted spurt, so they gave up.

Beyond the mild thrills of witnessing the single humble spout shoot its steaming load over a crowd of idiot tourists (there's one scalding a day in peak season), going to Geysir is like visiting Cheddar or Paisley or Cortina, a disconnected, rather meaningless pilgrimage to go somewhere purely because its name became attached to an international phenomenon. Disappointingly, there are even warning signs and ropes around some of the beguiling still pools, particularly the one with the enticing blue tint of a Capri grotto, which apparently claims thirsty dogs every year. Also, bitter experience has taught me that it is impossible to capture the eruptions on film without standing a long way away.

I knew this, but still I couldn't stop myself joining the multinational brigade tightly encircling the active geyser's sickly blowhole, cameras pressed to faces, fingers poised on shutters. What happens is that everyone snaps as the geyser does its unexciting preparatory belchette, and is then caught off guard by the following full splurt which sends them wheeling away into the steam in disorientated panic. I would not believe people's capacity to perform exactly this sequence over and over again were it not for the fact that my own learning curve has proved even more depressingly horizontal than most. I believe I can lay claim to an unrivalled photographic collection of the unfocused, vapour-fogged male Bavarian back – a dangerous boast, I accept.

Dufferin and his party waited three long days for the Great Geyser to do its thing, and by the end were wandering off around the mountains and surrounding plains in search of alternative entertainment. Fitz struck up such a close friendship with a local family that they invited him to stay over, thereby heralding a scene which must have incited a few trouser geysers when *High Latitudes* was published:

On rising from the table, the young lady of the house proposed by signs to conduct me to my apartment; taking in one hand a large plate of skier [*skyr*, a yoghurty sort of curd-like concoction which as Dufferin carefully points out is 'excellent when well made'] and in the other a bottle of brandy, she led the way to the place where I was to sleep. Having watched her deposit – not without misgivings, for I knew it was expected that both should be disposed of before morning – the skier by my bedside and the brandy-bottle under the pillow, I was preparing to make her a polite bow, and to wish her a very good night, when she advanced, and with a winning grace difficult to resist, insisted upon helping me off with my coat, and then – proceeding to extremities – with my shoes and stockings.

At this most critical part of the proceedings, I naturally imagined her share of the performance would conclude . . .

Not a bit of it. Before I knew where I was, I found myself sitting in a chair, in my shirt, trouserless, while my fair tire-woman was engaged in neatly folding the ravished garments. She then, in the most simple manner in the world, helped me into bed, tucked me up, and having said a quantity of pretty things in Icelandic, gave me a hearty kiss and departed.

On the fourth day they finally get a result, but only a 60-footer barely more impressive than the ten-times-an-hour Strokkur. 'I do not believe the exhibition was so fine as some have seen,' notes Dufferin curtly, before explaining, in the now familiar O-level diagram format, what should have happened.

The next day, after the mild excitement of a visit by Prince Napoleon and his vast entourage, Dufferin's party returns to Reykjavík. En route, Dufferin is 'violently hugged, kissed and nearly pulled off my horse by a tipsy farmer'; Wilson sustains a 'tremendous

High Latitudes   AN ICELANDIC LADY.

fall'. Again it seemed that I would be more likely to emulate the experience of Dufferin's valet.

The Geysir shop was the last commercial outpost before Kjölur, and so the last before Iceland's northern coast. Once again a misguided sense of frugality led us to restrict our resupplying to the purchase of a vast and incredibly cheap half-kilo slab of chocolate. This turned out to be spectacularly horrid. I'd say it was cooking chocolate, but that would imply a significant market for people who like their cakes to taste of linseed oil and palm lard. No matter how much we forced into our protesting mouths, the bar never seemed to shrink. Along with the awful, congealed turd-slab of slimy prunes, this came to be the leitmotif of the following days, the mouldy carrot not in front but behind, chasing us away, driving us on, on, northwards, to fresh foodstuffs and beer.

(As an afterthought, we also picked up a leaflet on five fun ways to eat mountain grass, in case things got really bad or scurvy set in. Fortunately they didn't, as when I got back to England I read the leaflet and wondered how we would have gone about preheating an oven to 200°C.)

4

The shortish ride to Gullfoss – the Golden Falls – marked our farewell to Dufferin. Returning to Reykjavík, he discovers that his crew have in his absence embarked on what may be history's sole instance of a mutiny inspired by indigestion.

> 'Dyspepsia and her fatal train' having taken hold of them, in a desperate hour they determined on a desperate deed, and rushing aft in a body, demanded of my faithful steward not only access to the penetralia of the absent Doctor's cupboard, but that he himself should administer to them whatever medicaments he could come by.

But I'm not sure if this peculiar episode was as funny as it sounds, because in a strange and stark entry headed '3 A.M.' (only three hours after his return), he writes: 'I give up seeing the rest of Iceland, and go north at once. It has cost me a struggle to come to this conclusion, but on the whole I think it will be better.'

His faltering justification for this – that time is getting on, and he doesn't want to miss out on the promise of a tow to Jan Mayen from Prince Napoleon's steamer – doesn't convince. Time isn't getting on – it's still only 7 July – and, in any case, why make such a startling snap decision? He'd had days in the saddle to ponder it, and heading 'right across the middle of the island to the north coast – scarcely ever visited by strangers' had been one of his main goals. It's clear to an eager fantasist like me that having seen what happened in his absence, he decides he can't leave the

Foam again. Where were Wyse and his twin revolvers when the crew rifled through the senna pods? He doesn't say.

So for the next 250 kilometres I was setting the agenda. Following in someone's footsteps makes a prospect less forbidding. Now the footsteps had shuffled about and turned back on themselves. I had lost my leader; we were on our own.

I still can't understand why Dufferin passed up Gullfoss: there is little in the natural world to match the awesome splendour of a bloody great waterfall. All the usual 'I heard its mighty roar and beheld the clouds of spray from many leagues hence' stuff applies to the falls generally accepted as the most stunning in a land spoilt for cascade magnificence. Maybe the commonplace appeal of a load of water rolling off a cliff just wasn't exotic enough for his purposes.

It's a sort of two-tier fall. First a broad current wallows down a boulder-strewn rapid, with the odd vertical crash. Then, just when it thinks it's all over, it's slammed at 90 degrees down a sheer chasm, well over 100 feet deep, which ferries away the quivering froth along a chiselled, two-mile gorge. In severe winters this extraordinary spectacle is frozen, a display of sinuous torrents arrested in mid-leap which I have unfortunately only beheld on an Echo & The Bunnymen album cover.

This was a humbling experience for the bussed-in Germans. You get drenched by spray even 100 yards from the falls, and picking your way along the slippery grass path towards the growing roar is an unsettling experience. There are no warning signs at all, just a low rope of the sort village cricket clubs put round their squares when not in use. You can therefore go, as Dilli did but I certainly did not, right up under a shuddering ledge, so that the water crashes over you just before it turns right into the gorge. The noise was incredible, the loudest thing I've stood so close to apart from the rotary saw in our school workshop.

How fondly I recall this splendid device. We used to get the hapless Mr Slee to operate it as often as possible, offering as it did the rare chance to stand right next to a member of staff – albeit an elderly and completely benign one – and bellow mid-pubescently that he was, say, a shitty crappy tosser, without redress. Interestingly, according to the same law of acoustics that dictates that you can hardly hear yourself when you yodel while hoovering, but everyone in the next room can in fact hear you perfectly, if you passed the workshop while the saw was on the volley of shamingly frank epithets rang out loud and true. Despite this no action was ever taken to curb the practice, leading me to assume it was reluctantly accepted as an outlet for pent-up juvenile energies. Or that maybe the headmaster simply could not bring himself to disagree: when all was said and done, the man Slee was a shitty crappy tosser.

Anyway, Gullfoss is awesome and majestic and ground-shakingly loud (though not, in fact, quite as loud as the rotary saw, as the party of outraged Swedish tourists who stood in front of us will testify). But unless you're talking to, or rather shouting at Dilli, there's nothing to tell you that a few years ago a German tourist disappeared here. He was last seen, camera poised, moving towards a narrow vantage point. No one saw him slip, roared Dilli, and that close to the falls a scream wouldn't be heard unless you cupped your hands round the ear of the person below you and bellowed into it as you plummeted past, and even then they'd probably gaze curiously down at your tiny, flailing form and wonder what you meant by 'Help! I'm falling to my certain desk!' But the German didn't show up when his party went back to their bus, and they never found a body. The awful prospect is that it's still there, trapped in the plunge pool, forever buffeted and bullied by the ceaseless torrents.

The only monument is for the woman who − shouted Dilli as we cycled up towards the start of Kjölur − saved the falls from being despoilt by a huge hydroelectric plant. Even now, Iceland produces vastly more electricity than it needs. There are perennial plans to send it by undersea cable to the UK's national grid, and a Swiss aluminium firm has built an enormous plant on the Reykjavík–Keflavík road − I got so bored once driving out to Keflavík Airport that I measured it on the odometer at over a kilometre long − to take advantage of the cheap power, huge amounts of which are apparently needed for smelting or refining or the Scalextric layout in the canteen or something.

Up we cycled, off the tarmac and on to rock. And there was the sign. 'Kjölur' it said, pointing nonchalantly across an unending moonscape that had suddenly appeared out of nowhere. We wordlessly dismounted to survey the prospect, and contemplate our foolishness. The scene was like a still from a Road Runner cartoon: a sterile sienna plain; great, caravan-sized, coyote-squashing boulders left randomly about its surface by long-gone glaciers; a tiny track that disappeared and reappeared around the barren hillsides before dropping off the horizon. To the east these hills swelled into aggressive spikes, row after row of lonely, forgotten peaks which you felt you could scale and be the first man to do so. 'Thirty thousand square miles in disordered pyramids of ice and lava, periodically devastated by deluges of molten stone and boiling mud, or overwhelmed with whirlwinds of snow and cinders – an unfinished corner of the universe, where the elements of chaos are still allowed to rage with unbridled fury,' writes Dufferin, no doubt rubbing his hands by the fire in his cabin and toasting his decision to leave it all well alone.

Nowhere in this humbling panorama was there vegetation, habitation, transportation. The scale was unsettling, confusing. Everything seemed massive yet tiny, distant yet in your face. It was like holding a magnifying glass to one eye and the fat end of a telescope to another. Even more disconcertingly, this scorched wasteland was also cold, around 5°C, and trouser-flappingly windy. I'd been rather disturbed to read in the summerhouse that Kjölur was the second largest desert in Europe (after its neighbour, Sprengisandur).

I might not have been aware that there were any deserts in Europe – the third largest is probably Clacton Sands – but even so this claim had a loftiness which suddenly threw the inadequacy of our preparation into stark relief. What, in fact, were we thinking of? Even the sign which said 'Abandon hope all ye who enter here' (or maybe it was 'Four-wheel drive vehicles only beyond this point') had been eased to the floor by some quietly omnipotent meteorological or geological force. 'In the interior of Iceland, the weather can change in just some few minutes,' the Icelandic Cycling Club leaflet had reminded us.

The track only opens to vehicles in July; by late September the snows and Arctic gales are back and it's closed for the next nine months. But in between there's still plenty of scope for unexpected catastrophes. On one of the hills a few miles off the track, the remains of three brothers and their sizeable entourage of livestock still lie where they were caught in an unseasonal snowstorm in 1780. Horses' skulls and worse still carpet the upper reaches of what is marked on the maps as Bone Hill.

Here I was on a one-wheel drive vehicle over which I had only partial control, my wellbeing dependent on things I didn't know how to use like chain-link cutters and spare spokes, things I was too frightened to contemplate using like survival bags and things I didn't even have like Kevlar tyres. But I had to do it. I had managed to convince myself that Dufferin's pretext for turning around – the tow from Prince Napoleon – disguised a fear. That's what it was. He came, he saw, and he ran away. In the same way that Dilli and I had built up an unspoken competitiveness on our bikes, so I'd come to accept that all along I had been pitting myself against Dufferin. Neither contest, of course, was in any danger of a photo finish, but here, laid out in an eternity of glaciated rubble, was a chance, my only chance, to out-Dufferin Dufferin.

Overwhelmed by the prospect, I sought solace in Dilli. He was an Icelander, and a doctor, and as such seemed utterly unperturbed. His only worry was that people would think he was German, like most of those who attempt this crossing. 'Really, it's not that bad. At this time of the summer it'll be full of tourists. If anything happens, a car will be along in twenty minutes.'

After an hour of total and increasingly unsettling solitude, I was only persuaded after an argument from turning back to find the right road. It was three hours until proof of intelligent life – any life – on earth appeared, in the form of a pick-up which popped up on the horizon behind us in a little ball of hazy dust and shot past, treating us to a brief Doppler-distorted bleat from the two sheep in the back.

At least it wasn't raining. It actually became quite hot. This, in combination with my habitually laboured progress, meant that I soon began to sweat like a dying carthorse. 'For the layering principle to work, you really ought to take that cotton shirt off,' said Dilli. 'It's just soaking up sweat and not letting it out through your fleece.'

I knew he was right. Every evening my collar-up Fred Perry was as wet and heavy as an old bathmat. But I couldn't help it. The Fred Perry stripes under my chin lent a welcome touch of amateurism. On my flash bike with its Goretex-sheathed cables and all this proper Karrimor cycling gear I was worried people might think I thought I knew what I was doing, despite a cursory glimpse at my teetering progress making it abundantly clear that I didn't. The last thing I wanted was some Arctic enduro freak from Hamburg coming up to compare granny rings.

More significantly, one of my many suburban phobias is an hysterical fear of wearing prickly wool or nylon next to my neck flesh. My purple Karrimor fleece, which neatly replicated the feel of prickly nylon wool, could not be tolerated. I tried, as I have tried so many times before, to confront this irrationality. Every morning I would boldly eschew the Perry, and, breathing deeply, sheathe my skin with fleece. Fine. No prickles. Okay. No need to tear this off in a great panic of revulsion or anything. Oh no. Great. Okay.

Sometimes I would hold out until we got out on to the bikes; more usually it was while I was still in the tent. This was worse, because the resultant flailing paroxysms, over which I had little control, often dislodged guy ropes or sent Dilli flying out of the zip end with a muddy knee-print on his forehead.

The one positive aspect of my extravagant perspiration was that it dramatically reduced my need to urinate, sometimes down to a single dribble of syrupy Lucozade wincingly extruded at the end of the day. Given the clumsy striptease demanded by fluid excretion, the benefits of this were not to be underestimated.

Less conveniently, it meant I was possessed by a permanently raging thirst. I would usually finish both my litre bottles before 'lunch', then start apologetically on Dilli's. We'd been warned that this was probably a stupid thing to do – however unlikely the temperature made it seem, we were after all in a desert – but in reality a tumbling river was rarely more than two hours away. Most, though, were of glacial meltwater, like the Hvítá – White River – a torrent the colour of Wash'n'Go which we followed for much of the second half of the pass.

How delightfully refreshing, I said to Dilli as we stopped our bikes on a plank bridge over it. 'Well, yes. But actually glacial water is undrinkable. There's so much mud and grit in it from the glacier. Everyone in Iceland always laughs at products which say "made from pure glacial water" on the label.' Oh. 'Also, it's probably about 2 degrees – if you slipped in you'd die of shock almost immediately.' Wash'n'Go indeed.

Shortly after we found a far less enticing mossy trickle, into which Dilli eagerly plunged his entire head. But I couldn't join him. I heard Wilson's leering whisper at my shoulder: 'Enjoy the waters, sir. It's just that I won't be partaking, sir, on accounts of the sheep's corpses what's lying drowned in it just upstream, sir.'

The temperature rose further, boosting morale to near-whistling levels. We even reached 53 kilometres per hour on a descent, which was stupid. Soon we learned that the track surface consisted of whatever rocks happened to be lying around, vaguely bulldozed into a line. Most steep declines ended in dried-up river beds, which tended to comprise a few millennia's worth of large boulders. Negotiating these surprise arrivals at speed on an overladen bicycle, and with sudden braking out of the question, never failed to fill the blasted apocalyptic wilderness with echoing shrieks. My reflex cry was 'Cocking bollocks', and the frequency with which this phrase burst involuntarily from my throat forced acceptance that should I meet a sudden and violent end these would be my rather unedifying last words.

Then things closed in once more, and we were pushing our bikes up gravelly Sisyphean inclines in mists so thick we more than once wandered off the track and had to consult our compass. Every so often an alarmingly humanoid rock would loom out of the fog into our faces, making me want to jump into Dilli's arms like Scooby Doo into Shaggy's.

With so much irregularly shaped stonework and so few people, it's unsurprising that lone travellers in Iceland have a long history of getting into a bit of a state and seeing trolls. In previous centuries the trolls were waving swords or milking sheep; now they're watching television or taking girly trolls from behind (as the second mate pointed out to me in a formation just above the harbour in Heimæy). But take it from me: travel about the Icelandic interior for more than a couple of hours and you'll never laugh at that elf-fearing 53 per cent again.

On my first visit, Birna drove me and a friend in late summer gloom across the lonely plateau of Kaldadalur. We'd already exceeded our daily excitement quota, having sheared the exhaust off Birna's mother's Daihatsu on a boulder and got stuck in a ford. With darkness closing in, we drove hesitantly down out of the fog to be presented with the cheery, welcoming spectacle of a dozen or so Icelandic ponies being herded along a valley.

But our sighs of relief were stillborn: my friend and I had both noticed simultaneously that the first horse was being led by a 12-foot-tall man. We exchanged pale glances, convinced that when we looked back some rational explanation would present itself: the man would in fact be standing on a wheeled stool, or the ponies would turn out to be rabbits. But when we looked back, we just saw a 12-foot-tall man herding some ponies along a valley. It is the closest I have ever come to a supernatural experience, one whose impact is only slightly tempered by the fact that my friend and I had drunk perhaps a third of a bottle of whisky each.

The mist cleared and I looked out over the scrappy nothingness. It wasn't just the supernatural which concerned me. It's like walking through a graveyard at midnight, when the rational part of your brain says that it's pointless to be frightened as no one would be hanging about here on their own. But then the same part of your brain realises that what you're saying is, *no one in their right minds*, and it's feet first into the vortex of terror. It is, to my way of thinking, a perfectly logical conclusion. No one could live out here in this unfinished corner of the universe . . . but, if someone did, they would certainly be grandiosely insane, the sort who would think nothing of forcing a man to rape his own bicycle before eating him.

After five hours or so, the road surface began to deteriorate. We had to weave about rocks so much that for the next three days our odometer readings were 10 per cent greater than the map distances. Then there would be great stretches of sand, so appealingly smooth as we approached, so uncomfortably abrasive as our wheels gently sank into the dune, stopping us dead before almost apologetically pitching us over. Shortly after one of these we freewheeled down a rocky descent and came to rest with our wheels at the edge of a river. We silently surveyed its freezing rapids. They'd told us all the fords on the road had now been bridged. The many three-point-turn wheeltracks suggested we weren't the only ones to be misled so.

'We'll just have to get wet,' said Dilli. I didn't mind getting wet, mainly because I was already bathing in my own sweat and wearing clothes that still hadn't quite shaken off yesterday's rain. Getting dead was more of a worry. I had heard umpteen stories of even quite large vehicles being swept away at these river crossings.

As we sat down on the rocks and prepared to disrobe, two identical black motorcycles, their engine noise blotted out by the roaring water, appeared on the opposite shore. Their identically clad riders dismounted in unison, simultaneously opened panniers on their respective machines, and donned identical pairs of thigh-high rubber waders. In perfect synchronisation they wheeled their bikes across the river and arrived with a businesslike nod of the helmet beside us. I noted their German numberplates without surprise.

Together they pointed in turn at our bikes, our shoes, their waders, the other shore. We blurted a volley of *Danke schön*s and nodded in vigorous supplication, then scrambled uphill to where it was possible for a nimble human to leap across on stepping stones without getting a toe wet. With my left leg consequently sodden to the thigh, we watched the black-leathered Christs on bikes carry our cycles side-by-side over the river, raising them overhead untroubled by the vast weight. With brisk, gratitude-forestalling gestures of the kind Batman and Robin make when they're urgently needed elsewhere in Gotham City, they deposited our bikes and crashed back robotically through the surf.

It was only later we realised how lucky we had been. Their bikes were the first vehicles we'd seen for hours, and the only ones equipped to help us. It was an exciting moment: something good had happened.

With the odometer reading 73 kilometres for the day's travel and my brain and lungs on empty, we cycled up to the Icelandic Hiking Association hut at Hvítarnes. It's an amazing setting. The two-floor whitewashed crofter's cottage with patchily turfed outside walls and a red corrugated iron roof is the only building for dozens of miles, stuck forlornly on a windy plain facing a wall of glaciers and Lake Hvíta, with its misty fleets of low icebergs.

It was unbelievably isolated for a suburbanite, but somehow cosy to think that we had the house to ourselves, with a Dufferinian sense of no one to trouble us for a day's ride in any direction. Except the ghost of an old woman whom Dilli said was supposed to pester guests on the upstairs floor.

Gaily we threw open the front door, only to be confronted with a heart-sinking scenario: three men in cagoules and dirty hiking socks, skulking around the dark kitchen in silence. One didn't even look up to acknowledge us. It seemed clear that each had come here to revel in the isolation, and like us was now seething with resentment at having to share the hut with strangers. Our arrival strained further what was an already fragile status quo.

The most cursory of introductions revealed that one was Icelandic, one Austrian, one Swiss. (Dilli and I fought manfully to resist the lure of crass racial generalisation and refer to the latter two as 'the Germans'.) The Icelander almost immediately retired to his room, the prime one at the front of the house with beds for six. The Swiss and the Austrian were in the back room. We would have to share with the ghost in the loft.

The house could not be described as well appointed. The only running water was provided by the stream outside, and there was no electricity, no fuel for the single wood-burning stove, no bedding beyond a stack of thin mattresses impregnated with the sour mushroomy damp to be expected from life in a house with grass walls. Recognising the house's affinity with the rude lava-brick shacks described by Dufferin, it wouldn't have been too ridiculous to find the ghost asleep in a box filled with feathers and seaweed, or even better, sitting in a horse's skull.

It was cold – the Austrian insisted on leaving the front door wide open as soon as the Camping Gaz stove began to make the kitchen almost comfortably warm – and, despite the persisting midnight sun (largely a theoretical phenomenon in the prevailing overcast gloom), oddly dingy. Given the frugality of the conditions, it seemed remarkable that payment of the nightly 800 krónur was to be deposited in an honesty box by the door. It would have been enough to encourage me to have considered reducing my contribution to the honesty box from 800 krónur to maybe no krónur.

The atmosphere in the tiny kitchen was tense as the Swiss and the Austrian washed up with boiled stream water, their careful preciseness contrasting favourably with our slap-happy preparation of enough just-add-water soya Beanfeasts to feed eight.

'The packet please.' The Austrian shattered the truculent silence, snatching a Beanfeast foil sheath before we could react. With this one brief sentence and deed he eased ahead of the ghost in the who's-going-to-hack-us-all-to-death-in-our-beds stakes.

He read intently for some time. We stirred congealing Beanfeast. The wind rattled the tiny, smutted windows. No one spoke. Suddenly the Icelander burst out of his room, arrestingly outfitted in thick socks, chunky sweater and underpants. He wore the desperate expression of a man in a cheap horror film about to try to convince an unwisely sceptical ticket inspector that he's just seen two dozen Tube commuters absorbed by a giant slug. If I'd had lapels he would have grabbed them. There was obviously something very important he had omitted to communicate.

'How do you like Iceland?' he demanded, nodding too fast and too violently at my faltering reply of approving truisms. Apparently satisfied, he grabbed a packet of skimmed milk powder seemingly at random from a shelf and withdrew to his lair with a slam, returning the kitchen abruptly to its damp silence. The Austrian did not look up from his – our – packet. He had obviously been involved in a similar exchange some hours earlier.

'Ja. Yes. It is as I believed. You see?' He pointed at the nutritional information. 'Here you have only three hundred-twenty calories in one hundred gramme. It is not good.'

'Er, okay.' It seemed reasonably clear that this was not intended as a two-way communication.

'I will show you.' He disappeared to his room, unzipped things a lot, and returned with a crisp sheet of paper covered in painfully meticulous hand-written calculations and tables. 'Here. I have some charts. It is important.'

'Yes,' I said with peculiar gravity. 'Yes it is.'

'See. Here foods, here energy in one hundred gramme, and here total gramme weight.'

'I see.'

He was becoming disturbingly strident as his fingers ranged over the chart. 'Yes! Here – muesli is good for walking holiday, not heavy and many calories. The best one I found is here . . . here! I call it Muesli II.'

'Right . . . What brand is that? What kind of muesli?'

He made an irritated dismissive gesture. 'It is . . . I am not . . . it is not important!'

He flustered off back to his room. By this stage I did not want to catch Dilli's eye. Then the Swiss finished reassembling his shiny titanium saucepan set, and turned to us. 'You are with bicycles.'

'Yes.'

'I am also with bicycle. There is a very bad river crossing to the south, yes?'

As nonchalantly as possible we told him there indeed was, but that with a great deal of courage and strength it could be managed. He withdrew a map, and asked us to indicate it.

'Here? At Kertlingafjell?' We nodded. He snorted. 'Not that! I

113

have done that – it is only a little stream!' This was to become a catchphrase.

The Austrian returned. 'Look now. Shaped pasta is also good in kilojoules. And see: Orient egg noodles – weight is just some few gramme. Your packets are *so heavy*. Why did you not make such a study?' This was to become another catchphrase.

'Okay. Listen up, lads. The thing is, we both really hate you two now, and would like you to stop talking straight away and go to bed,' I should have announced at this point. Instead we silently took our food up into the loft and ate ourselves to sleep.

The one good thing about sharing accommodation with lone hikers is that they've vacuum-packed their Muesli II, graced the visitors' book with a humorous German poem (I say humorous on the evidence of the exclamation marks at the end of every line, although on reflection it could just as easily have been a rhyming list of barked orders) and left by 5.30 a.m. This gave us a full free morning to wash up the communal crockery without Teutonic reminders that stubborn Beanfeast streaks are unlikely to be emulsified by chilled stream water and shampoo. And to visit the earth closet.

I read somewhere that a young Winston Churchill once asked a dinner party mathematician to calculate the cubic volume of a railway carriage, as he had often pledged to devote his life to consuming a Pullman full of champagne. Similarly, but perhaps less appealingly, I have often wondered whether my accumulated lifetime excretions would fill an Olympic swimming pool, though I've yet to encounter an associate with the magic combination of scientific know-how, numerical ability and base degeneration to help me out with the figures. But at least I now have a fair idea of what it might look like.

Dilli emerged from the innocuous triangular hut with a haunted look. 'That is worse,' he said vacantly, 'than anything I saw in seven years of medical training.' But with urgent Beanfeast-related messages from below, I had no choice but to take my turn in the dark pyramid. Inside, all initially seemed well. The smell was barn-like rather than anything more dreadful. There was a cosy-ish wooden bench framing a proper loo seat. Growing in confidence, I raised the seat cover.

If I had been playing the unwisely sceptical ticket inspector in the aforementioned low-budget release, this action would have been immediately followed by a single, deafening symphonic crash, and a close-up of my features vibrating with disbelief, blank terror and revulsion. But rather than gastropodic revelation, below lay Pandora's dirtbox, a Hieronymous Bosch vision of the terrible variety of man's excretory excesses, a dug-out pit the size of a large garden shed almost two-thirds filled by a vast conical mound of the remains of last month's *pylsur* and this morning's Muesli II. With a single, hysterical giggle I recalled the joke about drinking real ale and the world dropping out of your bottom. Then I was abruptly gripped by the conviction that my watch would slip off my wrist into the mouth of hell, and having removed it, voided myself more rapidly than I have ever done before.

Another day, another ford. After an hour's ride across the *One Million Years BC* rubble, now muddy after a midnight downpour, we reached the Svartá, or Black River. Instead of a bridge, there was a helpful sign. 'Use a strong rope when crossing. Always wear brightly coloured clothing.' In two brief sentences this managed to relay the information that wading across was not only demanding, but so dangerous that any slight slip would inevitably lead to a drawn-out downstream search for your bloated corpse.

We took off most of our clothing and Dilli carried over his bike, confidently predicting he would be able to hurl his ersatz wading trainers across the freezing 30-yard stream for me to wear. His failure to do so caused me to get wetter in the hazardous act of retrieving them than I would have done if I'd stuck on a snorkel and crawled across on my stomach. In any case, there was no possible way I could carry the bike, and despite the irrefutable evidence of my own eyes somehow managed to convince myself that I could wheel it across without the water level reaching the panniers.

A horse. That's what Dufferin had, and that's what these tracks were designed for. Icelandic ponies would think nothing of a cold knee bath, and their peculiar 'fifth gait' would soak up the awful bumps and rocks. Fifth gait? The standard horse has four gaits – walk, trot, gallop and . . . super gallop. Icelandic ponies have this fifth gait, which involves them running reasonably fast but taking very short steps, or something, so that despite the flurry of equine feet, the rider is transported along smoothly. On the other hand, it looks really stupid, a bit like the 10-kilometre walk at the Olympics when the athletes pump their chests forward and roll their pelvises and stick out their elbows as if someone just put on 'Do, Do, Do The Funky Chicken' at 78rpm and you keep wondering why they don't just run and be done with it.

But I've tried and failed with Icelandic ponies. The first time, the only riding hats the stable had to accommodate my bulbous, encephalitic cranium were sort of ill-fitting plastic Wehrmacht helmets like they might have sold in Woolworth's in the Sixties if the Germans had won the war. I bravely backed down on aesthetic grounds. The second time, I managed to climb into the saddle of one, which then reared up impressively in heigh-ho Silver style, shocking the farmer who said he'd never seen an Icelandic pony do that before. Somehow I avoided falling off, and shakily informed him that I was probably okay, but he was already patting the horse's neck and whispering sympathetically into its ear. It was his horse he was worried about. The occasional look of suspicious malevolence he cast round at me suggested he'd marked me down as a troll's nark, casing stables and sizing up beasts for later theft by my 12-foot-tall accomplice. His animal's sixth sense had rumbled me. I sort of rolled off the horse and drew a shaky line under my equestrian career. Only on a bicycle would I be able to claim that I had beaten Dufferin by riding across Iceland.

On we cycled across the desert, finally finding some sort of rhythm, our refreshment stops declining in number as a growing distaste for our provisions eased past hunger. Even the dried apricots, which had assumed an Ambrosian wonder during the dizzy malnutrition of Day 1, now held all the appeal of inexpertly crystallised Egg McMuffin yolks. Mere contemplation of the prune brick sent a series of nauseous shivers through me, shivers I recognised from a terrible incident just before I'd left home when it had become apparent that every open packet of dried foodstuffs in our kitchen was crawling with moth larvae.

The traffic declined, from one vehicle an hour to hardly any ever at all. Most were slightly over-the-top converted Unimogs with 15 feet of road clearance, but there was the odd family saloon, invariably issuing the roar of the recently severed exhaust and the gritted screech of the dust-filled wheel bearing, driven slightly too fast by young fathers wearing oh-well expressions. But all vehicle occupants were now starting to offer waves, some friendly, others – and these were particularly treasured as the only examples of the type I am ever likely to receive – of genuine admiration, accompanied by slow head shakes that said, 'You're crazy, you Germans.'

The clouds vaguely thinned out, exposing little distant puffs of steam on the horizon. These were the hot springs of Hveravellir, the only permanently manned outpost in Iceland's interior, where

High Latitudes   SNORRO.

a presumably placid and well-suited couple overwinters alone to provide uselessly exact meteorological details of just how howlingly Arctic the gales are in the uninhabited middle of nowhere. But in the summer, Hveravellir was a bustling truckstop, with a restaurant, hotel, bar and petrol station/supermarket.

The prospect of ingesting carbohydrate in both processed and fermented form fired us on as we pushed our bikes up an awful series of dusty ochre hills surfaced with Russian railway ballast. We'd already passed up the 14-kilometre round trip detour across raw lava to Bone Hill – poking about horse ribs and other pleasant holiday diversions were put to one side. It was now about staving off physical and mechanical collapse just long enough to complete our journey. So we pushed on towards the grandiose commercial delights of Hveravellir, past such forgotten remnants of civilisation as a roadsign and even, excitingly, litter. 'Germans,' muttered Dilli.

There was also a rough airstrip, marked out by big pyramids with numbers painted on the sides and windsocks on top. Now what is the point of this? There's one permanently occupied house here – one – with two people in it. And the airstrip is about 3 miles from the house anyway. Iceland's interior is full of these isolated landing strips, leading me to recommend it as an excellent drop-off place for consignments of drugs and weapons. Fly in the crack in the summer and you can even land without lights at 3 a.m. The only drawback is the minuscule domestic market, which is a terrible shame. They have the vast areas of wilderness required for the trouble-free disposal of rival cartel members and everything.

There isn't much crime in Iceland. Until a couple of years ago they'd never had a bank robbery. The single prison is so half-heartedly secured that inmates hop over the picket fence at will. The closest thing to organised crime are the gangs who make the hooch that in recent years has become the staple teenage intoxicant.

Homebrew is a way of life in Scandinavia, partly from tradition but mainly because of the monstrous price and scant availability of liquor. A bottle of spirits in Iceland or Norway is £20; even a truly horrid Lithuanian Riesling is £7.

Getting drunk on home-made wine and beer is one thing – the only harm you can come to is falling asleep in a sauna and all the excess yeast you've consumed rising and making your ears inflate. Getting drunk on distilled homebrew of indeterminate but generally alarming potency is another. One needs only to visit a Scandinavian town with more than fifty inhabitants on a Friday or Saturday night to see the effects.

In my nine weeks away I saw more deeply drunk people – people with no control of their necks, people arguing with seagulls, people so dangerously wayward that everyone weaved out of the way and stared back with horrified intrigue in the expectation that they'd imminently fall off a quay or steal a tram – than I think I've seen in the previous ten years in London. And they weren't crusties or Scotsmen, just smartly dressed fifteen- to seventeen-year-old boys and girls, optician's sons, travel agent's daughters. In Bergen I saw a terrible, vicious street fight breaking out amongst some very young and obviously well-to-do girls behaving like rival gangs of Tyneside tarts on glue. And it was only 8.30 p.m.

Scandinavia's youth does this twice every weekend for two years, and then stops. But in the meantime a disproportionately large number of them have drowned by reversing their parent's cars into hot pools and so on, doing the sort of things people don't often do under the influence of the more benign intoxicants of my youth such as Kestrel lager or Tesco's Lambrusco.

As we topped the hill, the wind changed. Our faces were stung by ancient, restless orange dust. Through slitted eyes the terrifyingly desolate scene was more than ever like the first pictures sent back by the Mars buggy, which I'd seen a few days earlier. The bronze boulders oddly stranded amongst the wrinkled lava, the looming black spikes on the horizon: it was all prehistory or post-apocalypse. It seemed farcically inappropriate to be crossing this landscape on something as stupidly mundane as a bicycle. A *Mad Max* motor trike or a saddled-up brontosaurus would have fitted the bill.

The outlines of shadowy buildings and parked cars penetrated the dust storm. Here it was. Civilisation. Our oasis. We had by now pieced together our snippets of knowledge of Hveravellir's summer attractions: pride of the town, and certainly our first port of call, was the Wild West theme restaurant, where sassy, chaps-clad cowgirls brought you trays of red-eye and racks of ribs, where blackjack was played in a cosy, smoky backroom casino. 'There was a bit of a fuss about the neon sign at first,' I said, 'but now it's a landmark – the planes use it when they land in summer.' Then there was the complementary adjoining hotel. 'It's not huge,' recalled Dilli, 'but most of the rooms are all done up with four-poster beds and those sort of cowboy saloon swing doors into the bathroom and stuff.' 'That's right,' I said. 'And if you ask they bring you one of those old tin hip baths and fill it with foam, you know, like they always had in *Alias Smith & Jones*.'

We freewheeled to a halt, realising straight away that something had gone wrong inside our heads. There was a campsite, a toilet block and two huts. Thankfully, as we'd both obviously been rendered temporarily insane by the dislocating landscape and hysterical fatigue, there was no need for a postmortem into this outbreak of mutual delusion. It simply wasn't mentioned as we trooped into one hut, saw the Swiss inside writing a poem in the visitors' book, turned around and trooped into the other. Besides, all was not lost. There was still the petrol station shop.

'Excuse me, where's the petrol station shop?' I asked a man as he emerged from a door marked 'WARDEN'.

'In the petrol station, I would expect,' he replied with the smug deliberation favoured by the unfunny when making a joke in a foreign language.

'Well done. That's really excellent,' I replied, 'but where might that be?'

He looked at his watch.

'If you drive well, you may be there in two hours. How do you like Iceland?'

At least the hut was a step up from the authentic discomforts of Hvítarnes. It was new, pine-clad and hot-housed to sauna levels by geothermally heated radiators. Best of all, we had the entire top floor – essentially a bank of mattresses forming two huge beds, each about 15 feet wide – to ourselves. Also, there was a natural hot pot by the front door. Having emptied the kitchen of middle-aged French couples with another Beanfeasts of the World jamboree, it was to there we eagerly repaired.

We lolled neck-high in the steaming hollow for an hour, oblivious to the blue and orange alien-snot-streak calcifications on the rocks behind our heads, the day's 73 kilometres slowly seeping out of our ravaged frames. My most interesting disability was now a sort of permanent pins-and-needles numbness in the fourth and little fingers of both hands, probably related to the boneshaking track and my habit of rigidly clinging to the handlebars for dear life. This was now having the effect of permanently twisting my hands round and up into two spastic, palsied claws. My left hand was almost useless, a single bone articulated only at the wrist, but the right was worse. It had assumed a terrible rigid glassiness, incapable of undoing buttons or holding cutlery. It would be two weeks before I could pick up anything smaller than a shoe, and the residual nerve damage persisted for a month after my return, rendering me a gormless spectator at the scene of even slightly demanding manual operations.

Emerging groggily, we let ourselves be flayed dry by the wind and, Dilli having helped me with my shoelaces, set off for a midnight tour of Hveravellir. The place is famed in Iceland as the home of the eighteenth-century outlaw Eyvindur, who fled a coastal village after being caught pilfering cheese and ended up with his wife by the then almost unknown springs. Here they stayed alone for thirty-seven years, rustling sheep, boiling mutton in the hot pots and pretending to be the Flintstones. Looking round the remains of his lava-brick cottage, I wondered why he didn't build the thing beside the springs rather than about 300 yards away – the winters here are almost inconceivably awful (100-miles-per-hour winds, 40-below frosts, stodgy corn pone at the Wild West theme restaurant and so on), and with not a scrap of combustible matter for days in any direction they would have been the only source of heat.

What's interesting about Eyvindur isn't that he did what he did but the fact that he's famous for doing it. There's a noted play about his exploits, which includes a scene where his wife, being pursued by the sheriff's men, improves her mobility by nobly chucking their baby down a waterfall.

Such reverence for someone who took on the Icelandic interior and won shows the awe in which Icelanders hold their nation's middle bits. The stories of trolls and mythical 'Thieves' Valleys' in the interior are all part of the mystery of the desolate, empty wildernesses. Birna's brother Aggi expostulates that the cult of the interior is the epitome of the Icelandic obsession with purity. The untouched language, almost unchanged from that used by the original Viking settlers from Norway; the racial purity these settlers and a millennium of almost total isolation ensured; some of the world's cleanest air and water . . . all this finds ultimate expression in the interior's frigid virginity, essentially unsullied as it is by man or beast. Or bush.

As we walked back across the steaming crusts, I concluded that despite all this, the Hveravellir springs are amongst the planet's most compellingly unwholesome natural phenomena. From the abnormally perfect fumaroles – miniature volcanoes permanently whistling out a high-pressure jet of superheated sour gas – to the unearthly sulphurous dribbles – Barclays blue, McDonald's yellow – coursing nauseously down the whole area's barren silica carapace, it was as fresh and pure as the effluent from an abandoned Chinese battery factory. Eyvindur probably built his cottage a healthy distance away because he was petrified that Satan would pull him into the particular fire and brimstone funnel reserved for cheese pilferers.

We returned, steamed and dizzy, and spread ourselves gratefully across the sprawling mattress plain. Then something senseless and awful happened. At 12.50 a.m. the hut door opened, and a dozen pairs of noisy feet began a slow, ominous ascent up to our haven. Soon our room was filled with morose, youthful East Europeans, all wearing badly pilled World Cup '74-style nylon tracksuits and the sallow, waxy complexions that come from a life of chain-smoking cardboard fags and waiting at 5 a.m. by tram stops near open-cast brown coal mines. We drifted to sleep to a curiously effective lullaby of ill-restrained giggles, belches and stage whispers, waking every hour or so to the welcome sound of a Slavic skull making heavy contact with the steeply pitched pine roof.

Packing as clumsily as we could in a vain bid to disturb their late-morning lie-in, Dilli noticed that his camera had gone missing. A recreation of its last known movements placed it either on the table in our room or by the hot pool; it was now in neither location, and the Slavs were the sole suspects in either scenario. Waving aside French protests at the state of the Beanfeast-streaked stove, we went outside to load our bikes and ponder the options. There we saw their cars, a spanking new Toyota RAV4 and a Land-Rover Discovery in 'Czech Republic Camel Trophy Team' livery. Busying himself about them was their leader, a cheery middle-aged grizzler with white stubble, brown teeth, and a round, red stomach curtained by open shirt flaps. He was clearly the one with the money. I delivered a faltering, qualified accusation.

'Er . . . hello. Um . . . did you or any of your friends see a camera last night? Because, you know, my friend had his camera, and . . . maybe, I don't know, one of your friends thought it was lost and wanted to take care of it in case it rained . . .'

'*Prosim?*'

In Scandinavia it's easy to forget that the whole world doesn't speak English.

'Er . . . a camera. Camera? Click-click? My friend – his camera? Your friend – take camera? Put in pocket?'

He gave me a look that initially suggested he had interpreted my mime as a request for my friend to take photographs of his friend's trousers, then smiled with the joy of comprehension. 'No, no! Iceland – people not taking camera here. No! Look – my cars, I have doors open in night – no key in Iceland!'

We'd recognised from the start that a return of the camera was unlikely given the limited scope for innocent appropriation; in any case this affluent, jolly fellow would scarcely have been party to such a petty, opportunist crime. No. He was probably here to pick up 50,000 tabs of E from the airstrip. There was only one thing for it: to irritate him by referring repeatedly to his country as Czechoslovakia, then pedal off into the desert muttering darkly.

At least the sun had come out, giving us for the first time clear views of the stark peaks on all distant horizons. Pedalling up the first of the day's many drawn-out inclines, we actually stripped down to our bare waists. But I could see Dilli was preoccupied. It wasn't so much the camera itself as the amount of time we'd expended doing elaborately staged self-timer shots on the film in it, balancing the camera on boulders and running back to our bikes just in time to see it get blown over.

I'd been more troubled by the fact that the theft had seemingly been endorsed by all eleven young Czechs; normally a sample of that size ought to contain at least one conscientious objector who would have vetoed the crime. I expounded my new scenario to comfort Dilli: it wasn't a theft they'd planned, but a drunken prank adapted from an urban myth.

'They waited until we were asleep, then borrowed your camera to take a load of photos of each other with our toothbrushes poking out of their bottoms. They were going to leave the camera for us to find the photos when we had them developed at home, but then the old guy came in and threw a fit and smashed the camera in outrage.'

We cycled on a bit.

'So, they, you know, just had to throw it away. The camera.'

A car passed, enveloping us in a gritty dust cloud.

'Maybe they chucked it down a fumarole.'

The sun was very nearly beating down now.

'In what single way is that anything other than far, far worse?' enquired Dilli at length.

A German guide at the Hveravellir hut had told us of a roadside café with an attached minimart. Though the persisting desolation suggested this originated from the same dark corner of the mind as our Wild West gin palace, the thought of it drove us on to previously unheard of average speeds.

As indeed did the flies, thriving on the delicious lava dust that was all there could have been for them to eat. No doubt lured by the soggy preserves and rancid undergarments now billowing from our panniers, they kept up with us at astonishing speed – after some time I was able to establish that only by maintaining a minimum velocity of 14 kilometres per hour could we outpace them. (Later, when I calculated that as 9 miles per hour, I realised how feeble an achievement this actually was.) Their irrepressible fondness for entering the unprotected orifices of the stationary cyclist reduced still further our stops for ingestion and excretion.

We gradually attained an almost karmic detachment, the constant aerobics and fasting combining to elevate our consciousness to a state above fatigue, a state where the rhythmical clocking up of kilometres achieved its own momentum. As the scenery became flatter, the road being diverted around a monotonous artificial lake created in the early Nineties as part of a hydroelectric scheme, so we narrowed our focus to the gravelled strip ahead of us, taking it in turns at the front to share the comfort of the slipstream.

Only out of curiosity did we briefly stop at the emergency hut that had been our planned overnight refuge if, as had seemed likely twenty-four hours before, febrile exhaustion had by this point gripped us (me). Inside, as in most Scandinavian buildings of any description, was a visitors' book, and, inside that, as in most Scandinavian visitors' books of any description, the bulk of the entries were of German origin. The most recent note was penned by 'Frederik, 17 years, cycling alone from Germany'.

These huts are only intended as refuges for those trapped by avalanches or with tibia stumps sticking through the flesh of their calves, and their casual use as free hostels, particularly by Germans, is frowned upon. But reading his disjointed stream of consciousness, it became clear that Frederik was a worthy guest. 'If you go south, the street is good for 10 kilometres, but then you have the worst street you ever seen. Fuck – I don't have bread or oats, and it's a sandstorm.' You could imagine the Dusseldorf coroner's clerk reading this out to his weeping parents.

On we pedalled. Forty kilometres, 50, 60. We weren't even excessively dispirited when we chanced upon the fabled café, only

125

to discover it boarded up. Soon after we spied the Swiss on the horizon, and inexorably reined him in, passing his aluminium superbike with a patronising wave then leaving him for dead. Our record daily distance – the day before's 73 kilometres – came and went. Beyond the hydroelectric plant, grass appeared. Then sheep. Then tarmac. We were back on earth.

The road gradually lowered itself into a mammoth, windswept descent of the sort Tour de France riders stuff newspaper down their shirts before tackling, and we covered the next 10 kilometres in only slightly more minutes. In this new, slightly unreal world, nothing seemed surprising. I didn't even bother telling Dilli when we next stopped that I'd almost met a suitably ridiculous end when a sheep ran out in front of me at 61 kilometres per hour. It seemed perfectly unremarkable when we shot past a roadside bust and inscription, and Dilli called out lazily that it was of his great-grandfather.

Then, abruptly, anticlimactically, there was a junction, and a sign marked 'Kjölur' pointing back to where we'd come from. It was over. We'd done almost 100 kilometres in a day.

Stopping to photograph this symbol of our achievement was, on reflection, a mistake. On the descent, we'd agreed that given our trouble-free progress, it would be not much more effort to continue to Blönduós, where we'd find food and a hotel. 'Fuck camping' was, I believe, the phrase used. But having stopped, and endured the recurring horrors of gelatinous desiccated fruit and that awful, awful vulcanised pork-knuckle chocolate, we found our bodies had belatedly come to their senses.

'What's all this about, then?' ratcheted my knees as I remounted. 'Don't you start, you're not the ones crucified on a red-hot cast-iron radiator,' rejoined my shoulder blades. Brief, random gastronomic fantasies formulated themselves in our stomachs and proceeded directly to our helpless mouths.

'Red wine,' I blurted. 'Chips. Grilled meats.'

'Licorice sherbet,' ejaculated Dilli, much to his own surprise.

We winced our way up to the ring road, Route 1. It was still 20 kilometres to Blönduós, along a dead straight, dead flat, dead dull road following Langadalur, Long Valley, the Blandá's vast flood plain. Right on cue, the drizzle picked up into driving rain, spawning small puddles which provided an irresistible target for Iceland's many bored and vindictive motorists. We hardly cared. I was now having to stop every ten minutes, lying prostrate on the verge to ease the crucifixion pains, and Dilli's pedal revolution rate slowed inexorably. Such was the fatigue that my usually exuberant flobbing was reduced to an ineffective wheezed-out dribble that invariably failed to clear my shoulder. After about seven months, we topped a final incline, and below us lay the damp huddle of Blönduós. The milometer read 121.07 kilometres. It was 9.32 p.m. I think I cried.

Now utterly drenched, we wobbled into a petrol station with an attached cafeteria. Inside normal people were doing normal things, things we had forgotten seemed possible, like using urinals without completely undressing and paying £6 for a hamburger. A line of customers queued in front of a cabinet of confectionery, crisps and carbonated beverages, yet none seemed ready to kneel with humbled gratitude that man's wisdom and the earth's bounty had combined to assemble such a cornucopia before them.

I dropped into a chair and sat there vacantly, idly stripping off most of my spittle-streaked outer garments and wondering how I could ever adapt to society again. This, I dully noted, must have been how Vietnam vets felt when they returned to Baton Rouge and Des Moines, outsiders, who had seen and done things that no civilised man ought still to see and do. Nothing in our suburban existences could match the extraordinary intensity of what we had experienced, the comradeship, the suffering. I smiled dozily at two toddlers, then felt a terrible urge to smother them. It was not right that such happy innocence should be soured and poisoned by fear, filth and hunger. The courting youths on the table to our right, the grandparents taking the kids for a treat on a Sunday? Wednesday? Doomsday? It was impossible now to look at these suddenly inane stereotypes without feeling an almost Nietzschean superiority.

'We are not as they are,' I croaked blankly to Dilli, who fortunately nodded in comprehension.

But, like time, chips are a great healer. The waitress clearly had an eye for the symptoms of dangerous malnourishment, and served us each with a shoebox of French fries. With most of these stuffed haphazardly down our gullets by trembling, wristless hands, we reappraised Western civilisation and our place within it, and took stock of more immediate prosaic considerations, such as the fact that our torsos were currently clad only in black silk thermal vests which, on account of the internal and external moisture, were now repellently, nipple-baringly sheer. Girls were openly pointing and laughing.

Drunk on carbohydrates, I weaved up to the waitress and asked for directions to the hotel. 'It's some metres distance.' 'How many?' I asked, knowing that any answer above 12 would rule it out in my current state. 'Maybe 2 kilometres. But there is a campsite here.' So be it. Our priorities were shifting. Sound sleep would not be a problem wherever we were. I could have merrily bedded down under the air hose compressor. Beer was now the thing. Beer, beer, beer. So urgent was this need that after sort of propping the tent up next to a soaking hedge in a soaking campsite, we cycled off and eventually ended up at the hotel anyway. It was the only bar in town.

Within its endearingly contrived airport-pub cosiness we despatched a succession of £5.80 pints in the sole company of a group of underage drinkers who kept stealing display miniatures of cherry brandy whenever the harassed bargirl ran off to answer the phone in reception. By this method they contrived advanced drunkenness, and as we slumped, empty-headed and silent, before our fourth pint, their inhibitions lowered to the point where it became important to involve us in their lives.

Dimly recalling that, in England, a group of drunk youths approaching two nipple-flaunting men in a pub would be the precursor to ugly and one-sided violence, I lethargically prepared myself for a crescendo of abuse and a sound thrashing. But I should have known better. 'How do you like Iceland?' their leader slurred.

Weaving home, we stopped on the bridge over the Blandá,

bikes propped against the railings, watching ducklings buzz about in the foam as the river broadened out and was lost in the sea. Somewhere, just beyond the horizon, 60 miles out, the Atlantic became the Arctic. Now, suddenly, came the sense of achievement. I had done this thing; I had crossed a whole country on a bicycle. I had conquered Europe's second largest desert, out-Dufferined Dufferin. I was clearly one of the best people in the world.

5

The next day began in accordance with the second law of camping, that an incline of 0.2 degrees will involve all parties present in the tent awaking on top of each other in a puddle. Drying myself down with an old pair of socks, I decided upon returning to Reykjavík by bus with Dilli forthwith. Apart from a determination to punish my tent before a large crowd in a busy town square, I was also lured by the arrival from England of my wife and children and a rumour that the impending Viking festival in Hafnafjörður (Reykjavík's Slough) would be (a) funny and (b) attended by a convoy of boats from Norway, offering hope of hitching a suitably Dufferinian nautical passage on their return voyage. He'd sailed from Iceland to Norway via Jan Mayen; in the absence of marine links to the marooned volcanic outcrop, I was having to do Iceland to Jan Mayen via Norway in the shape of a military flight from the Arctic Circle port of Bodø.

We drank two cups of two-quid coffee as we waited at the bus station, remarking how quickly and easily we had slipped back into our blithe acceptance of the perks of civilisation. Poking about critically at the collected grinds in the bottom of the cup, Dilli noted that only eighteen hours earlier we would have heaved aside nursing mothers for a chance of dabbing this sediment on our lips. Recent deeds such as the pointless theft of a box of teabags from the Hveravellir hut kitchen now seemed the desperate acts of two haunted, hunted men, men who bore no relation to the pair of humdrum, slightly grubby tourists now grumbling about the limited range of hot dog relishes at a bus station café.

Some 410 minutes later we were standing before Birna's parents' front door, gawping at it like something half remembered from a previous life. Within another ten I had pulled off half my clothes, eaten a lump of cheddar the size of a Harold Robbins and fallen asleep on the sofa, my ruined frame oblivious to my son's energetic slaps and pokes.

I stayed in my in-law's large and peaceful home for three nights, relearning my children's names, being wonderfully nourished with the grilled meats and red wine of my famished hallucinations and watching my calves belatedly swelling, as promised by Dr Dilli, into, well, cows.

For the first time since leaving Grimsby I now enjoyed the physical and mental wherewithal to continue my study of Harold Nicolson's *Helen's Tower*. Despite scoring a handsome and much needed victory over Dufferin in the indefatigability stakes with my trans-Icelandic trek, I was still uncomfortably aware that my unseemly spiritual collapse aboard the *Dettifoss* was certain to be repeated on the next maritime leg of my journey, whatever that might be. In this context, I was now desperate to notch up some more credit points over Dufferin before I set sail.

But the first chapters of *Helen's Tower* offered slim pickings: 'amused even at his own splendour . . . ambient gaiety . . . generosity of soul . . . florid, flamboyant . . . a man of unusual fastidiousness, sensibility and wit'. Buttocks. I got quite excited by the half-his-age marriage to the eighteen-year-old cousin, Lady Hariot Hamilton, more so when I read that the union was seemingly a cynical, loveless political deed contrived by Dufferin, ever the diplomat, to heal a 200-year-old family rift (the Hamiltons had been the original lords of Clandeboye, but through a series of disputed wills had been outflanked by the Blackwoods).

Then of course it's revealed that the couple shared a deep bond of love and respect. He was 'the sun around which revolved all the planets in her firmament'; she was 'the most stately of all Vicereines . . . who could enter a room like no lady in Europe'. On a unicycle. No? Double buttocks.

The only real hope of scoring character points over him was engendered by hints that he evolved into rather a pompous old sod. Harold Nicolson's first memory of Dufferin was as a five-year-old, visiting his sixty-seven-year-old uncle's residence, the British Embassy in Paris. Harold is given a small helium-filled balloon decorated with a rooster motif, and lets it slip from his grasp at the foot of a cavernous ambassadorial stairwell. The footmen are thrown into a lather, pelting the miniature dirigible with darts and swatting it with long broomsticks. 'I only hope,' quakes a terrified attache, 'that His Excellency does not emerge.'

Would Dufferin – who danced jigs on apothecaries' tables and was amused even at his own splendour, whose most prominent literary work, *Letters From High Latitudes*, scandalised many contemporaries with its accounts of drunkenness and inclusion of 'several quite common words' – really have been that bothered? After I read that his wife, during their time in Canada, once walked out of a New York theatre after 'she saw signs of the play taking an improper turn', it was clear that she was the humourless prude in the partnership. Though some of it might have rubbed off on him, I could only allow myself half a point.

The scoreboard clicked on monotonously: 'much too good-looking and captivating' (Queen Victoria on Dufferin when he became a lord-in-waiting); 'the only person of whom my father was ever known to stand in awe'; 'he mastered the appalling touchiness of the Canadians' (eh?) with his 'frankness and humour'; 'even in his seventy-fourth year he would navigate his little yawl *The Lady Hermione* through the deceptive tides of the Minch assisted only by a boy of fourteen'.

It might have been the 'much too good-looking and captivating' that did it, confirming as it did my conclusion during the seasick sulk that Dufferin, certainly by my standards, was too good to be true. You couldn't be fearless and sensitive, statesmanlike and flippant, wealthy and wise, fine and dandy. And you certainly couldn't be all these things and be charmingly modest about it. Accepting defeat with a wholly characteristic lack of grace, I lowered myself to claiming consolation points from the surprising revelations that Dufferin was short, went deaf in middle age and had a lisp. 'He smiled courteously, dropped his eyeglass and answered "Yeth, yeth."' Well, whoop-de-doop! That's 410–3½. Thee you in Thpithbergen, Marqueth! Dubiously buoyed up, I was ready to enter Valhalla. After the biking, the Viking.

The bi-annual Viking Festival in Hafnafjörður is apparently an embarrassment to Icelanders, with few locals among its hairy-coated delegates. As Birna's brother Valdimar drove me and my family into the Festival car park he sunk down in his seat. Icelanders are all Vikings, related to each other ten generations back, many able to trace their lineage right back to the eleventh century. They don't need to reaffirm their roots with a cringing display of playground pillaging. Viking culture is very much a part of contemporary Icelandic life. Birna's eldest brother, Asgeir, named his two sons after Oðin's ravens, Hugi and Muni, which doesn't sound too controversial until you learn that they mean Mind and Memory.

Most of the weekend-Norsemen originated from the invaded rather than invading nations. There were a few Norwegians and Danes, but the majority were Brits and Germans, come to emulate their ancient torments. So when Valdimar drove up to the car park attendant and said: 'I've got these two foreigners here to see the Vikings, who I don't want to see at all, but these two foreigners do, and I don't, and they do, and they're foreign, and I'm not,' I wasn't offended. Nor was Birna, who's not even foreign at all. I'd have done exactly the same if I'd had a French brother-in-law who'd asked me to chauffeur him to the Pearly King Festival.

It's easy to be glib and snotty about a load of assistant ombuds-men from Fleetwood and harbourmasters from Cologne running about a wet school playing-field waving pikes and trying to stop their jogging pants peeping out from under their tabards. Also, I am lazy – so hold on to your horned helmets for a deluge of glib snot.

The festival was laid out as a series of hemp-like tents and wooden stalls selling things like Viking honey and runic joke books. Wandering past Coke machines ineffectively camouflaged with fox pelts and *pylsur* grills hidden behind woven windbreaks, we stopped at a stall selling shiny bovine horns of the type Kirk Douglas blew to summon Tony Curtis in *The Vikings*. The proprietor was an imposing fellow, the effect of his matted auburn beard and carpet-stitched jerkin only slightly spoilt by the digital watch and Oscar Goldman glasses. A teenage Viking was pointing out the inadequacies of his wares in Germanic English. 'This horn cannot be used. The mouth hole here, it needs to be more deep inside. Have you not tried to make a noise?'

The owner had not taken exception. 'Not me, son. I only sell them,' he replied with a wink in cheery Black Country. Our own conversation with him, enquiring about the nautical Viking convoy, confirmed a suspicion that his heart wasn't really in Jutland, AD 948. 'No, well, there's not many come by boat. There's Viking events all round Europe in summer, and boats are really too slow. I think some Germans sent their merchandise over in a container. Not sure.'

Merchandise? Events? This was bizarre. Obviously this gentleman and many like him were little more than a tabard-clad division of those itinerant professionals you see at car boot sales, who travel the country selling product-recall job lots of mercury-plated Chinese screwdriver sets and poorly earthed Thomas the Tank Engine nightlights.

We ambled off, slightly disillusioned, past a sealed tent where a man with an M4 corridor accent was attempting to bring to order a palpably important briefing.

'Okay, okay. Right, after the tannoy guy's said his piece, the villagers – that's all you lot, and Dave . . . where's Dave? Dave? Okay – Dave: you're with the villagers. Look, can we keep it down a bit, *please*? Thank you. Right. So the villagers come running out round the back, into the battlefield area, shouting, "Oh no, it's Thangbrandur," that sort of thing. Whatever. Then it's as we've agreed. Okay?'

This we had to see. Within minutes four dozen Vikings were

embroiled in an anarchic mêlée with an equal number of Christian Thangbrandites, amid scenes of surprisingly raw violence. The swords were blunt but heavy, and swung with full arcs which smashed plywood chips from shields and sent them spinning into the retreating spectators. My three-year-old son was enchanted. 'Nice one, Dave!' yelled someone behind us. Strident though perhaps etymologically inappropriate Anglo-Saxonisms soon joined the Jimmy Connors grunts and Geoff Capes roars. One female Viking with a pike became enmeshed with an opponent under our noses. 'Christian . . . cunt!' she yelled. 'Sssh. Don't swear. No swearing,' whispered her enemy urgently, slightly too loudly to prevent about forty spectators hearing and bursting into a giggle, and an Icelandic teenager piping back, 'Ferck you, man!'

No swearing? You're Vikings, for pity's sakes! You rape! You pillage! You get drunk and don't wash! Who do you think you're going to offend? 'Well, I'm very sorry, but I was going to sign up to the Baby-Impaling module in your Mindless Slaughter workshop, but then I heard one of your colleagues say "cock-hole".'

The fight petered out. As the dead rose from their bus-lane Valhalla, the tannoy bid them in turn to identify their origins. 'All British Vikings!' it roared, and two-thirds of the fighters waved a shield. The crowd booed the Germans, many of whom had no doubt been drying their tents in local garages with only partial permission, and also the sole Icelandic Viking, who responded by screaming 'Thor!' in a voice maybe half an octave too high to get away with it.

'And finally, any and all other Vikings!'

'Ireland?' apologised a little voice beneath a meekly wiggled staff. I thought, not completely sympathetically, of Dufferin's liking for Vikings.

High Latitudes is stuffed with page after page of tales from the sagas, introduced by headings like 'Thured's Lover' and the excellent 'A Berserk Tragedy', detailing breathless accounts of Thor wrestling with a nurse and Arngrim boiling Halli to death. I suppose his fascination was partly down to his romantic idealisation of noble savages, and partly down to the theory, championed by

135

Dufferin at length, that Vikings travelled at will between Iceland and his native Ireland (the resultant interbreeding is said to account for Icelanders generally having darker hair than their famously blond Scandinavian cousins). As he gazed blearily at the sea of glasses before him at the Governor's banquet, Dufferin must have felt a reaffirmation of this across-the-water, under-the-table bond. And of course the Vikings' fondness for ghastly slaughter allowed full rein to his powers of understatement: Berserker massacres are described as 'moments of excitement'.

As we'd found on our bikes, the primeval landscape encourages epic fantasies to take hold. Apologising for 'becoming a little magniloquent', Dufferin explains that 'amid the grandeur of the colossal scenery' his crew had 'assumed the appetite of giants'. 'The pulses of young Titans beat within our veins,' he says. As the *Reine Hortense* towed the *Foam* out of Reykjavík harbour and set off north to the distant, lonely volcano of Jan Mayen, such sentiments were wholly in order. The voyage to Iceland, however uncomfortable, was a routine one; the trek across the interior had been replaced by a mere round-trip sightseeing jaunt. Ahead lay icebergs, uncharted water and empty wilderness. His adventure proper had begun.

If a Viking boat could indeed sail me to Norway (my military transport to Jan Mayen flew from Bodø in three weeks), it would clearly be perfect in terms of Dufferining, but every time I thought about the reality, the pulse of a young gerbil beat within my veins. And though I'd attended the Festival in the hope of gathering inspiration as well as information, I had wisely not set these hopes too high.

Walking pensively amongst the Thors-in-trainers it was difficult to feel appropriate sentiments. There's something about people who purport to adopt the demeanour and lifestyle of a forgotten age that makes you want to follow them about and eavesdrop cheap amusement from the inevitable anachronisms of their conversations.

'What's it like in the tents? We're staying up in the school gym with the Manchester lads.'

'Right . . . We went round the house where Reagan and Gorbachev met yesterday, but Harriet forgot to charge the camcorder.' Occasionally, though, authentic Viking sentiments emerged: 'Got totally mullahed with Chris and Hootsy last night. Totally. Jesus. Ended up being thrown out of two nightclubs.' Or this memorable exchange: Fat Viking husband: 'Why are you laughing?' Fat Viking wife: 'Because you look like a bag of shit and you always will.'

Browsing around a toy stall specialising in chainmail for dolls, we started talking to an American Viking who'd obviously kept quiet at the international roll call. He'd heard about the Norwegian boats. 'The PR women up at the school were telling me about it. They started out with forty-five boats from Norway, but then kind of left some guys behind, and I think they said there's ten actually arriving here.' Ten? That sounded an unacceptably high rate of attrition. 'Most of the boats turned out to be too small or something. Hey – do you want my card? I'm producing a multimedia Viking project.'

That evening, having abandoned my bicycle in their garage (where it remains to this day), I drove with Birna's parents to their summerhouse in dense fog which perfectly complemented my mood. I should have been glad that the Hafnafjörður tourist office was now attempting to get me a berth on the Viking convoy, but I wasn't. The whole endeavour was plainly both overambitious and disastrously inept. Of all the adjectives I could apply to boats in which I would not wish to cross the North Sea, 'small' and 'Viking' would come in the top five, just behind 'ablaze' and 'upside down'.

Again I was failing to Dufferin, and, as aboard the *Dettifoss*, I found solace in taking it out on my mentor. This time, though, as I contemplated that piloting an authentically unseaworthy Viking craft across the North Atlantic would have been precisely the sort of romantic yet incredibly hazardous jaunt Dufferin would have jumped at, my surge of anger towards him possessed a more rational basis. His whole voyage was ultimately pointless: it had no scientific or geographical significance; it cost money rather than made it. He was entitled to risk his own neck, but what right did he have to endanger the lives of twelve crewmen, probably each supporting a dozen kids and a wife with a big gin habit? 'No hatred is so intense as that which you feel towards a disagreeable shipmate,' he'd written at the start of his voyage. He'd been my shipmate, in a way, for the longest three weeks of my life, and for the first time I was starting to see what he'd meant.

We stopped at the geothermal town of Hveragerði, 45 kilometres east of Reykjavík on a snooker-table plain at the foot of a ragged Gothic slab. Here Icelanders went about harnessing their steaming soil, building the first geothermally heated greenhouse in 1940. Before that, said a tourist leaflet I picked up at the gift shop where Birna's mother bought some jewellery fashioned from sheep droppings, the mud pots were regarded as a nuisance. 'The most renowned of the hot springs in Hveragerði is Manndrapshver (the Killer), named so after a man fell into the boiling water in 1906 and died,' said the text, with the usual Wilsonian relish preferred by Icelanders when referring to most human catastrophes more than fifteen years old.

Now the area is aglaze with greenhouses, producing cucumbers, red peppers and tomatoes for the domestic market. Generally these are no less hideously expensive than imported produce. I was once compelled to pay £2.50 for a cucumber, which struck me dumb for two hours. But I recall one magical summer visit, when for a glorious week Icelandic tomatoes were the cheapest in Europe, a fact trumpeted by the national media every day until Holland nosed ahead. I expressly taught myself how to make gazpacho, and toiled inexpertly at the liquidiser almost constantly until begged to stop by Birna's scarlet-splattered family.

As we were unpacking the car at the summerhouse, a familiar voice came on the radio. My mother-in-law was introducing her Arctic Island Discs. An hour later a journalist phoned my father-in-law and interviewed him. Within two weeks Birna and Aggi would be profiled in the national press.

Someone once calculated that with such an active media and a diminutive population, all Icelanders can expect to appear on television at least three times. It can all be a little intimidating. I once found a book on the genealogy of my in-laws' extended family and was dumbstruck to find a bad photo of myself, with a caption hurtfully describing me as a computer programmer (at the time I reviewed PC games for the repellent Teletext), lurking near the index.

But it does have advantages. Set your heart on being Iceland's leading radiographer or animal impersonator or consumer terrorist and the limited competition implied by a population of 270,000 gives you every chance of success. People in Britain who really want to work in television spend eleven years photocopying autocue scripts at HTV for the chance to land a job arranging the prizes on the *Generation Game* conveyor belt. In Reykjavík, string a sentence together without being sick or pulling your trousers down and you're the evening news anchor within six months.

The next few days were largely spent lolling in the enclave swimming pool, a supra-heated open-air establishment affording fine views of Hekla. The Icelandic swimming pool is perhaps the nation's finest institution, and in my lazy basks I often pondered what a shame it was that Dufferin never got to experience one.

For the 700-odd years following their forefathers' shamingly non-sustainable forestry, the vast majority of Icelanders had almost no access to fuel. Hot water was so rare that Birna tells me most communities only had one bath a year, at Christmas. Today, the freedom to bathe outside in steaming tubs is an inalienable right, and you are never far from an immaculate, heavily subsidised establishment (entrance is generally less than £2). It is poetically rewarding, though sadly not remotely accurate, to state that Iceland must certainly be one of the few countries in the world where public baths outnumber public houses.

However, before plunging gleefully into a skin-blistering hot pot, it is important to have a solid grounding in pool etiquette. The first time I went swimming in Reykjavík, I was grabbed by an elderly attendant as I skirted past the exuberantly nude shower party and slunk towards the pool. People over the age of 60 are generally the only Icelanders with a less than fluent grasp of English, which was particularly unfortunate in this case as it rendered his gesticulations – pointing at my trunks with one hand and miming a vigorous frottage with the other – open to a disturbing variety of interpretations.

Most, but not all, of the more unpleasant of these were expelled when he led me to a poster, which with the aid of a shamelessly frank diagram explained the intimate bodily areas that were to be scrubbed with bactericidal soap before entering the pool.

Perhaps it's not only the dirt they're washing off, but the stubborn shame-stains of those centuries of once-a-year bathing. Whatever the reason, it's all reached the other extreme now. Birna and her parents came to live in England when she was four. After the family's first, shocked visit to an English swimming pool, her mother fulminated against the threat to public health posed by the unhygienic bathing practices. The unlikely bogeyman of Birna's childhood was not Freddie Krueger or a dalek, but The Old Man With The Badly Wiped Bottom.

You can always tell the tourists at an Icelandic swimming pool. They're the ones with their eyes closed and distant lop-sided grins smudged across their sagging faces, looking like they've just had a big hit of morphine. The cocoon-like warmth, and the knowledge that it has welled up from Mother Earth's own womb, lends the whole experience a dreamy sense of wellbeing, of man's happy symbiosis with nature, that inevitably starts me mumbling the choruses to 'Golden Brown', 'Across the Universe' and other selected musical paeans to the wonders of opiate abuse. Even if the water does smell of tramps' trousers.

A few days of lotus-eating – bathing, barbecuing, meeting relatives with funny nicknames, eating lotuses – came to an abrupt end with a phone call. The captain of the lead boat in the Norway-bound Viking convoy was offering me a place on board. 'What is your sea experience?' had been his first question, which elevated my misgivings to a whole new plane. I suddenly had a striking image of myself lashed to a rough plank bench, struggling to manipulate an oar the size of a telegraph pole as another wall of black brine dashed over me. 'It might be a little cramped,' he warned, thereby squeezing four drunken redbeards on to my plank and one on to my lap, 'but don't worry – we aren't having too many ceremonies on the way back.' This rounded off my mental picture. The leering pagan astride me was now branding 'Danegeld' into my cheeks with a glowing axehead while his four colleagues heaved my blazing rucksack into the foam to appease the Norse gods of the sea.

'Any questions?'

'Yes, I most certainly do have questions! Are you all insane? Have you any idea what you're doing? And, damn it all, do you place no value at all on a human life, man?'

All this and more I tried to imply in the following limp enquiry: 'Er, how big are your boats?'

'You are lucky. My boat is the biggest – 62 feet. We leave tomorrow from Höfn. Bring your passport and 1,500 Norwegian kroner. I will see you on board.'

I spent my remaining hours visualising things 62 feet long and what it would be like to be in them at sea. The summerhouse didn't seem nearly big enough to tackle the North Atlantic, with or without the veranda and another five feet. Nor did a coach towing a kebab van. My father-in-law did little to calm my accelerating unease. 'It will be very interesting. You will come back a man,' he intoned portentously over dinner. Jesus. I went to bed before he could place his hand on my shoulder and whisper hoarsely, 'Those about to die, we salute you.'

6

The convoy's itinerary would take them back to the Faroes and the Shetlands, with three-day stops at each, before arriving at Haugesund in Norway in two weeks' time. If I wished, though, the skipper of my boat would afterwards take me north to Florø, home of most of the convoy's prosperous skippers, from where I could catch my boat up the Norwegian coast to Bodø, and thence my flight to Jan Mayen. I supposed I did wish. However petrifying the vessel, however cock-eyed the route, at least I was back on a boat, back on the path to Jan Mayen, back on the lisping lord's trail.

Dufferin had thet thail from Reykjavík on 7 July, after a party on board the *Reine Hortense* where half a dozen sailors in turbans danced the can-can and he tried to chat girls up in Latin. 'The real, serious part of our voyage is about to begin,' he writes as the *Foam* is tied up behind the French steamer.

The next morning I savoured my last smelly shower – looming anointment by Viking urine notwithstanding – and felt a real affinity with Dufferin's statement as I waved what had suddenly evolved into a desperate farewell to my family. 'Daddy's going on a Viking ship,' said my son, sweetly, before rather ruining the placatory effect by following it up with his favourite battle cry from the re-enactment: 'Aaaargggh – Christians!'

Birna had helped me encase all my belongings in binliners to protect them from the brine and rain and slops swilling around the lurching open boat, and having wedged these into the family's Daihatsu, I was driven by Guðrún to Selfoss, from where I was catching a bus for the nine-hour journey to the southeastern port of Höfn.

'They are probably not real Vikings,' said Guðrún as we unloaded at Selfoss. No – but that'll be worse, I thought. All the beer-drinking and self-conscious boorishness – *ceremonies*, for pity's sakes – with none of the navigational expertise. In nine hours I would, apparently, start to become a man. Although I could not begin to imagine how this intriguing transformation would manifest itself, it did occur to me that, if I made a really good job of it, I could perhaps, in spirit at least, become a lord.

I made a mistake on the bus, attempting when purchasing my ticket to pronounce Höfn as the Icelanders do, which, unhelpfully, appeared to be 'Hurpn'. My staccato rendition of this had the conductress leaning towards me with worried compassion, and, if I hadn't followed it up with an instantly understood Anglo-phonetic 'Hoffen', she'd probably still be slapping me on the back and looking for obstructions in my airways.

After I returned home, I tried out my rendition of Höfn on Birna to prove how stupid the conductress had been.

'Hurpn,' I burped.

'Are you okay?'

'Hurpn!'

'Sure it's in Iceland?'

I was a beaten man. 'Hoffen,' I sighed, cravenly.

'Ah, yes,' she said, 'Hurbn.'

Scandinavians are so good at English that they even have two names for their own towns – one as pronounced by the natives, the other by idiot tourists. They are not programmed to deal with the possibility of an idiot tourist attempting the native pronunciation. I was rather taken aback, for instance, to hear that the correct Norwegian pronunciation of Oslo is actually the reasonably hilarious 'Oooshloo', but, on the single occasion I tried that out, the woman at the ferry terminal in Bergen gave me a leaflet about Newcastle.

The bus was busily peopled by Mitteleuropean neo-hippies, mostly, like the choice specimen occupying the window seat next to me, flamboyantly asleep. This saved them from fretting about the driver, whom I was horrified to note was not only laughing into a mobile phone, but also had a stupid-housewife jumbo crossword open on the dashboard. 'Please do not speak to the driver' read the multilingual notice beneath the rear view mirror, and it was a wonder a shaken passenger had not appended this with 'unless you know a better Norwegian joke than the one his brother-in-law's telling him or a three-letter synonym for "coach".'

As we motored steadily across Eldhraun – Fire Lava, the south coast's flat black lava fields – to a maddening chorus of passive Walkman hiss, it occurred to me that the closest I would get to a Dufferin-style discourse upon the classics was looking over the shoulder of the *Hair* understudy diagonally in front of me to garner snippets from his copy of *Colloquial Greek*.

This was becoming unsatisfactory. As some unseen Euro-crustie sparked up an illicit fag, I pondered that Dufferin wouldn't have put up with any of this. Or would he? I remembered that in his later years, Dufferin would light an after-dinner cigarette *'pour encourager les autres'*, but not actually smoke it. I supposed this fear of confrontation, of creating a scene, typified a man born for a career in the Foreign Office.

'That's why he's not known today,' Andrew Gailey had said. 'As a diplomat, he would have judged his own success by the extent he managed to stay in the background.'

True enough. The only surefire ways to ensure a place in political history are to start or end a war or to cock up on a grand scale (a category which, perhaps harshly, includes being assassinated). A long career of successfully defusing tension with charm and tact might have been thrown away by giving a single illustrated lecture on the history of the pornographic limerick, but to have done so would have greatly enhanced Dufferin's prospects as a candidate for posterity.

'Dignity was his job,' Andrew had said. 'And of course when he got married he became more staid and respectable.' Indeed. Looking through some of the transcripts of letters, I noted that his wife always addressed him as 'Dufferin'. I supposed this evolution fitted in with what I'd seen in the Internet image, the whimsical youth who matured into a grandee.

But could this transformation really just have been down to the passage of time? At the next comfort stop ('Thanks for that stop – it would have been really uncomfortable if I'd pissed all over your coach'), I stayed in my seat and, battling against the phlegmy snores around me, resumed my stuttering progress through *Helen's Tower* in search of an answer. And the answer was in the title.

As a young widow, Dufferin's mother spent the winters in Castellamare, overlooking the Bay of Naples, with her friend the Duchess of Somerset. In the winter of 1842, her thirty-fifth year, she struck up a friendship with a surprise visitor, The Old Man With The Badly Wiped Bottom. Actually, it was Lord Gifford, who soon began paying almost daily visits to her apartment.

Would the young Lord Dufferin, then seventeen, have been pleased at the prospect of a well-bred, well-heeled stepfather? Possibly. But not this one. Lord Gifford was eighteen and a friend of Dufferin's.

It's difficult to imagine how Dufferin would have coped with seeing his goddess entwined in such a relationship. Perhaps he hoped that Gifford's ardour would cool over time. If so, he was wrong. Gifford proposed to Lady Dufferin with tiresome regularity as he progressed into his twenties, entered Parliament, became the manager of his father's estates. Every time 'she begged him to dismiss from his mind so unsuitable a fantasy'.

Nicolson says that she could not bring herself to remarry until her beloved Frederick had paired off. Perhaps aware of this, he seemed in no hurry. When he finally did get hitched, at thirty-seven, he might well have been confident that his mother, now fifty-five, would hold diminished appeal for Gifford. Wrong again. After a twenty-year courtship, the couple were married in 1862, outraging his parents, shattering her son and scandalising society.

In fact, she had done her homework. Earlier that year he had begun suffering some sort of muscular pain; this got steadily worse, and the doctors, diagnosing an 'internal lesion beyond the resources of their skill', despaired. Before agreeing to marry him, Lady Dufferin established from the medics that (a) his days were numbered, and in a low-digit total; and (b) there was absolutely no chance of his withered loins being up to anything unseemly.

Sure enough, he only lasted eight weeks beyond the wedding. Six years later, Lady Dufferin, now Countess Gifford, succumbed to breast cancer, and was buried beside him in Friern Barnet.

How very odd. Perhaps Dufferin's trips to the Crimea and the Arctic were an escape not from social and political expectation but from the cringing shame of seeing his childhood friend run about after his mother, of seeing her cast by society as a proto-Mrs Robinson; maybe by dragging her away with him to the Mediterranean he was hoping to save her from Gifford's relentless approaches. And the frenzied career-forging programme he belatedly embarked upon after her marriage was as much as anything a distraction from the awful truth, a bid to blot out the scandal with his own achievements.

As I read on, Nicolson confirmed that the marriage had come as a 'lasting shock'. 'It was his undue sensitiveness to public opinion, his fastidious dread of ridicule . . . It was torture to him to feel that the gnats of malice might buzz even for a moment above that sainted head.'

The smellies reboarded, and we headed off into a suitably melancholic mist. Suddenly I understood why Dufferin had built *Helen's Tower* — an obvious memorial stuffed with epitaphs — six years before her death. When she married Gifford, his mother — or at least the sisterly virgin he worshipped her as — died.

The mist thickened, but in any case there wasn't much to look at. Just as the polychromatic run-off waters at Geysir and Hveravellir had overpowering sensory associations with illegal industrial leachate, so it is the misfortune of unvegetated lava deserts to call to mind dug-out opencast mines or hastily half-filled gravel pits.

I was momentarily intrigued by a lesson in — whisper it — Erosion In Action, as demonstrated by acres of craggy turf half torn away by the winds whipping across the plains, the black lava showing through the violent rips and rents like a literal earth's crust. Every couple of miles a neatly planted square of purple lupins sprouted comically out of the blackness, looking hopelessly overwhelmed by the size of their task.

Fat-nosed raindrops steadily spermed their way across the windows; the smeared flat blackness outside persisted. We had reached Midwest American levels of landscape verisimilitude and carriageway non-deviation. I picked at a handlebar blister on my palm. I learned that 'πEPIπTEPO' is 'kiosk' in colloquial Greek. I ate all my food. I drank all my drink. There was only one thing left to do: develop and nurture a growing hatred for the bloke in the seat next to me.

His carefree somnambulance had been irritating for some time, but I now decided he wasn't actually asleep at all, just pretending in order to justify spreading his fifteen gangly limbs across my seat and floorspace. To give you an idea of how alarmingly this delusion blossomed, at its peak I pulled a blank page out of my note book and carved upon it in vicious two-inch Biro capitals 'DEATH TO THE SLEEP-FEIGNING HIPPIE' before placing it for his perusal at the correct oblique angle on my lap.

Although I've since managed to convince my tortured conscience that the two acts were unrelated, less than a minute after issuing this statement the bus stopped at a Nowheresfjord petrol station, and my colleague jerked into life with a horrible hawking snuffle, bundling blindly past me down the aisle, out across the forecourt and off into the unending scorched prairie. At the time, however, I was merely elated – the only traveller with a double seat. I redden now as I recall that I actually hoped he'd just gone off for a pee, unaware that we would be roaring away without him before he could even shake off the drips.

I had still not become attuned to the disparity between the cartographic prominence of Icelandic towns and their actual size. Places marked with bold capitals and an impressive target of concentric circles – Hvölsvollur, Vík, Kirkubaejarklaustur – spoke of cashpoints and multiplexes, hatching elaborate comfort stop plans foiled when a clutch of wet bungalows and a boarded-up factory shop emerged out of the drizzle. (When I got home and studied the 1:1,000,000 representation of Iceland in my *Times Atlas of the World*, I found to my astonishment that, such is the dearth of features in the interior, not only did the map feature the Kjölur track, but the barely visible sidetrack off the track that we'd taken to the hut at Hvítarnes, and not only the sidetrack but the actual hut itself. It was marked with a circle and labelled 'Saeluhus' – refuge house – in the same size text as the larger scale map of the South of England used for Orpington.)

Also unsettling, although less so because of my minimal grasp of the language, was the way that every town, river and mountain has a baldly literal name. As I'd cycled across the land with Dilli, I'd been struck by the number of Horse Mountains, Flat Mountains, Dog Mountains, Blue Mountains and Sand Mountains. Lava fields present a recurrent problem: New Lava, Lamb Lava, Tongue Lava – more than once they've just given up and called an area Lava. Höfn just means 'harbour'. No one really knows how London got its name (yes, yes, but where did 'Londinium' come from?), which is rather a pity. But in Iceland, the original settlers saw a puff of geothermal steam by the coast and they called the place Smoky Bay – Reykjavík – and it means just the same today.

The weather improved with the scenery, just in time to stop me succumbing to Dufferin's poetic penchant for desperately conjuring up purples and mauves from the greyness. The glaciers weaved closer, sometimes slithering sinuously to earth like frozen rapids, sometimes crashing to an abrupt finale with towering, toothpaste-blue cliffs of ice. Off the unglaciated crests in between streaked a succession of little waterfalls – stringy, unassuming brooks caught unawares by 300-foot drops.

The lava briefly gave way to a great, luminously verdant plain which looked as if it should be the breadbasket of Iceland, but was obviously more of the wastebasket of Iceland, as the only signs of human intervention were abandoned turf-roofed crofters' huts.

Sheep were the only evidence of farming life, blithely perched up 1,000-foot cliffs cleaved into weird, tottering, crazy-paved blocks, like a Picasso Mount Rushmore. Still the scenery called to mind the sense that Iceland's primeval landscape was half finished, the mountains' lower ripples tentatively sprinkled with a thin layer of moss and lichen, like geological bumfluff. The harsh canyons and rogue boulders had not yet been absorbed and smoothed by the elements and camouflaged by forests. Looking now at the wet, windy hopelessness, it seemed impossible they ever would be.

Then it was once more back to the flat blackness, or black flatness, but this time, following my crappy little tourist map, I was excited. As a keen follower of natural disasters, I had noticed we were now on the Skeiðarársandur, a 50-kilometre-wide black-sand flood plain traversed by glacial melt-rivers.

I had flown over this area once, and been stunned by the hugeness of some of the brownish torrents leaching away from the peripheries of Vatnajökull, Europe's largest glacier. (Someone once told me that if it melted, something impressive would result, the details of which I have now forgotten – something like the world's water level rising by three inches or a tsunami flattening Clydeside.)

Twice in recent centuries, Skeiðarársandur has been visited by epic disturbances. In May 1783 one of the many sub-glacial volcanoes under Vatnajökull erupted, sending up a cloud of ash which caused nuclear-style winters as far away as London. Dufferin writes with awe of the devastation wreaked, the estimated 1,300 human casualties, the pastures 'irretrievably overwhelmed' by ash. Here, no doubt, were the origins of the abandoned farmsteads we'd passed.

Then, just a couple of years ago, another sub-glacial eruption caused a huge lake of melted ice to build up behind a natural underground dyke. For weeks the world's media circled in helicopters, hoping to capture the cataclysm. But eventually they got bored of filming the unspectacular footage implied by subterranean activity, and after learning of the minimal scope for human catastrophe (there's nothing like a regular history of volcanic eruptions to discourage settlement), slunk back home.

Almost immediately, the sub-glacial barrier was spectacularly breached, and an inundation five times the width of the Nile smashed across Skeiðarársandur unseen by the world's vultures. Fortunately for me, though, my in-laws taped the Icelandic TV coverage, and a month later I gawped at house-sized icebergs tossed like screwed-up paper down brown torrents, scything through bridges and towering electricity cables.

After weeks of waiting, the authorities had been inevitably caught slightly off guard; one policeman, patrolling a kilometre-long bridge, had to speed across it with the water already streaming against his wheels. He arrived, shaken, just in time to erect a 'Bridge Closed' sign at the next junction and cut off an unwitting German tourist.

'How long will I have to wait until it's open?' he enquired, wondering if he just had time to nip down to a local farm and dry something large and canvas.

'About six months,' replied the policeman. It was the sort of gently arrogant, don't-mess-with-Iceland quip that most native males would wait a lifetime to deliver.

Then came an unexpected stop at Jökulsarlón, Glacier Lagoon, whose silent grandeur shook away the miles of accumulated misanthropy. I say unexpected because though I'd seen pictures of it, I had no idea where it was, or indeed what it was called. The ice sculptures on sale at a little stall offered a clue, but it wasn't until I followed the Germans up a gravelly hillock that I realised. It is a truly arresting phenomenon – a 20-square-kilometre lake at the foot of the Breiðamerkur glacier, populated – and that is the only way to describe it – by an army of icebergs.

The still water was punctured by vast, imperceptibly drifting shapes: some minty fresh blue, some marbled with brown; some low and round, others the size of opera houses. None were crisp and jagged like the *Titanic*-style drift ice of my mind's eye. These, having fallen off glaciers (calf ice) rather than off pack ice, are smoothed by wind and water into outrageous undulations, with odd holes and smooth grooves and whale-vertebra appendages sticking out crazily. It was as if Henry Moore and Barbara Hepworth had been alien yetis with a tempestuous penchant for throwing their excessively abstract creations into a lake. If you had the time and money, which I didn't, little inflatable speedboats took people around the lagoon, right up to the massive overhangs. What I did want to do was to throw big stones at some of the more precarious bergs to see if I could knock a couple of hundred tons of ice off. I reasoned that this would not in itself have been gross vandalism – icebergs are by definition ephemeral phenomena, and the lagoon is, after all, constantly being topped up with more bergs dropping off the glacier face – but it would have been difficult to carry off with dignity before an audience.

Also, my adolescent urges were soon being overpowered by more uncomfortable emotions. It started with the thought that the ice and chill winds of Jökulsarlón were a good training ground for Spitzbergen; by stages I back-traced my planned journey there, arriving with a stomach-punching jolt at the reality – which I had successfully postponed for the last half a day – that within an hour I would be aboard a Viking ship, with 720 nautical miles of some of the planet's stroppiest seas before me, sharing a wet plank with the Four Norsemen of the Apocalypse.

Saddling up my front and rear rucksacks in Höfn, I stood rooted to the spot by the vast dead weight. I felt like I was giving Oliver Reed a piggyback home from the pub. Falling over wouldn't be a problem – weight distribution was almost ideal, and I could have remained upright in a hurricane – but I was slightly concerned that my ankles would simply crumble under the stress. I tottered away mechanically in search of the harbour.

Höfn, as I've said, just means harbour, so I didn't anticipate much difficulty in this task, but naturally enough it was only after a lengthy robotic march around the town's drab concrete perimeter that I rounded a corner and saw a clutch of Norwegian-flagged masts swaying above a warehouse. Masts. This was a good sign. It suggested, as was soon confirmed when I reached the quay, that at the foot of each mast was a . . . pleasure boat.

I know almost nothing about boats, but these boys – aluminium-hulled yachts, lovingly varnished converted trawlers – were very distant descendants of the Viking variety. A survey of the middle-aged boating enthusiasts aboard them – some even wore yachting caps – confirmed that their crews were similarly far removed in appearance and character from their pillaging forefathers. I was probably not going to be sacrificed.

Conflicting emotions enveloped me as I approached a grey-haired fellow on the quayside: relief, embarrassment, even a touch of regret at the farcical anticlimax of it all.

'Is this the, er, Viking convoy?' I asked, sensing the wavy shame-lines sprouting from my scalp like the victim of a practical joke in a cartoon strip.

'Of course. Do you like horseradish? I'm grating some for the meat sauce tonight.'

Directed towards my boat, the *Fridtjofen* – its jaunty but weather-beaten squat, grey superstructure at odds with the sleek executive hulls – I met my captain, Sverre Koxvold. Bright-eyed and grey-bearded, he had the look of a *Gardener's World* presenter, but, as he revealed by sliding down the bannisters into the galley, not the plodding deportment. What a lovely man he was. He made me a huge smoked meat sandwich and we talked in the *Fridtjofen's* cosy saloon, all dim lights, purple upholstery and panelling, like an Edwardian rail carriage. Here at last, in both size and ambience, was a reasonable approximation of the *Foam*.

The boat, said Sverre, had been built in 1955 as the University of Bergen's research vessel, with a laboratory in the saloon we were now seated in. My bunk, in a tiny four-berth cabin right up in the bows, had been slept in by the current Emperor of Japan, a keen amateur marine biologist. The *Fridtjofen* was now Sverre's home, as had been his previous vessel, a canal boat which he'd lived in for years at a mooring just up the road from me in Brentford. He knew all my local pubs. We shopped at the same Sainsbury's. For some time, decades it seems, he'd worked as finance director for a computer company's European base in Hounslow.

Then it had all gone wrong: his wife leaving him and taking their two teenage sons, his career wound down by mutual agreement. At 50 he'd suddenly found himself alone and uprooted, so he'd flogged the canal boat and bought the *Fridtjofen*, blowing four fingers of his golden handshake refitting her. Now his life was cruising up and down Norway's endless coast, his only steady income derived from occasional articles for boating magazines, the proceeds of which were largely swallowed up seeing his sons through university in England. He'd been drafted into the convoy, despite not quite fitting in with the Rotarian bonhomie, as at the last minute they'd been told by the marine authorities that they couldn't leave Norway without being escorted by a boat of the *Fridtjofen's* size.

Still lightheaded with joy at my skipper's warmth and my nautical home's unVikingness, I greeted the rest of the crew – ten of them – as they returned fresh, or rather drunk, from a farewell reception with the mayor of Höfn. (With an inward 'Oh, *right*,' I realised that polite civic events like these, rather than woad-daubed beard-burning orgies, were what Sverre had meant on the phone by 'ceremonies.') A bottle of Icelandic schnapps – Brennivin – was produced and, amid scenes more raucous than I am used to at 5.45 p.m., swiftly consumed.

Thus fortified, and in the knowledge that we weren't leaving for five hours, I set off to inspect the small areas of Höfn not covered during my packhorse wanderings. Foremost among these was a distant memorial out at the end of a curving headland, approached by passing the town's raison d'être, a fish smelting plant which permanently billowed a cloud of burnt herring fat.

Icelanders often tell you that their fish doesn't smell. Only fish that is rotting smells, as it were, of fish, and theirs is all too fresh. Unfortunately with regard to this maxim, the whole of Höfn stinks like a smouldering, month-old whale carcass.

To combat the stench, I drew my hood down over my face. This had a serendipitous side effect, because as I approached the monument I found myself under aerial bombardment from nesting arctic terns. This has happened to me once before in Iceland, and the routine was the same. First it's risibly pathetic, these silly swallow-sized birds trying to see off a grown man with feeble squeaks and bleats. But then, as you realise you've gone just too far, the attack develops into an assault of Hitchcockian intensity. Awful Stuka screeches and Dalek-like klaxons shriek out by your ears; beaks and claws make exploratory contact with your scalp; you laugh nervously, then stop laughing, then you turn back, your brisk walk breaking into an undignified, flailing gallop, arms windmilling crazily above your head, phrases such as 'Piss off, you little shits' emerging from your throat in a reedy, strangled whine. Locals parked sensibly in their cars with the windows up have a rare old time monitoring your wayward progress.

Dishevelled and sweaty, I sat on a quayside bench to recompose myself. I had once again failed to Dufferin. In my idle moments I had taken keynote Dufferin sentences and made my own translations: 'Guessing we were in for it, I sent down the topmasts, stowed the boats on board and reefed all down.' 'Guessing we were in for it, I chewed up a fistful of Stugeron and lay on the floor crying.' Regarding 'The certainty of being a good three hundred miles from any shore inspired a feeling of comfort and security difficult to describe', one could merely replace 'miles' for 'yards' and 'comfort and security' for 'bottomless desperation'. Alternatively, a simple 'shore' for 'boat' exchange would do the job. At other times it might be more appropriate to combine 'off-licence' with 'anger and inadequacy'.

What was certain was that not even Wilson would have been so visibly unsettled by a flock of small birds. It did not bode well.

Luckily, it didn't matter, because six hours later I was dead.

7

We'd cruised out of Höfn, Faroes-bound, in the comely 1 a.m. twilight gloom, our gay little convoy's mast lights winking, an echoing volley of foghorns bidding farewell to the land of my in-laws, and probably waking most of them up.

I'd been cruelly exposed when daftly dropping a rope into the harbour as we cast off, but had managed to suppress a yelp of anguish when Sverre presented me with a copy of the watch rota. 'You're on the bridge from 2 till 6 a.m., then again from 2 till 6 p.m.' Stugerons had been gobbled in advance, and the ocean seemed reasonably benign.

But then we headed out beyond the headland, and within seconds were all sliding about like a challenge in *It's A Knockout.* I would not be playing my joker. Feeling a gluey sickness sloughing up my body, I muttered nauseous apologies and retreated haphazardly past the crashes of mobile crockery to my heaving cabin, where I stripped off as many clothes as I could in six seconds (one shoe and my trousers) before completing an ungainly ascent of my narrow ceiling bunk. There I lay flat on my back, shivering, sweaty, my breathing fast and shallow, gazing in a blurred, feverish stupor as green–black froth swilled around the porthole by my shoulder. Every few minutes we would smack into a particularly large wave, and with a jerk my limp, useless head would whiplash towards the claustrophobically low ceiling. Once or twice I hit it.

There I stayed for eighteen hours, Wilson's ghostly mantra haunting my Stugeron stasis. 'They sometimes don't recover,' tolled a gleeful Victorian Cockney, 'They sometimes *dies*.' Once in a while one of my two cabin mates – schoolteacher Per and oil engineer Lars – came in, dozed briefly and departed. Occasionally they would tug my shoulder gently and peer up into my glassy eyes. 'Is everything okay with you?' they breathed sympathetically. I winced and grunted, waving them away. If I'd had the energy I would have told them to piss off. Seasickness makes you terribly selfish. It didn't even occur to me that someone was losing out on sleep to take over my turns on watch.

After ten hours or so, the diuretic side effects of Stugeron made themselves known to my withered kidneys. Our cabin had a little sink, but it was 4 feet below me. I couldn't make it. But I had to. Dialysis casts a terrible blight on a carefree lifestyle. Unfortunately, bending to drink from the tap was not a useful posture. No sooner had I straightened myself than I realised I had hopped off the Circle Line of steady quease and on to the Bullet Train chuck-up express. Lars was in his bunk, reading a newspaper with his feet up against the backs of my bent knees, but however regrettable his presence, there was no alternative. I was going to honk right there, into this little sink, brimming it with smoked meats and impregnating our airless cell with fetid, cloying vapours. Then, as I lowered my head to the porcelain, a little voice piped up above the discordant marching band of nausea, telling me it was too awful, too pagan, too *unlordly* to debase myself in company. Get up in your bunk, the voice said, undress, get your head down, you'll feel better. It'll pass, the voice said.

Foolishly, I heeded the voice, and having rescaled my bunk, spluttered two great mouthfuls of vomit into my polo neck as I was trying to pull it off over my head. It was not an ideal situation. Lars rustled his newspaper uneasily, but said nothing. No doubt he was thinking that I'd be compelled to retire to the shower room for a cold rinse. But he was badly wrong. I wasn't going anywhere. I pulled off my polo neck, splattering my sleeping bag and plastering my hair, and lay there, exhausted, sad and stinking. If Dufferin had described me, he would not have used the expression 'holiday face'.

After five minutes, Lars left me to wallow. I popped three

Stugeron and absently scanned the ceiling, noting splatters of unpleasantness three foot to my right, a trajectory that would certainly have sent stragglers down towards Lars and his paper. After maybe twenty minutes the drug trumpeted its arrival by presenting my subconscious with an image of Nerys Hughes in a bowler hat and pinstripes, intoning over and over again with simple dignity, 'Clive James is dead.' I embraced coma with a small, tired, inward cheer.

This episode mercifully proved to be the high water mark of my nausea. Over the next twenty-four hours I gradually returned to society, braving nibbles of pancakes made by our indefatigably entertaining cook, Sissel, and venturing up to the bridge. The seas were misty and desolate, the setting rather a daunting one for a little boat like ours. Even in the currently negligible swell we were all over the place. There were six of us crammed in the bridge, and only two seats, leaving four people at the mercy of the metronomic rolling, forever waddling unsteadily from one side of the bridge to the other like Pingu's mates on a piss-up. The only convoy member not lost in the mist was a small yacht we were towing. Its gearbox had broken down outside Höfn, and the prevailing wind precluded effective use of sails. Sverre had a word to describe the captain of this boat, who had apparently expressed minimal gratitude for our assistance. This word was 'Pissface'.

Back down in the saloon, Lars's thirteen-year-old son Torbjørn accosted me with the choice ephemera of his adolescence. 'Look – The Prodigy,' he said seriously, withdrawing a CD. 'Look – Liverpool.' A green and white away shirt. 'Look – Dracula candy.' A packet of dusty red sweets. Probably because I didn't have a beard or a yachting cap and plainly didn't know what I was doing, the lonely Torbjørn had alighted on me as a fellow child.

It was difficult to have a long discourse about Liverpool FC with someone who'd never heard of Craig Johnston, or to share a love of confectionery which turned out to be flavoured with salt, but I tried. Probably too convincingly, as 'Tobe' was soon delivering mock karate blows at my midriff, swinging his legs at me from doorframes and attempting to coerce me into other forms of juvenile horseplay. This might not have been so unwelcome had it not been for my still considerable physical distress.

There had been a nasty moment when Sissel triumphantly unveiled a bucket-sized crème caramel, and I was still struck by the perfect conditions for nausea-inducement in my cabin. 'To let: Vomitorium. Lurching waves, insistent diesel throb, brine-swill views. Planning permission for strobe-projected medical photographs of terminal skin conditions.'

Boats, I concluded, were shit. I was now obsessed with calculating what proportion of the Faroes leg of the voyage remained. In ten minutes it would be 60 per cent. But that was so useless – I could have flown twice around the world by now, not travelled half an inch on a small-scale map.

As I sat in the saloon being unwillingly serenaded by Tobe's latest self-penned rap, I found myself staring idly at the blown-up Hagar cartoon above the little staircase down to the galley. 'Son, there are only two sorts of people – boat people and non-boat people.'

'According to who, Dad?'

'Boat people.'

Although this wasn't funny, not even slightly, it was probably true. I was conducting a showcase demonstration of my non-boat-person credentials. But sod it – Dufferin, a feverish early-adopter of fledgling technologies, would never have put up with this. For his next voyage he'd taken a steam yacht, and when Harold Nicolson visited his uncle in Paris in 1892, he was stunned to find the Marquess had illuminations in his carriage. ('His Excellency's electric light,' oiled a footman triumphantly as he demonstrated the innovation. Presumably he wasn't the one who had to run behind the horses wheelbarrowing a battery the size of a fridge-freezer.) If he'd been doing his journey now, he wouldn't go on a boat. He'd have chartered a Stealth bomber, or partnered Richard Branson in a solar-powered balloon.

We were joined in the saloon by Sissel, Per and the three-man crew from one of the cabin cruisers I'd heard of, craft so puny they'd been coerced to leave them behind in the Faroes on the way out. This leg had been the most hazardous of the voyage from Norway, Per announced gleefully. And then everyone started telling jokes. Accustomed as I am to Scandinavians around me communicating in English as a courtesy, it can be awkward. The implication is you have to listen to everything that's said, and respond in order to show your gratitude. 'Yes – I've always found that spinnakers made from bri-nylon just don't have enough flexibility, too.' But the alternative – them conversing in their native tongue – can be worse. For a start, you inevitably begin to imagine they're talking about you. ('Then he honks up all over himself – and all over my bloody newspaper. Check out the hair above his ears – it's still got dried puke flakes in it. Jesus, what a pig.')

This is especially true if they begin laughing. No matter where you are in the world, if anyone within 100 yards says something you don't understand and then everyone else bursts into a guffaw, it is impossible not to start feeling the back of your scalp for yard-lengths of double-sided airport luggage tape or checking to see if your genitals haven't somehow worked their way en masse through your underwear and back out of a large split in the seat of your trousers. Once, in Athens, repeated outbursts of civic hilarity engendered such severe self-consciousness that I forgot how to walk, and had to sit down in a car park for twenty minutes.

But even if they tell you the joke isn't about you at all (don't believe them, it is), it can be worse if they then try to translate it. By the time they get to the punchline everyone has long since laughed themselves out and are all expectantly awaiting your reaction. It's like stand-up comedy in reverse, with you as the one-person audience. Sit-down comedy. Another difficulty is that they then expect you to reciprocate. This is unfortunate for me, as I can only ever remember one joke at a time, which in this particular case was unfortunate for everyone.

Here was the joke. An Eskimo is driving across the tundra, when steam hisses out from under the bonnet and the car glides to a halt. He calls up the Inuit AA, and a breakdown truck appears.

The mechanic opens the bonnet to be greeted with further spectacular vapour billows, and following a brief diagnosis looks up at the motorist. 'Looks like you've blown a seal, mate.' 'No,' says the driver, nervously fingering his upper lip, 'it's just frost on my moustache.'

I personally find this joke endlessly entertaining, but as the punchline tailed away before a sea of faces wearing inappropriate expressions – some utterly blank, some promptingly 'Please go on'-ish – I realised too late it had been a poor choice in the situation. It depended on an understanding of the twin meanings of the phrase 'blown a seal', both reasonably colloquial. My audience's failure to grasp either meant I would now be required to explain in detail an obscure act of bestiality and its graphic aftermath. These were people I had known for less than thirty-six hours. The closest I'd come to establishing a rapport was to be sick on one of them.

I think someone might have laughed, but it could just as easily have been the sound of my soul trying to eat itself.

The mist closed to a windless, *Flying Dutchman* fish-souper of the kind the *Foam* spent days becalmed within after leaving Iceland. We couldn't see more than about 10 yards. How could Dufferin, or anyone in the days before radar, not have collided with at least half a dozen moving or inanimate obstacles every time they set out to sea?

In a momentary clearing in the fog a couple of whale fins scythed gently out of the oily surface, and I saw my first puffins, as had Dufferin in Iceland, when he'd been so drunk he thought they were rabbits. Looking at them now – red-beaked, black-feathered, tiny – I realised just how very drunk this must have been.

Remembering this, I thought again of Wilson's night on the hen-coop, and my assumption that he must have been on the piss. Certainly the prospect of Wilson on a deep-potation bender wasn't an appealing one. He wouldn't have been a happy drunk. Why in fact was he so miserable? Thinking about it, his wayward history – Chiswick, South Africa, Australia, Ireland – suggested even more than Dufferin's a restless quest for fulfilment. There was never talk

THE MIDNIGHT SUN OFF SPITZBERGEN.

of a Mrs Wilson; no little Wilsons sullenly tripping each other up in the pantry.

Back in my cabin, I rooted out the notes on Wilson I'd made at Eton and Clandeboye, which Birna had brought over and given to me just before I'd left Iceland. There was one telling mention, from the journal coverage of the Mediterranean trip Dufferin took with his mother a couple of years after he returned from the Arctic. 'Wilson sent off on many difficult and dangerous missions,' chortles Dufferin in North Africa. 'Hunted crocodiles while Wilson employed in getting a block of stone out of the remains of a Roman wall with only a knife, chisel and hammer – all broken!'

The cricked neck/telescopes mockery was one thing, but this elevated my misgivings about Dufferin's treatment of his valet to a new level. That exclamation mark was too much to bear. Getting an aged (I never found out his date of birth, but looking at the etching in *High Latitudes* he was certainly over fifty) underling to plunder antiquities, giving him useless equipment, then dressing the whole thing up as sport for his master. It was bullying. It was sending a little nephew down to the hardware shop to ask for crumpet grease. It was getting the young conscripts to clean the urinals with a toothbrush then stumbling in drunk and pissing in their buckets. And the worst was to come.

'Sent Wilson to carry away a boulder from the top of a hill.' That was it.

He'd probably been the life and soul on those Australian steam packets, leading *Oliver!*-style knees-ups around the saloon and winking at bonneted babies. All that natural joie de vivre had been slowly wrung out of him by a decade of hard labour and mockery.

On the one hand, Dufferin's cruel Wilson-baiting showed at last that he was flawed. I had found his human failing. But on the other, I felt badly let down. Even in accepting my own feebleness beside him I'd only once or twice let bitter feelings get the better of me. I had still been Clark Kent to his Superlord. But now I'd found his kryptonite, and for the first time found myself contemplating an anti-Dufferin alliance with Wilson.

Time dribbled fitfully on, two seconds forward, one second back, as funereal as the torpid fog around us. Sverre did his best to alleviate the tedium, announcing in a sudden flurry that he was starting up a quiz over the VHF radio which connected the convoy. Before broadcasting his first query, he tried it on me in English. 'If I put a rope around the equator, then raised it by one metre, how much longer would it need to be to meet?' Either this was a trick question, or it would require detailed mathematical and geographical knowledge. 'It's a trick question,' I announced. Sverre broadcast. No sooner had he rogered and outed, a chorus of crackles jostled for airwave coverage. '*Sex comma otta meter*' they uniformly intoned, which suggested the question had been misheard as 'How did Tarka masturbate?' but actually meant everyone had immediately worked out the answer as 6.8 metres.

Another boat desultorily took up the baton. 'Name four famous Norwegian inventions,' translated Sverre. 'The ski,' crackled one skipper. 'Paperclips,' said another. There was a pause. 'The aerosol can!' came a triumphant blurt, closely followed by an apologetic 'Cheese slicer?'

I retired to my soiled bunk and skimmed through the bookshelf. There was a copy of Jerome K. Jerome's *Tre Man I En Båt*, a title which gave me such a surge of confidence in my Norwegian that I grabbed an adjacent Berlitz Scandinavian phrase book. But it was an outrage of shoddy scholarship. The year of publication was 1981, but the typography was redolent of my copy of *High Latitudes* and many phrases could not be described as current. 'Where are the telegraph forms?'; 'I want a permanent wave'; 'May I have some more tunny?'; 'The wireless is making a lot of noise'.

Most insulting of all was the following statement in the 'At the police station' section: 'I forgot to keep to the right (Norway, Denmark), left (Sweden).' Sweden changed to the right in, what, 1964? I had a mind to proceed directly to Stockholm, hire a car and drive the wrong way round a busy roundabout at speed, having a lawyer send the resultant bills and summonses to Berlitz. Hear now the righteous crowing of my bereaved relatives!

Throwing the book angrily into a fumarole, I passed up to the saloon from where I spotted Sverre on deck hoisting a series of signal flags. Puerile sniggers emanating from the bridge suggested there was no cause for concern. Being passed a signalling manual, I eventually decoded his flags as denoting letters AJ, meaning: 'I have a serious radiation incident aboard. Approach with caution.'

We were to derive plenty more entertainment from these flags, as were the other ships, but I think it is fair to say that we were more entertained than they. That is to say that none of the following signals elicited a response from them: 39 – 'Move closer to the Commodore and observe his motions'; FO1 – 'I will keep close to you during the night'; TO – 'I have a mine in my net'; and my own personal favourite, TE – 'I am bottom trawling'.

With Sverre hoisting 'Have you enough bunkers to reach port?' the mist reluctantly rose, and out of it loomed the improbably verdant flanks of one of the Faroes' twenty-one islands. Like most things dropped in the middle of seas, the Faroes are not as small as they look. Their total area, 540 square miles, is actually . . . well, does 'four and a half times the size of Malta' sound at all impressive? No? Singapore plus Madeira? Anyway, it was hours after seeing our first Faroe before we rounded another massive green promontory and beheld the gay, almost lurid, rooftops of Tórshavn, still brazenly purple and yellow in the 9 o'clock half-light.

Sissel, who could be said to personify brassiness in the nicest possible way, was in the middle of relaying her dalliances with early Seventies bad-boy football legend Frank Worthington when a sweet chorus floated up to the bridge. A male choir perched on a breakwater were singing us into port, a reception which perfectly complemented our approach to the charming little marina, filled with swaying masts and lined with chandlers, heaps of lobster pots and other authentic accessories.

I'd been to Tórshavn once before, but had somehow missed this rewarding vista, ending up instead amidst the stinking factory trawlers and oil storage tanks of the modern dock further up. Now I gazed enchanted as broad rowing boats traversed the harbour at speed, their six-man (or -woman) crews urged on by strident barks from the cox.

Before manoeuvring into the dock, we had first to strap the lame Pissface to our side, a tricky operation during which I did my best to hide. 'Tim – take that rope,' sighed Sverre through a megaphone out of the bridge window as I skulked about on the foredeck. He hated raising his voice. Whenever he had to communicate with someone more than 5 feet away he would whisper through the megaphone. I picked up a filthy hawser by my feet, and after standing with it stupidly for ten seconds realised it was attached to Pissface's boat, which was now drifting away from us towards a breakwater.

What was I supposed to do? Splice it? Bite it? Tie it round Per's ankle? Reason suggested I was expected to lash it firmly to some stout and integral part of our boat, perhaps not the twelve-carton brick of apple juice I artlessly attempted to lasso. Pissface's horribly, almost aggressively, professional-looking three-man crew addressed me with steady gazes as the rope tautened in my hands and pulled me helplessly to the edge of the *Fridtjofen*'s deck bars. With an idiotic grin I hastily dropped it, watching it slip into the sea. This sequence raised the activity level on both boats dramatically, the Pissface boys retrieving the rope, Per and Lars catching and lashing, Sverre easing both boats away from the looming breakwater, me running down to the cabin to beat my pillow in rage and shame.

But the *Fridtjofen* crew (if not the increasingly sneery Pissfacers) were as benign and forgiving as ever, and having tied up at the dock entreated me to join them in the happy institution known as the anchor dram. Whisky was produced, which was welcome, but then came further Brennivin.

I don't want to be rude about the traditional 'akvavit' of Scandinavia, but I'm probably going to have to be, because

Brennivin isn't really at all nice. It's essentially grain alcohol, vodka I suppose, but flavoured with – mmmm – caraway seeds. Why do that? Why not just not have the caraway?

Nonetheless, drink it I did, and presently the *Fridtjofen* saloon became a focus for the convoy's plentiful merry divorcees, and homebrew of both distilled and fermented varieties appeared in lemonade bottles and I fear that I may have sung 'Those Were The Days' in Norwegian.

Tórshavn, even to a man looking like a hospice patient who has just had two dustbin lids brutally clashed together right in front of his face, is an undeniably endearing place. It's not beautiful – for each turfed roof there's a muddy corrugated warehouse or knackered Fifties shopfront – but there's a sense of confident, laidback affluence quite out of keeping with the remote, storm-lashed setting.

Prawns and reckless borrowing gave the island's 41,000 inhabitants one of the world's highest standards of living, and, though the Danish-owned province actually went bankrupt in the early Nineties, there's no sense that they've learnt their lesson. Huge, 28-inch colour TVs sit alongside crisps as supermarket impulse purchases, and crappy-looking businesses which have the air of down-at-heel pet shops turn out to be selling digital cameras and multimedia notebooks. Last time I was here, seven years before, I saw my first portable video player, lost in a childishly random window display alongside shaver adaptors and electric foot spas.

Coughing horribly up one of Tórshavn's many steep hills, I got utterly lost and began an unplanned tour of the rest. It was like a mountainous extension of Reykjavík's old centre – wooden buildings, corrugated roofs, narrow streets – but painted from a more daring palette. It is oddly endearing that anyone over the age of seven should choose to live in a mauve house with scarlet window frames. I kept expecting to see Tinky Winky and Laa-Laa pelting each other with Tubby Toast on someone's porch.

Once I had managed to stop myself thinking about the concept of mowing your house, I became rather taken by all the turfed roofs, except when one topped off a modern concrete bungalow. Would you thatch a tower block? It just wasn't right. Still, this rather foolish anachronism has occasionally been taken to the pleasing extremes of parody. I saw concrete garden sheds with turf tops, and one balding geodesic dome.

But hangovers have a way of inciting inexplicable shifts of emotion, and suddenly all the conspicuous consumption took on a contrived, grasping air. It was Icelandic-model consumerism on an epic scale. Why have a Mercedes S-class on a series of islands with a handful of country lanes? And certainly, why fit *cruise control* to it? By the time you've looked down to activate it, you've driven right across the island and off a cliff. All the silly urban accessories – the Ford Kas, the pay-and-display bays, the card-only phone boxes – it all seemed so irrelevant, so desperate, so 'Look – we're not fish-faced peasants here any more, you know.'

We cast off from Tórshavn at midnight, having first taken delivery of a vast consignment of provisions which had been impounded by the Icelandic authorities on the convoy's arrival and sent on by ferry after our departure from Höfn. Relations between Norway and Iceland had not been good since the trawler-towing incident I learned of aboard the *Dettifoss*.

But what a lot of food there was. We already had a mountain of herring and apple juice in our hold, and now I watched as the delivery van disgorged a more improbably lengthy parade of large items than Mary Poppins' carpet bag. As we (they) stacked them around the deck, I began a rough inventory of our biblical-scale provisions. There were 7,000 portions of strawberry jam, 1,000 litres of apple juice, 300 litres of variously preserved herrings, 1,000 portions of Snofrisk soft cheese, at least 250 kilos of Jarlsberg, an unknown quantity of smoked meats and a single, forlorn box of liquefying celery. Sissel calculated that we had over a ton of food on board. The convoy numbered eleven boats with a total of thirty-five crew. A *ton* of food.

Coupled to this, most of the food required refrigeration, a requirement we had not met by shoving it all into the old fish hold behind the engine room. I was particularly concerned about the (can I even write this without dry retching?) herrings in cream. (No. I can't.) Most of the especially ripe provisions had to be given to seamen's missions in our various ports of call, which must have proved a boon to any involuntary euthanasia programmes they might have been running.

I didn't fret so much about this monstrous overstocking when I learned that all the food – and much else besides – had been provided by sponsors. I was bewildered by their munificence. Where was the commercial benefit of advertising Norwegian apple juice in countries where it isn't even sold? And it wasn't even as if the sponsors asked for much in return, just a logo on some promotional material which we never bothered to hand out. If this had been an English endeavour, recreating, I don't know, the voyage of the *Beagle*, any sponsors would have insisted the boats change their names to *Spirit of Uncle Ben's Rice* and *Anusol Endeavour*, and at the Galapagos we'd have all had to leap out on to the dock dressed as Pot Noodles.

We sailed down the coast between tall green cliffs, the mid-July sun now dipping momentarily below the horizon for the first time since I'd left England three weeks earlier. Lars, Torbjørn and half a dozen others had flown home from the Faroes, leaving just me, Sissel, Per and Sverre. This was handy as all three were fluent in English, although Sissel's pronunciation sometimes caused alarm. Once she was telling me of the diligent faithfulness of her boyfriend back in Norway.

'Everywhere the convoy has stopped he has been sending me letter and presents. When I went into the harbour office in Hafnafjörður, there was a fox lying on the desk for me.'

I remembered the French consul in Reykjavík giving Dufferin a fox. Maybe it's an Icelandic tradition. But didn't the harbourmaster mind? How was it delivered? She eyed me quizzically. 'It's not hard. You dial in the number in the fox machine in Norway and put the letter in and it prints it on the fox machine in Iceland.'

Still, in this company I could speak with Level 1 English, for use with foreigners of advanced linguistic ability. Level 2, suitable for other convoy members, meant enunciating more crisply and stripping planned sentences of easily misunderstood colloquialisms such as 'taking the piss' and 'Please don't throw me that rope unless you want it dropped in the harbour'. With Level 3, the English speaker must talk in a stilted, deliberate way using only simple verb constructions and no adjectives. It can be helpful to imagine you are reading out a fabricated police statement. 'I then asked the Czech man about the camera. He said that he had taken it, and he laughed. He added that he did not wash his behind before public bathing.' The desperate mimes of Level 4 will be familiar to visitors in emerging nations or France, but are thankfully not applicable to Scandinavia.

But the reduced crew roster also meant my scope for duty evasion was severely reduced. The shifts were now eight hours; I was due on with Per at 4 p.m., but as ever, as soon as we emerged into open waters I became very unwell. My Stugeron habit was having increasingly worrying side effects. At some point in the early afternoon, I found myself in a jungle hut strewn with Silk Cut packets, lying on a straw palliasse, my bowels vividly out of control. Too weak to move, I watched as a shifty, rag-dressed native approached, issuing unintelligible pacifying mumbles and stroking my leg. Soon I realised he was actually attempting to steal my boots, and summoning up my last reserves I managed to force out a parched, drunken bellow.

'I've just shat myself . . . FUCK OFF!'

I awoke with a start, my hoarse cry still ringing around the tiny cabin. Relief that I had not, in fact, shat myself turned to despair when I glanced down and saw the recumbent figure of Per, who'd obviously popped in for a pre-watch nap, his one visible eye wide with alarm. This incident was not subsequently mentioned.

My presentation at this stage was not of the highest calibre. I hadn't eaten for a day, hadn't shaved for six, hadn't showered for two (the *Fridtjofen* only had hot water in port) – all these were close to my own records for physical deprivation. I had no idea of date or day. As on the *Dettifoss*, I felt the world shrinking to my bunk, and, as the oceans calmed, the bridge. One of the odd things about being at sea is that despite the empty horizons stretching away into infinity the sensation of claustrophobia is almost as strong as that of agoraphobia.

But Per, Sissel and Sverre were all immensely understanding. We got to know each other: Sverre, the sometimes preoccupied, sometimes indefatigably cheerful Anglophile who loved P.G. Wodehouse and Frankie Howerd and even Andrew Lloyd Webber, captain, chief engineer and provider of smutty innuendo; Sissel, cook and raconteur with a nicotine guffaw and an unnervingly colourful history of murdered husbands and minor celebrity lovers; Per, the painstaking and precise French teacher who agonised over tiny mistakes in his English and was always asking me to translate the names of nautical hardware of which I was utterly ignorant (in the end I just used to make names up: 'Those posts you tie the ropes round? Yeah, they're, well, they're usually known as . . . as coilers. In West London').

As is often the fate of the obsessively vigilant, Per was also tremendously accident-prone. Every time we went out on the *Fridtjofen*'s bikes he would manufacture some spectacular abrasion, usually while trying to evade non-dangers such as a lorry turning round in a petrol station 200 yards away. He was also possessed of a splendidly gleaming pate of the sort nature intended to impact frequently with overhead impediments. Lying on my bunk, I could always monitor his progress about the *Fridtjofen* by the thuds, bongs and partially suppressed profanities associated with its low doorways and swinging kitchenware. And, as I did so, I sniggered. I was really getting into this Wilson thing.

8

My three days in the Shetlands marked the lowest point of my short career as an adventurer. I was going south when I should have been going north, back in Britain drinking Tartan in breezeblock pubs when I should have been standing, proud and alone, at the foot of Jan Mayen's volcano, improvising an ode to the vicious floe-strewn sea. Many convoy members acquired a taste for strong cider, and as their behaviour became increasingly unpredictable I more than once heard mention of my name being followed by harsh laughter. As we cruised out of Lerwick harbour at noon, I felt a surge of relief. This represented a serious lack of judgment.

Having guided us past the Bressay lighthouse and set course for Norway, Sverre popped down the bridge ladder. I hadn't noticed Sissel and Per drifting away earlier; I was now alone. I felt like Manuel when Basil leaves him in charge of reception, and jumped eagerly into the skipper's chair, playing with the binoculars and wishing I had a pipe. But then, as with Manuel, everything went awry. The autopilot had never inspired total confidence, and it chose this moment to completely lose its head.

When, from time to time, it corrected its line, a loud hum and a click told you the rudder had been moved a degree or so. But now, suddenly, one hum-click was followed by another, then another, and in a minute or so we were humming and clicking right round, 180 degrees round. Unable to switch the autopilot off, I grabbed at the wheel, only to find it immovably locked. We arced past a small fishing boat, which seemed to have its nets out. A concerned face stared out of its wheelhouse, a face that I could only too easily imagine shouting: 'Didn't you read my flags, you daft wee shite? I said I was bottom trawling!' I was now in total panic. 'Er, help? Hello! Help!' I quavered down the bridge ladder. There was no one to be seen or heard. The autopilot had now decided it was happy with our new course, which, I noted with something beyond disappointment, was directly towards the towering bird-cliffs of Noss. We had been bringing up the convoy's rear, and, as the rest of the boats noticed our change of direction, Norwegian messages began to crackle in over the VHF, first sounding amused, then curious, then genuinely fearful.

'Cocking *bollocks*,' I whined, unaware at the time that this signalled my preparation for death. Gannets circled like vultures. The cliffs beckoned. After the birth and death of a thousand civilisations, Sverre re-appeared. 'Oh,' he said, dispassionately noting the massive solid obstacle ahead of us. He flicked a large and obvious switch to disable the autopilot, and eased us round with the wheel (which he had just been down to unlock). Then he picked up the binoculars. 'Did you put these here, next to the compass? You should not. They're metal. It confuses the compass, and so also the autopilot.'

Feeling that my feathers were all stuffy and brown, I went and sat out on the deck. Happily, it was a lovely evening. I was able to sunbathe after a fashion, something that had seemed a risible impossibility in the cold Fisherman's Friend mists of Iceland and Tórshavn. Also, I realised I only felt very slightly queasy. Had I finally beaten my mal de mer? Perhaps. But, despite the languid seas, I wasn't brave enough to forego Stugeron, and so it wasn't until 4 a.m. that I joined Per on the bridge for our 2 a.m. shift.

We were now fairing steadily through the North Sea oil fields. In the thin dawn the blazing palaces of the Norwegian Frigg rigs (yes, yes) towered terrifyingly around us. Not for the first time I was struck by just how lucky we'd been with the weather, fog not-withstanding. The deck thermometer told us that even now, at 5 a.m., it was 17°C. Perhaps I would salvage a summer after all.

At length, low, hazy peaks poked up in the distance. The convoy, which had been fanned out across the horizon, closed together behind the *Fridtjofen* for our final approach. As the little line snaked through southwest Norway's coastal archipelago, parched and dusty after a record summer, it was impossible not to feel a little jolt of pride. The adjective 'plucky' loomed large. With the gold evening sun burnishing our strings of signal bunting we foghorned our way up the confidently prosperous quayside of Haugesund, where a little band of dignitaries and children stood waving, even when I dropped a rope into the dock.

It was a most satisfactory evening. On the quay pennants were exchanged between mayors and skippers and marketing managers' wives, and anchor drams copiously downed. I had bought a bottle of pink fizz in the Shetlands, having planned to accompany it with a touching and humorous address upon the friendships forged amongst the *Tre Man* (and *Ein Woman*) *I En Båt*. But then we were boarded by a gaggle of landlubbing convoy wannabes whom even I felt entitled to regard with haughty disdain, and the moment passed. Sissel came round asking if anyone wanted one of the complimentary hotel rooms she'd managed to wangle, but sadly failed to interpret my 'Well, I'm not really part of the convoy, so . . .' as 'YES. BURN PUKED-IN SLEEPING BAG. DO IT. GIVE ME BED LINEN. GIVE ME ROOM NOW.'

A walk round the town, still balmy at 9 p.m., restored me. Ambling through the Friday night crowds of well-dressed, well-oiled youths, I reacquainted myself with cosmopolitan delights such as nightclub bouncers and photocopier repair shops. It was good to be back. Haugesund might only have a population of 47,000, but this was the same as the Faroes and the Shetlands combined.

I'd just reread the chapter where on his return journey Dufferin reaches Trondheim, his first civilised outpost after a month in the uninhabited desolation of Jan Mayen, Spitzbergen and the ice floes. It was a reasonable parallel for my recent travels, and I'd hoped he might have shared some of my sense of celebration.

'I cannot tell you with what eagerness I drank in all the features of this lovely scene,' he writes, having described the city's cathedral and palace and docks. Well, I thought, I could have said that.

Substituting 'scene' for 'beer', anyway. But then, launching into a romantic account of Trondheim's bloody Viking roots, he says this eagerness is nothing to do with the current cityscape and its 'signs of a modern humdrum prosperity':

> As I gazed from the schooner's deck, the accessories of an elder time came to furnish the landscape . . . armed galleys with rows of glittering shields . . . and the snug, bourgeois-looking town shrank into the quaint proportions of the huddled ancient Nidaros . . . and the old marauding days, with their shadowy line of grand old pirate kings, rose up with welcome vividness before my mind.

Oh. All I wanted *were* the signs of a modern humdrum prosperity. The only thing that rose up with welcome vividness when I gazed from the deck was the late-night supermarket to which I would shortly repair to buy two bottles of local ale and a vast sack of own-brand paprika crisps.

An hour later, feeling one-dimensional and spiritually inadequate, I was crunching and swigging disconsolately on the *Fridtjofen*'s bridge deck. But Haugesund was busily pursuing aimless thrills and it was infectious. If I was stupid, I might as well celebrate the fact. This was my first proper urban summer evening of the year. The quayside thronged with vibrant youth. Badly customised old Volvos cruised about noisily. After one bottle I started to smile benignly, after the second I was absorbed in happy voyeurism. If I'd been Ray Davies, I'd have got my acoustic guitar out and written 'Haugesund Sunset'. And B-sided it with 'Dedicated Follower Of Fishing'.

Even the squalid aspects assumed an innocent bacchanalian charm. I watched a succession of drunken girls weeing behind parked cars while their glazed consorts shambled about trying to knock into passers-by. Crappy Continental techno pulsed out from quayside clubs. Another Lars from another convoy boat joined me, and as we exchanged nautical anecdotes (not a very fair exchange, it should be said) and rum, a blonde head of wavering big hair appeared at the top of the deck ladder.

Its owner was in such an advanced state of intoxication that she managed to talk with or rather at Lars and I for half an hour without noticing I was English. All I could translate from her disjointed monologue was that she had a Danish boyfriend and a garden. Eventually she slid down the ladder and staggered away, and we tutted and laughed and Lars apologised for his nation's youthful excesses.

There is nothing like depressing news from home to make one consider one's own surroundings in a new light. Having phoned Birna the next morning to be told I'd lost my unfair-dismissal industrial tribunal with Teletext, I suddenly pondered moving here, to Norway, where the air was clean and the water clear and there's a 60-billion-dollar petroleum fund waiting to be lavished on 4 million souls.

Yes, I thought as I roamed Haugesund's quiet and sunny afternoon back streets, I could live here. The estate agent window ads offered dealboard houses, many with gables and scallopy roof slates, for around sixty grand. The weather was sufficiently clement to grow roses, and the locals sufficiently clement that they apparently didn't mind if you chose instead to decorate your property with broken lawnmowers and large cable reels. If the immediate scenery wasn't as fjordish as I'd have preferred, then the plunging verdant chasms of Bergen were only a brisk drive up the coast. Decisively, there was the prospect of getting my hands on a slice of that petroleum fund. In the meantime, if I shopped around I could (and already had, twice) buy 200-gramme packets of crisps for 75p. The only real barrier I could see was the towering arched girder bridges that, as in almost all Norwegian towns, linked Haugesund's various islands together.

To my mind, vertigo doesn't count as an irrational phobia. Cockroaches and spiders are generally unlikely to cause me real physical harm in the same way as falling 200 feet on to a barge full of bottles. It is right and proper that a fear of heights should be in direct proportion to the height itself and the sense of exposure to the height.

Thoughts like these did not help mental preparation as my iron-rigid limbs bore me jarringly towards Haugesund's loftiest span. It arced up like an Evel Knievel ramp, and the footpath was composed of loose metal plates which bounced – actually bounced – every time a vehicle passed. The reverberations from one especially heavy goods vehicle put me to my knees.

Then, as a slick, palpitating palm took hold of the spindly handrail and the first dizzying peek of fjord shimmered distantly below, a ridiculous thing happened. With a firm, wet slap, I was hit square on the top of the head by a hand-sized cellophane packet of crustacean detritus: crab claws, prawn noses and so on. Wiping at the smelly smear on my hair I looked up, but there was nothing – no bird, no bat, no bored balloonist. Probably the package had been dropped by a seagull – there was a fish market on the quay below – but at the time I was happy to interpret this as an omen from some angry or concerned Nordic deity, and turning on my heel I ran right back down the slipway with eager, liberated bounds.

With the convoy disbanding, the rest of our day was taken up with farewell activities. We trooped in to a multi-screen presentation of Haugesund's claims to fame (the brochure regularly left the 'c' out of exciting, giving rise to such treasures as 'See Haugesund's crowds of happy exiting people'). After a starring role in Viking days, it seems the town has suffered a lengthy lean patch, forcing it to rely perhaps too heavily on a limited appeal as the birthplace of Marilyn Monroe's father.

Then it was down to a small jetty, where the elite convoy committee (headed by its now openly hostile leader, Ole) were led into a proper Viking boat to row themselves over to a nearby island. They splashed, they shrieked, they giggled. Watching from the deck of a more conventional tourist craft, I marvelled at the bathetic gulf that lay between this farcical facsimile of Viking behaviour and the pagan horrors I had imagined ten days before. It was over.

The following two days, almost drifting northwards towards Florø, where I'd be catching my boat to the Arctic, were as lazily whimsical as any I can recall since entering paid employment. Freed from an itinerary, the *Fridtjofen* could now stop whenever and wherever we liked. In the archipelago's protected waters, seasickness soon became a distant memory, a joke ailment about cartoon characters turning green and running about with pouched cheeks and their hands over their mouths.

The sun was crisp, giving the area more than a hint of the Aegean: bleached rocks with cool, dark crevasses sloping out of the calm blueness. After the fog and drizzle and convoy politics it was gently intoxicating. For an hour the four of us just gazed about with knowing fixed smiles and slow nods, like people sharing a mildly euphoric drug experience. Per didn't even strangle a curse when he barked his shins falling down the last four rungs of the ladder.

We cruised up the Rannefjord towards Bergen's steep hills and suspension bridges, passing a trio of overgrown horizontal silos on the right-hand shore. 'Norwegian torpedo batteries from the war,' said Per, who was Bergen born and bred.

It seems the military did not give a very good account of themselves in the initial stages of the Nazi invasion. Hitler had ignored the counsel of his generals by ordering his fleet directly up the open fjord to Bergen, which should have been suicidal, and would have been had the Norwegian mines been primed, the torpedo batteries manned and news of the encroaching German forces been radioed to Bergen rather than sent by post. The letter arrived two days after the locals had surrendered.

The occupying Nazis built a rather more effective military infrastructure, and Norway's coastline, at 45,000 kilometres famously the longest in the world, is still littered with their pillboxes and airfields. Per said Hitler's original retreat plan had been to withdraw here for a last stand, and if he had they'd probably

still be rooting out octagenarian guerrillas from forgotten sker-
ries today.

If the earlier archipelago had presented an Aegean picture,
Bergen's seven verdant peaks, bright houses and terracotta roofs
hinted at Mediterranean connotations infinitely more convincing
than those fleetingly suggested by Tórshavn. Then again, it wasn't
raining, which I'd been told was unusual for such a notoriously
moist city, the wettest in Europe.

'Once a tourist, soaked into his skin, asks a local lad whether it
never stops raining in Bergen,' said Per, eagerly. '"I don't know,"
the boy says, "I'm only twelve." Only twelve! It's a somewhat
witty pun.'

I nodded cheerfully at this appraisal.

'But not true,' he added. 'The rain here is not so awful as some
have said.'

'Achghhghgcch!' hacked Sissel derisively at Per's efforts to pour
cold water on the rain issue. 'There is one valley just north of
Bergen where in one year they had five metre rain, and one
metre in one month!'

Per rolled his eyes.

'That's an inch a day,' I said.

'That's Bergen,' she said.

'No it isn't,' he said.

But then it started to drizzle.

Still, I liked Bergen. As soon as I saw its sprawling suburbs and
funicular railway and Burger Kings and strolling sophisticates, I
realised just how parochial the teenage drunks of Haugesund
had been. Haugesund had given me a little fix of urbanity, but
here was the hard stuff. This was a city. It had a population
which you could sensibly measure in fractions of a million, and
the expansive civilised anonymity that I craved after a month of
shabby, communal claustrophobia. I wanted to go where nobody
knew my name.

Going off alone to track down a long overdue pølse, I had a
foretaste of the weeks of solitary travel that lay ahead. The pølse
shop was particularly un-Nordic, a squalid kiosk with a broken

drinks-fridge, a single buzzing fluorescent tube and, it seemed, no staff. After I'd hummed for a bit, and begun to wonder about stealing some warm Coke, two voices – one male and breathily entreating, one female and placatory – made themselves heard backstage. Presently the owner of the female voice appeared, rearranging her extravagantly dishevelled blonde locks and pulling her skinny-ribbed T-shirt back into shape. I ordered a 13-kroner hotdog and tried to avert my eyes as she prepared it with hands that had plainly been recently blurred about her beau's love-pølse. But to her credit, though clearly eager to continue with the matter in hand – every few seconds a soft but urgent moan suggested her partner was in the process of finishing the job himself – she presented me with some waxy, varicose bratwurst the size of a fireman's torch and blithely demanded 24 kroner.

I paid without protest, accepting that this was the sort of shoddy tourist-bullying I had forestalled by aligning myself with natives. In a way it showed I was at last on my own, and as such gave me perverse comfort. Yes, this was Norway, so as a lone traveller I was only likely to be inconvenienced by rare instances of casual fleecing rather than by being necklaced or framed for sedition. But I wiped off the remoulade all the same.

We left Bergen the next morning and proceeded north, picking our way through an endless and happy procession of barely inhabited islands. Late in the afternoon, the *Fridtjofen* passed the lonely lighthouse, its white stone reflecting the late sun like a Greek church, which marked our approach to our final destination, Florø.

They'd all spoken of the town in reverent terms, but there was little to excite me beyond the moderate thrill of visiting a town with an 'ø' in it. It seemed an unassuming and slow-paced community, the sprinkling of light industry and humble, messy quayside hardly explaining the wealth its commercial grandees had lavished upon their nautical hobby. Nor indeed the huge BMWs and Mercedes estates behind whose wheels they now sat on the quayside, the convoy's top dogs come to ferry away the doggy bags festering on our decks – 10-kilo Jarlsbergs and vats of apple juice.

As they strode out to greet us, all expensive dentistry and Ralph Lauren, it occurred to me just how distant their lifestyles were from those depicted in the shanties they'd drunkenly roared in the Faroes about herring fishermen pining for fair young Helga back at home pickling rams' bollocks.

The rural Norwegians of Dufferin's time were medieval in their lifestyles and superstitions. He reports how, only a few years before his visit, the inhabitants of Alta, near Hammerfest, convinced that a boat wrecked outside the harbour was in fact the Kraken, assembled on the beach to mow down bedraggled survivors with volleys of musket fire. As in Iceland, where at the turn of the century over half the population lived in turf-roofed huts, it's intriguing to note how rapidly and completely these barely self-sufficient crofters and fishermen have developed into prosperous technophiles, and how troublefree this transformation has been.

Having crossed the 'ø's and circled the 'å's, the big cheeses drove off with their big cheeses, leaving Sissel, Per and I to share a farewell Bergen Pimms (rum, apple juice and celery). They had homes to go to. My boat didn't leave until 4.20 a.m. It was a poignant moment. These people had taken me in, a complete stranger, a foreigner; they had nursed me through my protracted nausea and its concomitant delerium, tolerated my artless incompetence, and they had done it all with good humour.

I would miss them. I would miss Sissel with her 'tree or four sheeps and fishes' and 'my first husband was a terrible bad man' and her stories of picking berries wearing only sunglasses and gumboots. I would miss Per with his 'So it is. This ling or heather is most particular to this commune' and his helpless self-mutilation.

Sverre helped me do some last-minute laundry, which would fail to dry in time draped about the *Fridtjofen*'s still warm engine room, and I retired for a pointless two-hour nap. As I teetered off the peerless *Fridtjofen* into the chilliest and thinnest of dawns, he emerged on the deck in trackpants and bare feet and called me back.

'You haven't signed the visitors' book,' he said cheerily, brandishing it and a Biro. A lifetime of filling such volumes with surreptitious vulgarities had not prepared me well for this moment. I can't remember what I wrote, which is to say that I can, and it was inadequate. To atone I gave him a brisk hug and headed off to a soundless grey quay where I waited for my boat with a bloke on a forklift and four pallets of rooftiles bound for Tromsø.

9

The Coastal Express, or Hurtigrute, is an institution. For over a hundred years it has ferried mail, cousins and rooftiles all the way up Norway's flank, or at least from Bergen to Kirkenes, next to the Russian border. If that doesn't sound impressive, measure it on an inflatable globe with a toothbrush handle, by which means you will establish that this is as far as Southampton to Lvov. I'd only be going as far as the rooftiles, to Tromsø (with a stopover in Bodø for my Jan Mayen day trip), but even that was a Land's End to John O'Groats job.

Nowadays, the Hurtigrute has two distinct roles: to offer foreign pensioners with crumbs round their mouths The World's Most Beautiful Voyage; and to give the natives a rare old time listening to tourists trying to pronounce it. It was one of the tragedies of my time in Norway that the two indigenous nouns I was most regularly unable to avoid were the two I was least equipped to enunciate. Norwegians say 'Sverre' as if they are trying to down a pint in one, and 'Hurtigrute' as if they've spectacularly failed. Not once in perhaps three dozen attempts was my rendition successful. I knew how Dufferin felt when, at a ball in Trondheim, his partner is introduced to him as 'Madame Hghelghghagllaghem.'

As the boat was ten minutes late and nowhere in sight, I tried a quick 'Hurtigrute?' out on my fork-lift friend. He replied with a look that said, 'Look, mate, it's 4.30 a.m., I don't want to be here, you don't want to be here, so let's just shut up and wait, and could you get your stupid purple rucksack off my pallet.' So we stood and watched the black mountains across the fjord become gradually fringed with dawn, the silence broken only by the buzzing of reefers and the occasional wet slap of a cavorting fish.

After twenty minutes, by which time I was more or less convinced some starkly basic misunderstanding had been made, probably by me, a black and white razor-sharp bow cut through the thinning mist. Slowly, very slowly, the stately bulk of the *Harald Jarl* slid up, and, with a great churning of water, eased herself to the quayside, where she promptly blasted Florø out of bed with a single, mighty trumpet on her foghorn.

I was very glad it was the *Harald Jarl*. The Hurtigrute comprises a dozen ships, nearly all glitzy and soulless modernities, double-gin palaces. Only two 'traditional ships' survive, and the *Harald Jarl* is one of them. Built in the mid-Fifties, she's a sort of quarter-scale model of the *Queen Mary*, with balconies meant to be waved from and a shiny-planked flagdeck and a little crane for winching aboard pallets of rooftiles. There was a four-square, Royal Yacht *Britannia* look to her.

Waiting on the quay I'd felt so itchily, dirtily unrested that I'd decided to book a cabin whatever the expense. Within reason. But as I presented myself at the purser's office, I remembered that all the Hurtigrute boats were well booked in the summer, and that the *Harald Jarl* was the smallest of them. Cabins would be at a premium. It was important to make a good impression, and my rucksack/anorak/stubble presentation got me off to a bad start. I would have to talk my way into favour.

Fatigue makes some people depressed, others delirious. Unfortunately, my rather one-sided interchange with the chubby purser revealed that he was of the former persuasion, while I listened in horror to the inanities that unmistakably identified me as one of the latter.

'My name? Yes. It's Tim. Hello!' I raised a hand. 'But you probably don't want to know that. You probably want my surname, which is Moore. Like James Bond. The old one. One of the old ones. Roger, in fact. But there's plenty more – of my name, you know, middle names and . . .'

I trailed away, curious at the aristocratic falsetto I had somehow developed. Then he spoke. 'We have no cabins,' he said heavily. 'No cabins today at all.'

He printed me out a ticket for Tromsø. For £200 I would have to sleep for three nights on a sofa in the bar and be awoken at 5 a.m. by having my face hoovered. I could have suffered no greater discomfort and saved £150 by disguising myself as a pallet of rooftiles.

I toted my weary load blindly around the dim corridors, catching sight of the odd pregnant silhouette endowed by my front pack in the art deco mirrors. There were two newly plush saloons, each speckled with the inert forms of fellow itinerant scum. Many had their T-shirts pulled up over their heads to blot out the persistent daylight. It was a dreadful sight.

I retired to the café, deserted but for the cleaners. Behind us the landscape was retreating at unheard-of speed. The day before, aboard the *Fridtjofen*, the distinctive claw-shaped peak just south of Florø had guided us for a whole afternoon; in less than an hour the *Harald Jarl* had rendered it a tiny nose on our rear horizon. No longer would we be at the mercy of the big ships' bullying wakes. Now we made the waves. Make way for the Wavemaker! I am the Wavemaker!

Delirium gave way to a deep and unsightly sleep, a sleep interrupted, as is often the way, by the awful whining of an over-indulged French infant. '*Maintenant! Maintenant!*' he screamed, a chorus I was not surprised to notice was punctuated with regular flicks of a felt mouse into the face of his gently cooing mother. To escape this appalling tableau I rotated my neck to the window gingerly – sleeping for two hours with your chin on your chest is never a good idea, as Wilson had discovered in Reykjavík – and saw layers of receding peaks rising out of early morning mist like the label of a cheap Irish liqueur. And for the first time since England, there were trees – not just the odd one sheltering apologetically behind a barn, but whole forests of pointy greenness completely enveloping the mountains' nether regions. I was sorry to have passed my lifetime taking trees for granted, and to atone I spent some time thinking up slogans for timber exporters. 'Isn't It good? – Norwegian Wood' was the obvious one, closely followed by the Shaman-inspired 'Trees Are Good'. But, if I was in charge, it could only be 'Arctic Spruce – It's Fir-Cone Excellent!'

Nesting down in the cafeteria, I attempted to settle into the Hurtigrute routine. Every couple of hours the boat stops at some forgotten backwater just long enough to take on a couple of pallets of frozen cod cheeks and exchange four lank teenagers for a confused uncle. Perhaps twice a day there are longer stops at larger towns, when everyone troops off and engages in some extended milling about and unnecessary shopping.

The timetable told me I would have to wait until our stop at Ålesund for a more economical alternative to the cafeteria's five-quid cheese horns. At noon the tannoy burst into life with an airport ding-dong, heralding some administrational banality in Norwegian. I nodded sagely. The only hope of excusing my presentation was by passing myself off as a local fisherman or son of the soil. Then, with an apocalyptic convulsion from the engine room, we reverse-thrusted to a halt.

Ålesund's main role in the three hours it spent in my life was to provide me with a supermarket, and in this it succeeded admirably. Provisioned, I went down to the ugly and functional harbour to watch Russian ratings from a visiting tall ship busking in the drizzle. As the accordionist struck up 'Those Were The Days' for the third time, I bit into a slightly fizzy two-days-past-sell-by supermarket hot dog. Unscrewing my new guest condiment, a bottle of barbecue sauce, I was briefly disturbed to see that its neck already sported a grotesquely blackened foreskin. The Russian passing round the hat approached, then wheeled away in alarm.

Uncharitably, I wondered how much of the money they would spend on drink, having read that the average Russian male drinks half a bottle of vodka a day. The *average*. That means that for every man who doesn't drink, there's one who gets through a whole bottle. Christ, I thought, shaking my head and wandering off to find the beer store.

I had discovered that only certain supermarkets have dispensation to sell beer of greater alcoholic strength than 2.2 per cent, and Ålesund did not possess one. 'There is a beer shop near the harbour,' said the checkout girl. But the harbour was a sizeable entity. I roamed aimlessly. The boat was leaving in twenty-five minutes. I broke into a jog. Asking for directions to a beer shop isn't a self-enhancing activity at the best of times, and being slightly breathless and sporting the dirty stubble and hooded anorak of a passing terrorist captured on a security video does not represent the best of times. I puffed into the tourist office, my tawdry monomaniac request eliciting who's-just-farted faces and uselessly vague information. Twelve minutes to go. Driven on by the thought of the *Harald Jarl*'s 4-quid pints I now broke into a ragged trot, hoarsely accosting sport's shop assistants and young mothers until I was pointed towards an unmarked shack I had careered past half a dozen times, taking it for an abandoned whelk stall.

If class-A drugs are ever legalised, their sale will take place in harsh, sterile outlets based on Scandinavia's state-run alcohol stores. Strip-lit crates of beer sat stark and forlorn on streaked institutional lino, all the same strength, all the same price. I snatched up four two-quid bottles and hurried over to the unmanned till. Two men were eyeing me from a back office with a wearily revolted air that said: Here comes another user. At any other time I would have felt shame. But now I could only think: Four quid a pint. Six minutes left. Four quid. Five minutes. I actually clicked my fingers at them and beckoned. My damp boots slithered and scrambled up the gangplank just as the *Harald Jarl*'s foghorn blasted Ålesund farewell.

Naturally enough, my cafeteria nest was soon invaded by cuckoos, French cuckoos, the youngest of whom I presently discovered dining noisily upon the nectarine that had been my bulwark against deficiency disease. The mist smudged out the view. I got out my hot dogs, mustard and barbecue sauce, and rolled them up in some Ålesund flat bread like a series of crap crêpes. It was difficult to assemble these covertly, and some of the glances I got from the neighbouring Norwegians suggested I might just as well have been hollowing out a well-used dildo to make a crack pipe. I could now add two more phrases to my tiny

Norwegian lexicon: 'Mummy, what's that dirty man eating?' and 'Ignore him, dear, I think he's the one we saw running around shouting about beer'.

The terrible thing about my almost Zen-like sense of frugality is that it involves little sense of deprivation. Spending almost no money on anything at all is just something I do. When I went to Malta to write an article for the *Independent* on how it was possible to live off £4.87 a day, I didn't go on a holiday of nightmarish discomfort and self-denial. I just went on a holiday.

We stopped for an hour at Molde, an almost entirely modern town of grandiose banality, curfew-empty at 5 p.m. The wet streets were clean, the civic lawns Astroturf perfect. There was no graffiti of any kind, not even on a town hall so insipid it deserved it. The abandoned taxis parked funereally by the port were all spotless new Mercedes. It was suddenly easy to imagine whole townfuls of Norwegians toying with bits of wire until someone accidentally invented the paperclip, like the monkeys typing Shakespeare. I got so bored wandering up and down its immaculate and anonymous main drag that I almost bought a pair of binoculars.

But two good things happened when I reboarded. Firstly, the sun came out. Secondly, I got a cabin. An efficient-looking female purser had taken over from my glum fatty, and I thought I might as well chance my arm. Of course, there were in fact dozens of cabins, and probably had been all the time.

My £18-a-night kingdom down in the bowels was a bijou delight. I had a porthole, two bunks and a washbasin. Somehow its tininess – I could have touched all four walls with the tip of a limb had I been slightly fitter and perhaps 9½ feet tall – made it all the more appealing. The bed linen (my first for exactly 104 years), the abundance of varnished wood and chrome – everything was a delight. I could eat crap and drink beer in privacy, and so I now did, each bottle rendering the nostalgic romance of my surroundings more wondrous. This was sea travel. This was a voyage. I'd never get the 1850s, but at least I'd made it back to the 1950s.

★

We'd already been docked at Trondheim for three hours when I awoke, leaving me only a couple more to wander what I recalled from a previous visit seven years before as a friendly, liveable town with the tallest wooden something in Europe. Ski jump? Cathedral? Puppy? I couldn't remember. Norway's capital until 1380, it was still larger than Oslo when Dufferin pooh-poohed its vulgar commerciality. Its centre is much the same today, rebuilt in the late seventeenth century after one of those big fires they were so keen on.

Some time ago I depressingly concluded that I could not live in any city not sufficiently large and plebian to support both a Burger King and a McDonald's. Trondheim had both. Could I relocate here? It was possible. The cradle of mountains offered a pleasing backdrop, and the brown grass outside the bunting-festooned public buildings spoke of acceptably warm summers. Certainly my Norwegian was coming along. I was delighted to have translated this vital notice on the door of a tattoo parlour: 'No piercing until August 5th'.

But then I discovered a Dirty Nelly™ Irish Pub, and that the fish market was a concrete garage selling reindeer burgers to the Frenchmen off the boat, and I went slightly off the place. Finally, damningly, I learned as I reboarded the *Harald Jarl* that the bunting marked Trondheim's 1,000th birthday. That did it. Relocating here next year would be a terrible anticlimax, like moving to Hastings in 1067 or spending Boxing Day in Bethlehem. I would be history's nearly man.

As we cruised towards the Arctic Circle, I set out to explore the *Harald Jarl* with the new freedom of a paranoid man who has a lockable room in which to store his belongings. The night before, I'd overheard a Norwegian telling his transatlantic interrogators, 'I never take the new Hurtigrute. This is a *boat*.' I could not disagree with his verbal italics. There was a little panelled library. Elderly passengers sat out on the deck with shipping company blankets over their laps. An open door on the starboard promenade deck exposed the engine room, with its vast and shiny pistons hammering away like a demonstration at the Science Museum. Dinner, for those not chasing slippery tubes of processed meat around the floor of their cabin, was heralded by a gong, albeit a rather ethereal tannoyed reverberation. There was a seating plan in the dining room, and you could order port by the bottle.

The night before, buoyed up with port-out-starboard-home colonial nostalgia, I'd unearthed *Helen's Tower* from its fetid rucksack dungeon and repaired to the library to read up on Dufferin's plum diplomatic postings. The relentless splendour revealed put the *Harald Jarl*'s ambience in perspective. In Canada, an average week includes 'picnics, receptions, "drums", dinners, balls, torchlight processions, garden parties, bazaars and regattas'. All are paid for by Dufferin himself. 'I hear terrible things about your expenditure,' writes the Duke of Argyll.

In India it was different. As perhaps the most powerful man in the world, you didn't have to worry about paying for your own 'drums'. During a state visit by the Amir of Afghanistan in 1885, Dufferin's entourage sets up camp at Rawalpindi. This operation involves rather more than a couple of sleeping bags and a built-in groundsheet: 'The Viceroy's Camp,' records Lady Dufferin, 'consists of thirty-six tents for staff, and these form a street, eighteen on each side, with a broad strip of grass in front broken with fountains and rockeries and ferneries. At the top of this double street is our tent palace . . . His Excellency's office, her bedroom, his bedroom, with dressing-room and bathrooms . . . my boudoir opens onto a little square, full of pots of flowers and a little fountain . . . In all the rooms there are Persian carpets and sofas . . . the "street" has lamp-posts all down it; there are telephones and a post office . . .'

After annexing Burma in 1886 (two years later, he picked the name of its old capital, Ava, as the support act for his new title), he steams into Rangoon to find the stupendous welcome decorations include a life-size trompe d'oeil painting of the gatehouse of his wife's family home, Killyleagh Castle. He had twenty-four chandeliers in the ballroom of his Calcutta palace; one of his favourite pastimes was assembling a procession of rajahs to pay homage to him as he sat in his solid silver chair of state. Every time he leaned forward and gently touched 'the proffered nazar', a battery of guns outside would thunder in salute. As Nicolson says, 'he was not a man to despise the pomps of power'.

I thought again of Lindy's dinner-table comment: 'Of course, I was already quite grand, but when I became *very* grand . . .' It seemed an apt description of Dufferin's middle age. The Wilson-baiting revelations notwithstanding, it was difficult to equate the lisping, baggy-shirted poet of the crayon drawing with such haughty arrogance. Perhaps it was the influence of his wife's I'll-call-you-Dufferin stiffness; perhaps, ever the professional, he realised that affecting imperial omnipotence was his job, a way of letting any mutinous rajahs know who was boss. But somehow I felt there was more than that, and again it seemed likely that the shame of his mother's second marriage, her betrayal, had killed in him the sense of fun and self-mockery that had been such a feature of their friendship.

The weather improved as the scenery flattened out. Trondheim sat in glorious sun at the apex of our flat, blue wake, but soon it was gone, and the tannoy woman became increasingly desperate. I had begun to notice that all Norwegians begin their sentences with an uncertain 'Ja . . .' followed by a long, wondering pause, giving the impression they have no idea what they're actually going to say. Usually they do, of course, but she didn't. 'Ja . . . Gentlemen and ladies. Ja. In ten minutes we are . . . passing a . . . lighthouse!' There was always a triumphant flourish of relief as she thought of something. 'Ja . . . a little bit ahead and . . . right? . . . you can notice a . . . sea eagle! . . . This eagle in fact has disappeared now, but there will be more. Here in Norway we have one fourth of the number total of sea eagles!'

At length she was saved by the gong, and the deck emptied once more as the silly shimmer summoned the fortunate to dinner. I was left to savour a glorious evening, alone but for two bottles of Trondheim ale. At this latitude, the evening sun wasn't going anywhere. From 9.30 p.m. onwards it squatted on the horizon for hours, burnishing the sea before slowly rebounding back upwards.

Only once before, in Haugesund, had an evening on deck been feasible, and yet I was now as far north as Arkangel. For the first time, my £200 ticket seemed not just good value, but an impossible bargain.

I stayed up in the cafeteria to see us cross the Arctic Circle, in the company of two super-geriatric, baseball-hatted Americans. They had fag ash on their chins and breathed more loudly than they spoke. At 1 a.m., it was a sad but inevitable anticlimax. There was no ceremony; not even an announcement. I'd stayed near the Americans because one of them had a portable GSM receiver into which he stared so constantly I at first thought it was a handheld telly. As we crossed the Circle, he inclined his head to one side and issued a wheezing, low-key announcement: 'Yip. Well, that's it, Dave.' Dave reciprocated the head movement. 'Yip,' he said.

Was that it? It was sad to compare this mumbled exchange with the deranged initiations on board the *Reine Hortense* as it towed the *Foam* into the Arctic:

> Amid unearthly music, and surrounded by a bevy of hideous monsters, a white-bearded, spectacled personage – clad in bearskin, with a cocked hat over his left ear – presented to the officers of the watch an enormous board, on which was written

> ## 'LE PÈRE ARCTIQUE'

> by way of visiting card . . . there then began a regular riot all over the ship. The yards were manned with red devils and black monkeys . . . officers and men promiscuously mingled and danced the can-can . . . the Arctic father flung down hard peas, as typical of hail, while the powdering of each other's faces with handfuls of flour could not fail to remind everybody on board that we had reached the latitude of snow . . .

It would have been remarkably invigorating to rub flour into Dave's face, but he and his friend had abandoned their vigil the second we'd crossed the line. The barmaid shuttered herself in with the bottles, so I had to toast Dufferin's bumper of grog with the Coke Dave hadn't put in his whiskey. Then I went out on to the empty flag deck and said aloud, 'It's like the bloody Arctic out here.'

I wasn't expecting the Arctic to look any different, but somehow it did. Next morning, the coastal peaks had dark serrations which recalled Dufferin's etchings of Spitzbergen; even the gentle islands on our seaward side seemed oddly bleak. But it was still hard to think that out there, miles out there, lay Europe's single most isolated community, the improbable volcanic pillar of Jan Mayen.

Dufferin's approach to the island was perhaps the closest he came to disaster. Right on cue after the Père Arctique lunacies, the thermometer plummets and dense fog descends; it begins to snow. 'Whatever else might be in store for us, there was sure henceforth to be no lack of novelty and excitement,' he writes with typical understatement, and is unashamedly jubilant when following contact with 'an innumerable fleet of bergs', the captain of the *Reine Hortense* admits defeat, chalking up '*Nous retournons à Reykjavík!*' on a blackboard slung over their stern.

'It seemed so very hard to turn back . . . it could not be much above 120 miles to Jan Mayen.'

So, untying the tow rope and unfurling the sails, the bold Brits leave the feeble Frogs, and set off alone through the floes. Dufferin, obsessed with reaching Jan Mayen ever since seeing a Shetland whaler's sketch of its monstrous volcanic needle four years previously, will not give up so easily.

Turning to approach Jan Mayen from the east, the fog thickens, and what little of the ocean they can see is littered with icebergs, 'glimmering round the vessel like a circle of luminous phantoms'. Listening for waves breaking on the shore ('it was easier to hear land than to see it'), they drift in foggy silence for hour after hour.

'To relieve the tedium, I requested the Doctor to remove one of my teeth,' he writes preposterously. Finally, at 4 a.m., alone on deck, Dufferin catches a glimpse of Jan Mayen's peak, Mount Beerenberg, through a gap in the clouds.

But the 8 miles of sea which still lie between the *Foam* and the island are crazy-paved with pack-ice slabs. Three times they try to snake through; three times the bergs encroach and force them back. 'These unusual phenomena had begun to make some of my people lose their heads a little, so I stationed myself in the bows while Mr Wyse conned the vessel from the square yard. Then there began one of the prettiest and most exciting pieces of nautical manoeuvring . . . Every soul on board was summoned upon deck . . . all hands, armed with spars and fenders, rushed forward to do combat with the bergs.'

Even so, there are 'two or three pretty severe bumps', and Dufferin finds himself 'leaning forward in expectation of the *scrunch* I knew must come'. Jesus. They were 500 miles from anything useful. One puncture in those two inches of wood and they'd have had it – drowning, hypothermia, or, worst-case scenario, making it across the ice to the shore of Jan Mayen and settling down for a drawn-out wintry starvation.

Giving up on a proper landing, Dufferin weighs anchor near the northeast foot of Beerenberg, beneath a 1,000-foot cliff, and sets off in the *Foam*'s gig with the old figurehead, a white ensign and 'a tin biscuit-box, containing the schooner's name, the date of her arrival, and the names of those on board'. He hauls these mementos out of the boat and props them on a rock, 'the superseded damsel grimly smiling across the frozen ocean at her feet'.

I was suddenly glad that the only way of reaching Jan Mayen these days was by air.

Over breakfast I read the Jan Mayen appendix of the *Bradt Guide to Spitzbergen*. It seems to have been discovered by a Venetian, Nicola Zeno, in the late fourteenth century, but the first confirmed sighting isn't until 1614, when the Dutch captain Jan May, despite being aboard the fourth boat to land that year, somehow bags the place for himself. Within a dozen

FIRST GLIMPSE OF JAN MAYEN.

High Latitudes

years the island is crawling with Dutch whalers, whose insatiable blubberlust, as in Spitzbergen, does them out of jobs within a generation. Things peter out thereafter, and Jan Mayen is almost forgotten by Dufferin's time. By the end of the century, though, polar scientists begin to visit; the first successful overwintering is in 1882.

Then things get interesting. Between 1916 and the end of the First World War, an extraordinary succession of Norwegian loons arrive to stake claim to the island in a touching (which is to say Mickey Mouse) parallel to the race for Africa. One claims the southwest coast; another the north; another the mineral rights. The Norwegian state, considering Jan Mayen no man's land, ignores some claims and buys others out (one chap receives a lifelong pension of 100 kroner a month); eventually, the only two players left are Ekerold in the south, and his northern adversary, Jacobsen. Jacobsen's feeling pretty good – the only fuel on the island is driftwood, nearly all of which washes up in the north. But Ekerold's trump card is his radio station, from which he bombards the government with trumped-up anti-Jacobsen propaganda. A bitter Jacobsen retreats, perhaps peeing on the logs as he packs. But Ekerold, consumed with triumphalism, overplays his hand by claiming the whole island, thereby jolting the vague and evasive Norwegians into assuming sovereignty in 1930. No other country seems to notice. Jacobsen, or at least his family, has the last word – ten years after his death in 1942, the government pays his descendants 170,000 kroner to renounce any claims.

After the brief alarums of the war (two Nazi planes crash; the reasonably pristine wreckages are still prominent on the treeless mountainsides), Jan Mayen becomes home to a small radar and weather station as well as a predictable series of fishing-limits rows with Iceland (Jan Mayen is far nearer to both Greenland and Iceland than Norway). Life settles down. In 1950, one of the technicians is blown to death (outside during a storm, rather than inside during a gay orgy). In 1959, in a triumph of boredom over reason, they open a post office. In 1989, a polar bear visits aboard an ice floe. In 1992, one technician asks another whether he is

195

aware that Jan Mayen is the only active volcano on Norwegian soil, and the other one says that yeah, he is.

Standing on the flag deck it was difficult to imagine the unlovely inhospitabilities of Jan Mayen. It was still T-shirt warm, and the air was invitingly pine-scented. The only sign that we were entering an area that considered itself frontier country was the way every settlement displayed huge placards boasting their latitude: 'SANDNESSJØEN 66° 03 21'. Not that the bare numbers held much significance. For all I knew they could have been the vital statistics of a deformed seal.

At lunchtime we glided towards my destination, Bodø, in piercing sun. As was becoming usual with distressingly adventurous prospects, I managed to suppress acceptance of my looming Norwegian Air Force flight until, with a shattering rip of afterburners, a quintet of fighter jets shot up from behind a battery of camouflaged hangars and radar domes and screamed away at awful speed over the mountains. The whole town quivered and shimmered in their wake for a good minute afterwards, like Tom after Jerry puts a dustbin over his head and belabours it with a baseball bat. It was a little too exciting.

Soberly, I slogged off across the dusty marshalling yards of Bodø's modest hinterland, my feet once again pressed to the ground by the double-rucksack burden. It was very hot, and Bodø was very dull. Bored-o in Bodø. Drenched in sweat, I walked along crumbling pavements past deserted regional insurance company headquarters and sundry other squat and dowdy mid-height Fifties blandnesses, before swaying unstoppably down a short flight of stairs and into the tourist office. There I was directed towards the Hotel Norrøna (one of the advantages of looking like an itinerant roads protestor is that you are always forwarded to the cheapest hotel without the embarrassment of having to ask for it).

Thirty-five quid a night may not sound an outrageous bargain, but let me assure you that for Norway that's almost a loss-leader. And because it was in Norway, the Norrøna was no worse than blandly comfortable. My room was hardly expansive – the decision to bless it with a three-piece suite meant a trip to the loo in the dark inevitably began with a mouthful of Dralon – but after a month in cabins, tents and huts I felt strangely agoraphobic. Out of instinct I piled my belongings against the bed in a tight barricade, peering timorously out of the window at the flat, sad concrete opposite.

But then I noticed the telly, and all was forgiven. Dear, sweet telly, with your live football and your Swedish Disney Club! Also, with less straightforward appeal, your three pay-per-view porno channels!

Hotel porno channels are an interesting social phenomenon. My only previous experience was during a Californian motoring holiday with my father and grandfather. My poor grandfather. A compulsive traveller brought up on Fleet Street expense accounts, his already advanced appreciation of luxury was becoming honed as befits a man in his eighties who has no belief in the afterlife.

The nightly quest for accommodation was consequently fraught. After a week he came to accept that there was often no alternative to a motel, but having accepted this, he insisted on a quality motel. Every time his failing eyes picked out a 'Best Western' sign he would say, 'Might I make a small plea that we stop here?'

I feel awful about it now, but when my father and I get together, niggardly money-grubbing evolves from a mere blighting character trait to an obsessive, all-consuming competitive sport. Every morning, while my father staggered off for his sixth visit to the complimentary breakfast buffet, I would pore over maps and accommodation guides, planning our day's travel around reaching the very cheapest motel in a generously broad radius from our intended destination. The words 'Best Western' were from an alien vocabulary, alongside phrases such as 'Keep the change' or 'This is the life'.

So we would ignore my grandfather's quiet pleas, or even, I am ashamed to admit, fob him off with false sightings of 'No Vacancy' signs. On this particular evening, our budget goal didn't seem too bad – I recall none of the parasitic or scavenging fauna that had often shared our beds that fortnight – but our room's mirrored ceiling panels and the pinhead caretaker's lazy eye should have alerted us.

My grandfather joined us in mine and my father's room for our usual pre-prandial carafe of Paul Masson Hearty Burgundy, and while I flicked through the TV channels in search of news, it happened. Suddenly, inescapably, the screen, the room, the world was filled by a large and lazy phallus being hysterically fellated to erection. The musical accompaniment, I distantly registered, was the theme from *Sale of the Century*. For perhaps fifteen seconds, three generations of Moore males stood in arrested animation, tilted toothmugs of wine frozen near parted lips. Then my grandfather edged towards the action, squinted up at the wall-mounted television, and announced almost disappointedly, 'Well, you'd think he'd come.'

Though this partly defused a situation of urban myth-scale embarrassment, it left me with a confused and guilty terror of piped porn. Throughout my stay at the Norrøna I was convinced that somehow, probably while trying to get to the loo in the dark, I'd stumble on to the remote control and activate the sequence of button depressions that would unleash the adult channel, and in a great cacophony of klaxons and neon alert all fellow guests to my lonely, rapacious lust for filth.

It was 10 p.m., but still the sun beat down. The street below was dusty and sterile, but it remained cosily, familiarly urban. There was a hardware shop. There was an English theme pub, the Piccadilly. It seemed difficult to believe that in ten hours I would be on a military transport plane taking me 1,000 kilometres across the empty Arctic to the ridiculous, pointless, terrifying island of Jan Mayen.

Unwisely, I read again the passage where Dufferin struggles away from the island through ice floes so dense that there is 'not a vestige of open water to be seen'. He delivers an explanatory lecture, one which he presumably didn't shout out across the deck prefaced by a 'Now, crew . . .':

These bergs frequently acquire a rotary motion, whereby their circumference attains a velocity of several miles an hour; and it is scarcely possible to conceive the consequences produced by a body, exceeding ten thousand million tons in weight, coming in contact with another in such circumstances. Numerous whale vessels have thus been destroyed; some thrown upon the ice; some torn open, others overrun by the ice and buried beneath its heaped fragments.

After umpteen return trips down cold culs-de-sac, the wind shifts, loosening the ice and opening a clear vista to 800 miles of open sea between them and their next stop, Hammerfest, near Norway's northern cape. It had been a close call, and the lesson was clear: Don't mess with Jan Mayen.

With this in mind, I sat down and looked over, for perhaps the thirtieth time, the letter the Norwegian Defence Communications and Data Services Administration had sent me six weeks earlier:

Our reference: 97/01705–002/NODECA/D/RNS/KG/kg /005

1. Mr T. Moore has been given permission to follow the transport to Jan Mayen August 1st.

2. Meet at the old military air terminal in Bodø, 0800 hours. This is 300m from the civilian air terminal.

3. The ground stop is scheduled to 3 hours only. Your passport has to be presented at Jan Mayen.

4. Enclosed please find some information about Loran C.

5. Your point of contact with NODECA will be: Senior Engineer Kaare Gulbrandsen.

By authority, Chief Operations Division

The first time I read it, and for the following twenty-eight times, this curt missive had seemed risibly arcane. But in the light of

Dufferin's brush with icy death, it wasn't funny. Now it was stark, confidential, authoritarian. It was like my call-up papers or a coded letter a young Michael Caine might find in the exhaust pipe of a Wartburg near Checkpoint Charlie. I imagined unmarked jets plunging into the sea and my family receiving terse notification that I had died serving Norway. I imagined NODECA hoods tying me to a chair while the quietly terrifying Kaare Gulbrandsen asked repeatedly what I knew about Loran B 12 and advised me to choose my next witticism very carefully.

Having committed further crimes against gastronomy I went to bed early, before Liverpool had rounded off a 3–1 victory over Norway, and spent a restless night worrying about fog and lava and my alarm clock failing to go off. Which, of course, it did.

But – and this still disturbs me now – at 6.25, only ten minutes after my Remington Traveller had silently demonstrated its impotence, I was abruptly awoken by a blast of Scandinavian. I sat up and found myself blinking at a painfully polychromatic testcard, accompanied as is the regional custom by a radio broadcast. The TV alarm had gone off. I hadn't set it. I hadn't even known it had one.

Ploughing through a free, and therefore enormous, breakfast I tried very hard to convince myself that this arresting incident was Dufferin urging me on, working in mysterious ways to keep me on his trail.

It was a glorious morning. My twitchy restlessness had allowed ample time to stroll through Bodø's sunny, deserted Pleasant Valley Sunday suburbs, but, as I headed out of town across the lower folds of my map, it occurred to me that the distant, top-left Biro cross with which the receptionist had marked the military terminal was rather further away from the civilian airport, by a factor of perhaps fifteen, than the 300 metres described in my call-up papers.

I took the NODECA summons out again. It was like one of those exam nightmares. Somehow, despite my almost hourly rereading of this brief document, I had not previously noticed the crucial adjective 'old'. The *old* military terminal. I had gone in completely the wrong direction, and now had, what, seventeen minutes to cover the 2 kilometres back. All right. Bad. But not impossible. I set off at suitably military jog, and arrived at the civilian terminal, humid but presentable, twelve minutes later.

'*The old military terminal?*' said the girl behind the Braathens SAFE desk with what I should have recognised as excessive deliberation. 'It is the big, tall, green building down there,' she concluded, making big, tall building signals with her hands. I emerged from the glitzy new terminal and looked. There I saw it: tall, green, big – but not particularly military-looking and certainly over 300 metres away. I puffed into a steady lope.

The closer I got, the less military-looking the edifice became. It became round-sided, and lime green, and nowhere near the runway. Then, as I stood by a chainlink fence right in front of it, it became, unmistakably, a cement factory.

With my watch showing 7.59 I stormed through a car park to accost incoherently two men leaning out of a canteen window, then having been directed back towards the airport – 'No, no – not tall. A small building. Round roof, and green' – I careered raggedly up the road. My heart pounded behind my eyes; spurts of fizzy breakfast pumped up into my mouth. At 8.07 I saw a door in front of a matt olive hanger, reasonably clearly stencilled 'JAN MAYEN MOVEMENT CONTROL', about, what, 300 metres from the civilian terminal. As I wheeled towards it there was a harsh, whining growl, which grew, roared, then faded.

I gawped stupidly as a transport plane lumbered off above the buildings and arced out to sea. I stood bent double with my hands on my knees, hissing out breathless expletives, sweat and saliva mingling at my feet. There wasn't another plane for eight months.

'Hallo?'

A bronzed, craggy man in a blue shirt with epaulettes had emerged from the door. I wheezed what I could, which clearly wasn't enough as he began to witter apologetically in Norwegian. '. . . Eng . . . lish.'

'Ah! Okay. So. No. The Jan Mayen flight is not . . . flying. Today. We have some problems with some pilots. We try at the same clock tomorrow.' He strode away, straight-backed, brisk.

Disaster had been replaced by mere inconvenience. Yes, I would now have to spend another night in the Norrøna; yes, I would now have to fly to Tromsø to catch my Spitzbergen boat, and yes, this would mean my paid-for Hurtigrute connection from Bodø to Tromsø was now useless and worthless. But at least Jan Mayen was still on.

This should have made me feel better, but I have to report that it did not. I don't think I have ever sworn so loudly and with such stubborn persistence. I have little trouble in excusing myself from all blame in these situations, and it was days – no, months – before I was even distantly aware that the whole thing was completely my own fault. A simple call the day before would have sufficed. No matter. I cursed the daft arses of the Norwegian armed forces. This was just one more grandiose balls-up from the people who brought you 'Let's send the news of Hitler's invasion by postcard.' As I booked my Tromsø ticket from the same girl at the Braathens SAFE desk, it was difficult to staunch the flow of epithets directed at her childlike grasp of scale and geometry which had carried me along for every one of those fateful 300 metres. This despite the fact that she was ineffably cheerful and probably beautiful, and that the ticket she sold me was an inexplicably cheap £50.

Bodø was belatedly coming to life, and the harbour was busy with yachtsmen and prawn vendors. But I hadn't finished. I stormed furiously down to meet the midday Hurtigrute, where I hoped to obtain a refund on my Bodø–Tromsø passage. 'There is no possibility of this,' said the shiny-faced purser. As I gathered myself to protest, he cut me off with a Fawltyesque 'Thank you!' It was the last straw.

'Okay, the thing is, I'm writing a book,' I began, already adopting the wayward bass falsetto of an aggrieved adolescent, 'so how would it be if I write down that you are rude and . . .' (here, as is often the way in extremis, my vocabulary shrivelled) '. . . awful, you rude, awful man?'

This was hardly a statement likely to bring him round, and he replied with a verbatim reiteration of his opening gambit, most of it delivered to my retreating back.

Spent, I returned slowly to society. Cheered by being long-changed in the beer shop, I picked up a tourist leaflet on Bodø's history and sat on a bench by the marina amid the middle-aged couples wordlessly devouring sacks of prawns.

In other circumstances, this publication would have been an unlikely candidate for the most stimulating work of literature available in a town of 40,000 souls. I read with mild astonishment of the circumstances behind the town's rise to prominence when, in 1796, it became home to the region's first public healthcare centre. 'Veneral diseases were spreading rapidly and the hospital was sorely needed,' the leaflet stated matter-of-factly. A pity they couldn't have somehow incorporated this into the town crest. I skimmed through the customary herring booms to the arrival of the railway in 1962, an incredible feat of engineering which burrowed right through Norway's mountainous innards. With the world's second most northerly rail terminus, Bodø's ship (or rather train) came in; today it processes 1.5 million travellers each year. But then I read on, and discovered that even without this logistical significance, Bodø had proved an irresistible target for the Luftwaffe.

In just two hours on 27 May 1940, a bomber raid destroyed 400 of Bodø's 600 buildings. At a stroke the lazy stacks of frumpish Fifties concrete became monuments to Bodø's lost heritage and its plucky inhabitants' stout resilience. (It seems that all the less appealing towns I had Hurtigruted through – Molde, Kristiansund, Måløy – had suffered similarly.) Feeling guilty, not only for my own mockery but Britain's wartime abandonment of Norway, I suddenly lacked the appetite to smirk at the account of Bodø's annual highlight: the Grannies Festival. 'The week-long festival, which attracts 15,000 worldwide participants, is dedicated to making a fuss of Granny.'

The next day began unpromisingly. Again the testcard and radio awakening; again the dangerously excessive breakfast; again the

Day of the Triffids deserted streets. But there was one difference. The vertical, squinting sun of the previous two days had gone, replaced by a distant glow hiding translucently behind an even Polyfilla skimming. I hoped this wouldn't be significant.

Inside the formica and lino Jan Mayen Movement Control were a dozen silent civilians visiting the radar base's inmates: girlfriends, mothers, snivelling Rodney Trotter little brothers in too-tight, too-short trousers, blinking at the floor under village-idiot fringes. These were veterans; only I seemed impressed by the large, squat, four-engined Norwegian Air Force Hercules transporter whose grey bulk blotted out the light from the windows as it lowered its massive rear loading ramp.

A camouflaged tanker arced slowly around, depositing hoses and a Lee Marvin officer with metallic hair, gleaming toe-caps and an attaché case under one arm of his ironed flak jacket. He briskly inspected the Hercules, then marched in and said many things in Norwegian. The only one I even partially decoded was something to do with tickets. Tickets? Crap it. I had no tickets. Then he started reading a list of names, names like Kennetsen and Nyhamar and Steinbakk. It seemed impossible to believe that such a list would feature my name. Why hadn't I called to confirm anything? I was already rehearsing a pathetic little 'Excuse me, sir . . .' speech when his confident delivery faltered.

'Tim . . . Mour. Mourrr. Tim Mooerrr.'

He handed over a little computer-printed chit, a simulacrum of an airline ticket for a simulacrum of an airline. Airport codes usually bear some relevance to a condensation of their names: LHW for London Heathrow, CDG for Paris Charles de Gaulle. Bodø's, I was delighted to note, was BOO. But Jan Mayen's code served only to confirm its arse-end-of-beyond credentials. It was ZXB.

He motioned to me to fill in the back, whose text, I was glad to note, was in both English and Norwegian. But then I was not so glad. 'Next of kin'? Please don't say that kind of stuff. 'In the event of death, Norwegian Armed Forces will apply the following limitations of liability . . .' Well, now they were all set. After we'd smashed into Mount Beerenberg's volcanic flanks, they knew exactly where to send the sorry-love NAAFI coupons.

We trooped across the tarmac, and up a ladder into the plane's dark and cavernous belly. There was a Jonah and the Whale quality to the experience. Exposed pipes and cables, the plane's arteries and capilleries, twisted in impossible profusion across the distant, dimly lit ceiling. The flight-suited crew lined us up on two hammocks running the length of the fuselage, and asked us to attach ourselves with Amy Johnson leather seat-straps.

Everyone else put on thick jumpers, buckled up, and immediately set to work on their puzzle magazines. If they were affecting nonchalant bravado, they were doing a very good job. I couldn't even decipher the seat-belt, and had to ask my heavy, bearded neighbour to delve about in my groin.

It was incredibly uncomfortable. Our backs were up against a cargo net loosely restraining pallets of wank mags for the millennium and other uncomfortably angular Jan Mayen supplies. The Beard's left thigh bullied my right. My knees brushed a lever which I was reasonably sure would jettison the undercarriage or fill the cabin with a metallic cloud of radar-deflecting chaff.

The engines started. Everyone delved for earplugs. Well, come on, I thought. Conversation was off, but it was only about as loud as a Tube train. A conscript in road-gang ear protectors proffered a shrinkwrapped pair of foam cones. I smugly dismissed them. He raised his eyebrows in an 'Are-you-sure?' way. I had obviously overestimated their hardiness.

Then they started the other three engines.

We bumped off across the tarmac, my brain curiously registering a sound which transcended sound, swamping at least two other senses. As the engines roared and howled and whined up to maximum revs I wanted very much to be somewhere else, preferably a somewhere that didn't make me feel like a woodlouse under the nozzle of an Aqua Vac.

As we lumbered – I don't believe a Hercules ever does anything else – off the runway, clouds of vapour hissed from a pipe above my head. Then the pilot settled into a drawn-out ascent, during which the seating layout inclined me, gently but insistently, into The Beard's cushioned flanks. I resisted gravity at first, but soon realised his lavishly insulated shoulder restricted my aural distress to a monophonic assault, and presently began to nuzzle shamelessly.

An hour passed. It got very cold, then very hot, then very cold again. A burly para conducted a sign-language beverage service, dispensing Max-Pax coffee and broth from a machine lashed cavalierly to a stretch of webbing. Having done so, he rather disconcertingly returned to film everybody with a camcorder. Why had he done that? Few of the possible explanations reassured.

We levelled briefly, then lolled into a descent that was to last a further hour. Norwegian follicles insinuated themselves forcefully towards me. Through a tiny head-high porthole, I watched as we descended into the clouds.

Suddenly we banked sharply, the engines roaring desperately as we lurched right and up. Everyone was strained forward or backward in their harnesses. I craned up at the porthole and was presented by an image so unexpected that at first I couldn't decode its significance. But once I had, I almost burst into tears. Even those regulars who'd seen it could only manage the wannest of smiles. It was a mist-tinted, vertical close-up of a seagull, bobbing on the crest of a grey wave.

The clouds weren't clouds, but fog, horrible thick brown fog that had congealed nicely at sea level. We'd dropped down gently, and suddenly something had loomed out of it, like maybe a 7,500-foot volcano, and the pilot had taken evasive action so extreme and last-minute that we'd come a few feet from slamming into the Arctic. Later I was able to feel that I had at last empathised with Dufferin. Like him I had almost been claimed by the thick mists of Jan Mayen. But at the time I was just aware that I had at some recent point grasped, and was still grasping, a fistful of The Beard's trousered thigh.

After twenty minutes of banking, we levelled out and started to descend again. We were giving it another go. A more circumspect approach was demanded, but the pilot seemed unable to resist a succession of abrupt turns. Everyone was now trying to peek through the webbing-obscured portholes.

During one violent left-right-left combination, I saw it. Flattened under the fog was a long stretch of low, smeary black undulations, and one vast stocky haunch cut off at ankle height. Jan Mayen; Beerenberg. It was much longer than I'd expected. Just as Iceland, marooned in the North Atlantic, looks on an atlas about the size of the Isle of Wight, so Jan Mayen, a forlorn comma on a huge blank sheet of blue foolscap, seems like Rockall's abandoned runt. In fact, it's 35 miles long.

We continued our wayward descent. Again there were awful porthole cameos, wingtips almost scything the breakers, the reds of a fulmar's eyes . . . then a flash of grey and rock. The airstrip, I had read, was made of lava gravel, and since its construction in 1961 had hosted fewer than 300 landings. It was a surface you would only wish to approach at exactly the correct trajectory, and, since we were perhaps 30 degrees away from this, I was neither surprised nor distressed when once again the engines raced and we moved heavily up and around.

For the second time, the flanks of Beerenberg came momentarily into focus; for a moment there was the sensation that up there in the clouds was a lonely mountain so massive that someone in the Icelandic Meteorological Institute had told me it disrupted the weather over half of Northern Europe. A second more and it fuzzed back into the mist and was gone.

This time there was no circular banking. We rose gently, the engines settling into a head-filling drone, and after a couple of minutes the Max-Pax commando appeared. He embarked on a charade. An apologetically downturned mouth, head shaking and repeated hand-crossing motions were the first instalment; the second involved pointing back over his shoulder and mouthing a word that seemed to be 'Bodø'. It was all reasonably unequivocal, but I could not allow myself to believe it. The lobotomised indifference with which my fellow passengers had greeted his

performance encouraged me to entertain alternative interpretations. 'Don't bother with the southern border.' 'Kindly refrain
from throwing powder.' 'Never return to a sad poodle.'

Twenty minutes passed. We were not trying again. That was
it. No Jan Mayen. The last flight of the year. I mean, there *is*
a bloody great weather station here. Couldn't they have radioed
over before setting off? 'Oh, by the way, the visibility is about
7 inches so you can't possibly land.' If we'd gone yesterday,
like we were supposed to, the skies would have been clear
and blue and we'd have seen Beerenberg from Bodø. And
what was wrong with the bloody passengers? They were all
poring over word squares with imbecile placidity. I've seen
travellers looking more aggrieved when they're told to mind
the gap. Was it a national trait? A British party would have at
least tutted amidst the engine roar. A dozen Frenchmen would
have stormed the flight deck, and whipped up an impassioned
chorus of the 'Marseillaise' before smashing blindly into the
volcano. But only one of our number seemed at all distressed,
the housewife down the end of the opposite bench, who fid-
dled bitterly with the black bra strap that inveigled beyond her
cardigan's neckline.

I suddenly had an awful thought. The lone wives were visiting
their husbands for the first time in six months. I'd been told
to expect a three-hour stay on the island; the arrangements for
occupying this time weren't clear, but the efforts Black Bra had
made strongly suggested that for many the visit would incorporate
a frenzied venting of pent-up conjugal rights. I imagined the
Jan Mayen runway flanked by a dozen libidinous technicians,
waving furious erections and bellowing in primal frustration at
the retreating Hercules.

In contrast with the day before, my anger melted quickly
into acceptance. There was an air of predestination about the
whole endeavour. I should have known better than to have
genuinely thought I would ever emulate Dufferin. It was just
another inevitable victory for him. If he'd been our pilot, you
can guarantee we'd have gone back for another go.

Soon I was entrenched in the comforting melancholy of heroic failure. Never, after all, would I stride alone on Jan Mayen's wreck-strewn black sands, stand dwarfed beneath its seven mighty glaciers, talk to its funny men. The *Foam*'s old figurehead would continue its timeless vigil on Jan Mayen's bleak northern shore undisturbed. It was my fate to join the happy band of travellers who had seen Jan Mayen looming primevally out of the fog and opted to leave it well alone.

Two hours later we made a ridiculous landing at Bodø, one whose substantial sideways element made me rather less distressed that we hadn't tried again at Jan Mayen. We taxied up to Movement Control and cut the engines, and five hours of accumulated decibels began dribbling hissily out of my ears, a process that took the best part of three days. There was a brisk debriefing, which an Air Force johnny gamely translated for me. It hadn't been the fog at all.

'The wind was . . . bad. Bad wind. From the bad side. Fog is normal. In one year, only three days without fog. To see Beerenberg is not easy. Three days in one year.'

People started to file out. The Beard kindly told me that we'd try again in an hour. Conditions around Jan Mayen changed in minutes, he said. Yes, I thought. One minute you can't see your hand in front of your face because of the fog, the next minute because it's been blown off.

I followed the herd to the civilian terminal, paid £3 for a hot dog and bought a couple of five-day-old English papers for the flight, more in hope than expectation. But ambling lethargically back, I saw Black Bra and a couple of others driving away. The Air Force johnny shrugged his shoulders in cheery resignation and handed me a souvenir pair of earplugs. 'It is no good today. We will try tomorrow. 8.30?'

To be honest, at that moment I was delighted that my timetable precluded this re-run. Tomorrow I had to be in Tromsø, boarding a ship bound for Spitzbergen. I was even quite glad that we hadn't tried for Jan Mayen again that day. Five hours strapped to a net with a man in your lap and the last remaining memory of your O-level General Studies syllabus trickling out of your ears might no doubt command a high price in some circles, but it was not an ordeal I looked forward to repeating with enthusiasm.

10

I did a slight double-take as the *Nordstjernen*'s pitted monochrome hull loomed up on the Tromsø quayside. She was another *Harald Jarl*, identical in design and decrepitude. But, as I boarded, it was clear that this was an even more 'traditional' vessel. Victorian-workhouse plumbing echoed distantly away with an ethereal salutation to Davy Jones's Locker; the only recent additions, I was disturbed to note, were the Bullworker springs tethering all the furniture to the floor. Poor *Nordstjernen*. Forty years as a coastal cruiser, and then instead of comfortable dotage as a marine library you get the Death Run: out across thirty-six hours of the world's foullest seas to the icy, treacherous sounds of Spitzbergen.

But the thought of the Northern Arctic at least fired within me the realisation that after weeks of circumlocutory dallying and the abysmally abortive Jan Mayen outing, I was back in Dufferin's wake.

From Jan Mayen he'd sailed uneventfully to Hammerfest, a harmless fishing village he picks out for some uncharacteristic bullying. 'Hammerfest is scarcely worth wasting my paper upon. When I tell you that it is the most northerly town in Europe, I have mentioned its only remarkable characteristic. Its population is so-and-so, its chief exports this and that . . . it produces milk and bad potatoes.' I suppose this outburst was an equivalent of the superhuman superiority I'd felt after the Icelandic cyclethon. In the aftermath of his Jan Mayen ordeal, little fishing towns and their funny-hatted Lapp gentlemen seemed pathetically twee.

They buy jerseys, take delivery of a goat and exchange dinners

with the Consul. Preparing to set sail, Wilson accosts the Doctor
with a 'look of gloomy triumph in his eyes':

> 'Do you know, sir?' This was always the preface to tidings
> unusually doleful. 'No – what?' 'Oh, nothing, sir; only two
> sloops have just arrived, sir, from Spitzbergen, sir – where
> they couldn't get, sir; such a precious lot of ice – two
> hundred miles from the land – and, oh, sir, they've come
> back with all their bows stove in!'

Wilson was never one to underestimate a cause for alarm, but on
this occasion he isn't exaggerating. Dufferin examines the boats,
walrus-hunters, and finds their hulls suitably ravaged. 'Nevertheless, I felt it would not become a gentleman to turn back at
the first blush of discouragement.' Surveying the *Nordstjernen*'s
battered hull, I experienced an unwelcome affinity with Dufferin's
recognition that his voyage was on the threshold of true peril.
Struggling to unstove my bows, I puffed out my chest, headed
for the purser's office and demanded a cabin upgrade.

It was, in fact, the second upgrade. The only possible function
of my first home, a windowless cell with rusty taps, seemed as
the famous 'brighouse' solution to the age-old quandary of what
should be done with the drunken tourist. I wasn't paying £700
for an eight-day reign as The Cooler King. The purser, who quite
simply *was* Martina Navratilova, had sourly offered an alternative.
'It is bigger,' she said, without looking up. And it was, in the same
way that a shoe is bigger than a foot. If you had cared to make a
nest of cabins, these two would have intersheathed snugly. In a
rare display of authority, I returned and expressed dissatisfaction.

'Well, that is all I have in that category. If I upgrade you, everyone else will want to be upgraded.' 'No . . . not at all,' I countered
uncertainly. 'You know, it'll just be . . . *our little secret.*'

I tailed off, aware that my jovially conspiratorial tone had been
some way wide of the mark. It was like unsuccessfully attempting
to bribe a policeman. She gave me a splendidly withering look,
then proffered another key. 'Take it. Cabin 354. It is in the

same category, but larger somewhat.' She cut off my thanks. 'But understand this: you will have to share once we arrive in Longyearbyen.'

The cabin was not in the same category, of course. That was just her little lie to try and forestall the angry mutiny of aggrieved and jealous cell-dwellers whom I would be unable to resist frogmarching around my expansive quarters. True, there was still no porthole, but it had a desk, its own shower and loo, and the lower bunk converted into a sofa – ideal when entertaining aggrieved and jealous cell-dwellers. The ensuite alone was larger than my first home, and I felt very pleased with myself.

The lifeboat drill offered an early chance to allow my fatalist Wilsonisms full reign, and also to survey my seventy-odd fellow passengers, mostly twentysomething Italians, fortysomething French couples and sixtysomething Germans. Standing with our lifejackets on back to front while the purser explained how to tread water offered a demonstration of the pan-Continental refuge of nervous laughter. This was a proper voyage, across proper seas, and with a risk of a proper disaster. I wondered if anyone else had read coverage of the cruise liner which a few weeks earlier had run aground on Spitzbergen's lonely northeastern coast, stranding 150 elderly Americans for three days with the ship listing at 20 degrees.

And then, having perilously hoisted aboard a couple of Mercedes minibuses and lashed them to the foredeck, we were off, steaming up the Grøtsund past a gaily blazing warehouse, cutting a lazy, viscous wake in the still black water. As Tromsø petered out, I added the final spices to my definitive recipe for a Norwegian coastal town. Take one fishing settlement. Add in a wooden cathedral. Regularly raze to the ground and rebuild. Stir in one Nazi bombardment, a vast concrete bridge, and a small forest of oil storage tanks. Garnish with a white concrete Toblerone church, 400 shoe shops and . . . oh, enough. I *liked* Norway. Had I not pondered relocating in at least three of the places I had visited? No. Not seriously. But it was a homely land which retained a sort of pre-modernism, an innocent Fifties optimism and community spirit, like Iceland but with trees and a summer. I had a strong sensation that in a week I would be missing it enormously.

So used was I to my previous Hurtigrute existence as a self-catering semi-stowaway that I didn't respond to the dinner gong (this time an inane xylophone jingle like a Cold War radio jamming signal) until it was too late.

'Stop!'

The young maîtresse d' waylaid me as I homed in on a table whose animated occupants were making more noise than all the others combined. They were gesticulating and uncorking bottles, almost visibly sucking away any residual fun that may have been lurking amidst the sullen, mute pensioners.

'No! Please! That is the Italian table!'

'But there are many empty seats . . .' I began in Level 2 English as she led me away to her apartheid seating diagram.

'You can maybe go to German Table Three,' she offered, poring over her ledger like a governor offering a trusty a sought-after job on the prison farm. She indicated a distant couple. The idea of dining with Mr and Mrs Erich Honecker did not appeal. I gave her a bleak look.

'Perhaps,' she said, abruptly adopting an unctuous wheedle, 'you would like to go on the first dinner sitting?' I explained that it was a little early for me, without adding that only people in hospices and borstals eat at 6.30 p.m. 'But there are two nice Swedish girls . . .' She winked. 'Asa and Iris. Dark and blonde – like Abba? Very nice. Young girls. Swedish.' Jesus, what was this? I felt like asking her if they were, you know, *clean*.

In the end I was seated with the odds 'n' sods – a nice middle-aged French couple and an old Swiss bloke. He was a Hurtigrute groupie, having been up the coast four times in recent years. 'Now I have had enough of these bloody fjords,' he said in an oddly poncy Germanic voice as our Polar Platter arrived. 'I want to see a spot of ice. I say, might this meat be reindeer?' He had worked for Nestlé for years out in the Far East and had picked up incongruous colonial colloquialisms. Everything was 'pretty good' or 'perfectly revolting' or 'a bit thick'.

We turned off the normal Hurtigrute route and headed north out to open sea, though by then I was heavily asleep. This was probably for the best, as, shortly after seeing Norway off, things seemed to have become rather lively. I was dimly aware of the wastepaper basket rolling about, and the corridor was filled with the distressing sound of a retching female. There were a couple of booming sounds from deep in the hull that were easy to interpret as iceberg collisions, and as I awoke an extravagant lateral heave flung me straight off my ledgeless bunk.

After a half- (or more accurately quarter-) hearted buffet breakfast with the French couple in an almost deserted dining room, I weaved queasily out to the deserted flag deck. A restless swell loomed around the *Nordstjernen*, arrogantly smothering its puny bow waves. It was also getting cold, down to 9°C, and a thin skimmed-milk mist was bedding down.

Whenever I spent too much time looking at the Arctic I'd become haunted by the fate of the seven volunteers – *volunteers* – who had over-wintered on Jan Mayen in 1633 to assess the viability of a year-round whaling station. So was Dufferin, quoting at length from the journal that was discovered when the relief ship arrived the following June, eight months after leaving them.

On the 8th of September they 'were frightened by something falling to the ground' – probably a volcanic disturbance. A month later, it becomes so cold that their linen, after a moment's exposure to the air, becomes frozen like a board. Huge fleets of ice beleagured the island, the sun disappears . . . On the 12th of December, they kill a bear, having already begun to feel the effects of a salt diet . . . On the 25th of February, the sun reappeared. By the 22nd of March scurvy had already declared itself: 'For want of refreshments we began to be very heartless, and so afflicted that our legs are scarce able to bear us.'

On it goes, the clerk dying on Easter Day, the last two pullets being fed to the only two volunteers left in health, then one by one they pop their clogs (Dutch to the end), the last survivor dutifully recording the weather and so on until 30 April, when 'his failing hand could do no more than trace an incompleted sentence on the page'.

That ought to be enough. But not for Dufferin. I was slowly realising that, as with his gleeful accounts of Viking unpleasantness, he was lapping this stuff up.

> On the 4th of June, up again above the horizon rise the sails of the Zealand fleet; but no glad faces come forth to greet the boats; and when their comrades search for those they had hoped to find – lo! each lies dead in their own hut – one with an open prayer book by his side; another with his hand stretched towards the ointment he had used for his stiffened joints; and the last survivor, with the unfinished journal lying by his side.

On one level this comforted me, as evidence that Dufferin in fact shared Wilson's (and therefore my) ghoulishness. But on another level, it suggested that all the tales of epic suffering were devices to shore up his own indefatigability. The subtext of each account of Arctic deprivation was 'See? This is the kind of bad shit that goes down up here. But I take this bad shit on!'

I recalled the Bodø Air Force johnny telling me that Mount Beerenberg was only visible three days a year. A month ago I would have put Dufferin's lone sighting of its mist-wraithed peak down as a lucky break. Now it was just a great big lie, a memorable and epic scene he'd simply made up for effect. Stick that in your stovepipe, Freddy.

I was realising the extent to which my faith in the Dufferin cult had melted away. He had seemed so unimpeachably perfect, exemplifying all that was good about Victorian Britain, the grand visions, the self confidence, the philanthropy; I could only look at myself and wonder where it had all gone wrong. But then there had been the *Foam*'s near disaster at Jan Mayen and the general use and abuse of Wilson, and I'd decided that Dufferin was just a more refined version of those daft squires in TV costume dramas, to whom the pursuit of idiotic dares and challenges passed for a career, to whom staff were the dispensable slaves who bore the brunt of the dangers.

Probably no less important a factor was that Dufferin had been my only constant companion: as such, petty character flaws were magnified to global irritations. How else could I explain why Dufferin's fondness for the word 'lilac' caused me to tense with outrage? Dependence on a solitary guide through hostile and remote lands can easily lead to a build-up of feverish resentment as real as if the author were there in person. Once, in Romania, Birna and I spent a week choreographing the dance we would force the author of the Lonely Planet guide to perform as he yodelled a prepared confession at his showtrial.

That was part of the reason why, despite knowing almost nothing about him, I'd latched on to Wilson. He was someone else; he wasn't Dufferin. And wouldn't he have been a superb steward on the *Nordstjernen*? 'Oh, madam, you *do* look bad! Perhaps something so as to settles your constitution, madam? Cook tells me the boiled fox tongues are very good.' 'Italian, sir? Well, sir, happens that you'll be a little trepidatious, sir, on accounts of the big 'ole in the bow what's letting the Arctic in.'

With the swell growing and a steady stream of whey-faced passengers retiring shakily to their cabins, the morning's *This Is Spitzbergen* slide show accelerated to flash-frames accompanied by staccato bursts of disjointed commentary . . . Barentsburg, Russian mining town, horrible Azerbaijan brandy, workers not paid for nine months, polar bears in the top fjords for the last three weeks, world's most northerly waffles, last outpost of Europe to be discovered – 100 years after America, more snow-scooters than people, cats prohibited, 'Do not caress the walrus', Europe's largest parish, priest has a helicopter, fossilised dinosaur footprints, whole place was once near equator and moved north, Amundsen, driftwood, fox, reindeer, rabies, whaling . . .

By the time it became too much for me, there were only four of us left. As the slide carousel clicked forward faster and faster, flashing lurid images on the sliding screen, I was uncomfortably reminded of Alex's subliminal aversion therapy in *A Clockwork Orange*. They called lunch, and I was forced to concede that though I'd paid for the food, turning it down was probably preferable to throwing it up. I stumbled below to 354, and with a queasy sigh once more surrendered my soul to Stugeron. It seemed there still wasn't quite enough salt on my sea dog.

Bran-mouthed and disoriented, I re-emerged at 5 p.m. If anything, it was worse. The furniture slid about in ragged unison, straining at its spring tethers as the boat was eased aloft, then squatted down obliquely, squeezing out angry gouts of churned foam. A couple of elderly Germans ricocheted off tables as they crossed the deserted rear saloon. Making nonchalant headway was indeed impossible. After studying the crew's approach, I discovered the trick was to get up a reasonable speed and trust to momentum, treating the decks like the rolling mirrored logs in the *Gladiators* eliminator.

'We are at 74 degrees and 40 minutes,' announced the tannoy in four languages to the three of us braced against various fixtures about the saloon. 'The captain's cocktail party in the Blue Saloon has been delayed because of the bad sea.' Blue, blue, blue, sa-loon, I sang to myself. However much it was due to the drugs, I was delighted to be alive and above deck.

The dinner gong theme sounded for the second sitting; the maîtresse d' sidled up as I wandered into the dining room. 'You do not like the Swedish girls?' I said again that 6.30 was just a little too early (I didn't say that I'd seen the girls in question and had noted that while they had indeed resembled the two from Abba, sadly I'd never really fancied Björn or Benny).

'Couldn't I just sit on . . . [here I indicated one of the dozen or so deserted tables] . . . that table?'

'That one? Of course,' she said, with a sour gurn.

We took our seats amid slapstick crockery smashes echoing out of the kitchens. The Italians made it, all fag smoke, chatter and white teeth, as did most of the French, the chic wives disgraced by pot-bellied husbands sweating into their cardigans. Happy to be dining alone, I expansively ordered a pint of beer and a £15 bottle of wine, which had no sooner been uncorked when four of the remaining seats on my table were suddenly filled. One by the old Swiss guy, the other three by a pipe-smoking German woman and her two associates, a cancerous dinner lady-type with crooked lipstick, and a moon-faced, prematurely bald thirty-year-old who for no obvious reason other than perhaps his own appearance immediately launched into a protracted, Muttley-style cackle.

Publicly shamed by my alcoholic provisions, I looked out of the window. The swell was still swollen, but the sun now poked through little pouches in the mist, spotlighting distant circles of ocean. 'The weather is good,' tannoyed Martina, 'so we can watch for whale sprouts.' Everyone scurried for their camcorders. They knew when they got home they'd be asked four questions: Did you see a whale? Did you see a polar bear? Did you see an iceberg? Did you see that drunken Englishman being pushed overboard by the head waitress? The chance to tick any of these off made up for all those hours of prostrate nausea.

'Is someone sitting on your table in error?' The maîtresse d' was hovering around Pipe Lady with an eagerly vicious smile.

'No . . . well, there is one place for my husband, but he is ill in his cabin.'

'Yes. But I remember that you asked for a seat by the window, yes?'

I was of course sitting in the seat by the window, in which I now shifted uncomfortably.

'It is not any matter. I am preferring not to look from the window!' said Pipe Lady good-naturedly, as a fringe of spray heaved up from 20 feet below and spanked the glass. I suddenly realised how ludicrous it was that having traversed some of Northern Europe's more prosaic seas on container ships and Rotarian convoys, I now found myself atop its most lonely and hostile ocean aboard a supremely banal tourist vessel.

'But . . . it . . . the window seat . . . it is . . .' stammered the maîtresse d', fixing me with a pantomime-villain 'I'll have you yet, sonny' look before retreating.

'I'm sorry. I didn't realise it was your seat,' I said to Pipe Lady, glad that she'd taken it so well. But she wheeled round and jabbed the stalk of her pipe at me.

'Yes! It is my seat! Tomorrow you will have another seat, and my husband will be here also!'

But I never once saw her husband. The three were dangerous fantasists, I decided, and never again dined within pipe-jab of their table.

It was calm now, and quiet, but it had been a bad night. For hours I'd lain crucified, grabbing the sides of the bunk to avoid being rolled on to the floor. Just as well I'd succeeded, as illuminating the cabin revealed a bloody and distressing bookwreck crumpled soggily beside a prostrate bottle of red wine that had been a quarter full.

Having showered, I rushed up to the flag deck to catch my first sight of Svalbard. This is the correct name for the archipelago comprising Spitzbergen and a load of smaller and even more desolate islands whose names I never got around to remembering. It's a shame. Spitzbergen sounds distant and intrepid; Svalbard sounds like a Swedish hardware chain.

Call it what you like, though (and later I certainly did), it wasn't there. Not at 9 a.m., not in the freezing, heavy mist that squatted on the sea. Not even after breakfast, when the tannoy told us we'd turned into the Isfjord and were passing the masts of Isfjord Radio, Spitzbergen's (well, sod it) first proper habitation if you don't include (and nobody does) the nine Polish scientists cooped up 150 miles from anyone else at Hornsund.

I had set great store by this first sight. Dufferin, as ever, elevated the loss of his Spitzbergen virginity to a cloyingly poetic experience.

> The belt of unclouded atmosphere was etherealized to an indescribable transparency, and up into it there gradually grew – above the starboard ice – a forest of thin, lilac peaks, so faint, so pale, that had it not been for the gem-like distinctness of their outline, one could have deemed them as unsubstantial as the spires of fairy-land.

For once, it wasn't so much the lilac. It was the indescribable transparency. Later, in fact, I was to see exactly what he meant. The air is so haze-free that a shore which appears to be no further away than the Isle of Wight from Cowes can turn out to be 100 miles distant. But at the time, in the heavy fog, it seemed just another of his fancies.

Perhaps fittingly, there was of course no dramatic, Dufferin-style unveiling. At about 11 o'clock, through eyes streaming with cold, some fuzzy outlines in the sky slowly loomed out as ranks of Icelandic-issue squat, loaf-shaped mountains. Though I'd come up the same southern route as Dufferin, when he does eventually sneak through the ice it's 80 miles north of Isfjord, above Prins Karls Forland, where the land rises into those evil gothic shards that in 1596 inspired Willem Barents to name the place Spitzbergen, or 'spiky mountains'.

Slowly, though, vast, wet cliffs appeared through the mist, and insinuations of Spitzbergen's mighty desolation were aroused. The archipelago is half the size of England, but only 2,800 people live there in five settlements, and since anyone who willingly opts to relocate to any of these is clearly too mad to be counted, you can safely reduce this figure to 310, the number of children under eighteen. Odd (very odd) lone trappers and the brief whaling interlude aside, it remained uninhabited from the dawn of time until the turn of the century when coal was discovered. Spitzbergen did not witness the start of a human life until 1913.

The temperature drops to well below −40°C in February; the average in June is a snug 1.8°C. The climate, and indeed glaciated scenery, is apparently a very close approximation to Britain's in the last ice age. Given this, it's not surprising that the first attempt to overwinter here, around the same time as its Jan Mayen counterpart, was an even jollier fiesta. Both endeavours enjoyed an impressive 100 per cent fatality rate, but the Spitzbergen contingent suffered more grandiosely appalling deaths. Again, Dufferin gloats:

As well as could be gathered from their journal, it appeared that they had perished from the intolerable severity of the climate – and the contorted attitudes in which their bodies were found lying, too plainly indicated the agony they suffered.

And, as in Jan Mayen, he couldn't resist the chance to follow this up with an indirectly self-glorying account of the climatic dramas faced by visitors:

No description can give an adequate idea of the intense rigour of the six-months winter in this part of the world. Stones crack with the noise of thunder; in a crowded hut the breath of its occupants will fall in flakes of snow; if iron touches the flesh, it brings the skin away with it; the soles of your stockings may be burnt off your feet before you feel the slightest warmth from the fire; linen taken out of boiling water instantly stiffens to the consistency of a wooden board . . .

I particularly enjoyed the Victorian understatement of 'intense rigour'.

'Sir, the Light Brigade has returned.'

'Splendid! How did they get on?'

'Well, sir, there was the charge, of course, but then they ran into a spot of intense rigour.'

The permafrost ensured that the contorted remains of those pioneers barely decomposed over the centuries; Dufferin says that 'in Magdalena Bay, there are bodies of men who died 250 years ago, in such complete preservation that, when you pour hot water on the icy coating which encases them, you can actually see the unchanged features of the dead, through the transparent coating'. (When you do *what*? Good God, man. See what Spitzbergen does to decent human behaviour?)

In the face of such inclemency, the best the tourist board can do is bravely trumpet an annual rainfall level of less than 7 inches, while conceding in a footnote that this places it amongst the ranks of perhaps the least enticing climatic classification, an

'Arctic desert'. For this and many other reasons, I would be one of only 1,500 annual visitors who do more than just cruise about the archipelago.

Its tip is as far north of the Arctic Circle as Milton Keynes is south. Nowhere on earth can you get nearer the Pole without huskies, support teams, frost-flecked beards and other expeditionary essentials. There's no farming, and the only industry is coal mining. Everything is imported, and only the island's tax-free status keeps prices in check, particularly with regard to fags and drink, which are unsurprisingly consumed with remarkable efficiency.

Iceland is Wilderness Lite compared to this Mother of all Wildernesses. Or perhaps the Grandmother, as some rocks date back 3 billion years, making it 150 times older than Iceland. I loved the idea of Spitzbergen being wafted by continental drift from below the equator (400 million years ago), passing Spain (250 million years), cruising beyond the first lava bubbles of a nascent Iceland with a patronising wink, then, having ended up wedged in the pack ice, realising with an awful shiver what Spain had looked so smug about.

I was out on the flag deck with the Italians, immaculate as ever in their moleskin trousers and snow white puffa jackets. 'Camping,' one announced bleakly, and I looked across at a sorry clutch of tents staked out in a bog between a coal mine and an airport hanger. A pulse of gleeful relief surged through me. I had intended to stay at the campsite as an economy measure, only changing my mind after hearing that a French company used it as a testing ground for extreme-weather tents, and that a few weeks previously a polar bear had been seen on top of the toilet block.

Everything got uglier. The Isfjord turned a cold-coffee brown, and the granite slabs gave way to huge, bald stacks of slate and rubble; the devil's Jenga set; dark, satanic hills. The temperature settled at 6°C – naggingly uncomfortable without being hand-rubbingly bracing. Finally, there was Longyearbyen – shortly to be my home for what I now saw would be the longest ten days of my life.

I had negotiated with Martina to leave the *Nordstjernen* when in three days' time it passed back through Longyearbyen on its way home, reboarding it when it returned with its next cruise intake a week and a bit later. Now I wished I'd stuck with the standard option. An afternoon here would be ample, perhaps excessive.

After all those almost tediously trim and pretty fishing villages, it was a jarring shock to imagine Norwegians holed up in this grim, lost gulag. Hemmed in at the sides by scree slopes littered with abandoned mine workings, and at the back by a filthily skid-marked glacier, the town's 1,200 inhabitants were largely housed in three-storey concrete barracks lined up beside a culvert-like brown river which seeped from the foot of the glacier. Corroded carapaces snaked along every street, housing the sewers and cables, which can't be buried on account of the unstable, impenetrable permafrost. There wasn't a speck of vegetation to be seen. Everything looked muddy and filthy and rubble-strewn and rusty and dead. It was like the site of an over-ambitious bypass scheme that had run out of money.

As we tied up, I saw my first two Spitzbergeners, marvelling that they showed no obvious resemblance to the in-bred descendants of transported convicts, the only form of humanity whose presence commonsense would permit. 'You will stay here for five hours!' barked Martina, making it sound, with some justification, like a sentence.

The long, wet walk into town bore several reminders that I was not in a normal place. The cars (surprisingly numerous, given that the road to the airport is the only one outside town, and driving on the grand total of 33 kilometres of tarmac is impossible for six months a year) had special yellow and black numberplates. Mounds of Edwardian mining hardware lay about, eerily well preserved by the cold and (theoretically) dry climate. Most of the buildings stood on stilts to raise them clear of the mobile permafrost; those that didn't, we'd been told, had to have refrigator units in their foundations to keep the ground beneath them frozen solid. Not a single bike was locked up; generations of teenagers had somehow endured grandiose tedium without once succumbing to temptation by torching the old wooden mine buildings up the hills around town. Also, the whole place was ghost-town empty.

Whatever there was to do in this place, which at first, second and all subsequent glances appeared to be a hyphenated expletive, could wait. For now I would satisfy myself by buying tax-free depressants, in quest for which I found myself drawn towards the town's incongruously glitzy shopping centre.

Even here, though, the veneer of familiarity was paper thin. Having decided that the sign outside a boutique selling sealskin waistcoats – 'No loaded guns in this store – by which we mean no guns with cartridges' – was a wind-up for tourists, a teenager with a heavy rifle over his shoulder squeezed past as I slushed up to the supermarket's automatic doors.

Before I could recover my composure, I found myself face to face with a matching pair of posters, one in Norwegian, one in English. The latter was headlined: 'It attacks without warning – KEEP YOUR DISTANCE!' Beneath was a photograph of a haughty, muscle-bound polar bear. Snatches of text, now petrifying, now farcical, loomed in and out of focus: 'the only mammal to actively hunt man for food . . . attacks without warning . . . blowing violently through its nose like an angry bull, gnashing its teeth with a smacking sound . . . great, supple leaps, directly at its prey . . . throw flares . . . fire warning shots . . . throw down your hat, mitten, scarf – the bear will sniff the garment, giving you more time . . . report to the authorities if you have had to kill a bear . . . find out what sex it is, and take care of the skull and skin . . .'

My blithe assumption that the polar bear stuff had been puffed up to contrive some tourist-friendly mystique was completely undermined. This wasn't gamesmanship. This was big gamesmanship. Even on the shelves there was no escape. Looking for postcards I was confronted with images of crimson-snouted polar bears dining with gusto upon unidentifiable mammalian remains which bled like raspberry sorbet into the surrounding snow ('Having a lovely Tim, wish you were here'). A bland-looking pamphlet entitled *General Information About Longyearbyen and the*

Surroundings 1920–1991 kicked off with 'Accidents (Fatal)'. Here, in Wilsonian detail, were the case studies to flesh out my fears.

Amid the bald accounts of snow-scooters plunging through the ice and runaway wagons doing the business in Mine 6 were regular entries such as this: '18th July 1977. Austrian camper, thirty-three, killed in Magdalenafjord. The man was bitten repeatedly and received several blows before the bear crushed him with the full force of the front paws. Death was probably instantaneous.' It was twenty years aț o almost to the day. I was thirty-three. I would be in Magdaler ɩfjord tomorrow.

I had imagined myself spending my time in Longyearbyen on long, solo rambles over the fjord to pick about in the eerily well-preserved remains of seventeenth-century Dutch sailors and so on. Now it seemed the brochures hadn't been joking about 'taking a rifle of a calibre of at least 7.62 on all trips outside Longyearbyen'. I read in despair that 'three or four bears are shot every year in self-defence'. Given that the total human population is less than 3,000, this represented a statistically unacceptable risk. It had all been spoilt.

I thought again of the bear upon whose yellowed, gristly pelt I had trodden at Clandeboye, and Dufferin's encounter with it. The *Foam* is moored up by Prins Karls Forland when Dufferin, up on a hill returning the endearing curiosity of a flock of ptarmigan with volleys of musket fire, hears a commotion aboard. Wilson greets him: '"If you please, my Lord, there's a b-e-a-a-a-r!" prolonging the last word into a polysyllable of fearful import.'

Of course, the bear has already been shot half a dozen times as it swam harmlessly across the water, though not before the sight of it had compelled Wilson, busy taking photographs on the beach when it was spotted, to spend some time hiding in a barrel. Even as a corpse, though, the bear gets its revenge. 'To have killed a polar bear was a great thing – but to eat him would be greater,' writes Dufferin, adding once more to the growing anthology of phrases I am least likely ever to utter. But having butchered the bear and strung up the choicest morsels in the rigging, one is fed to the pet Arctic fox, which promptly goes into convulsions. The meat is wordlessly thrown overboard.

The *Foam*, it occurred to me, was not a good place for an animal to have been, or even to have been near. One of my favourite sentences in *High Latitudes* is Dufferin's aggrieved assertion as he introduces the ptarmigan/bear bloodbath: 'We had killed nothing as yet, except a few eider ducks and one or two ice birds.'

Not directly, maybe. The ship's cockerel had been first to go, before they even reached Iceland. Troubled (claims Dufferin) by seasickness and the absence of night, 'he crowed once or twice sarcastically . . . then cackled lowly, and leaping overboard, drowned himself'. The fox's convulsions were presumably fatal, as he's never subsequently mentioned, and shortly after leaving Spitzbergen, Dufferin decides that the goat they'd acquired in Hammerfest is looking depressed. 'The butcher was the only doctor who could now cure her,' he declares confidently before her remains are flung overboard.

The most disturbing incident occurred on the first leg of the voyage, when Fitz sees an Icelandic solent goose asleep on the water, like Noah's dove a cherished sign that they have neared land. So what does he do? Whips out his rifle, only to be driven 'nearly lunatic' when the bird 'flew away at the moment the schooner hove within shot'.

But as I stood in the supermarket reading of .22 rounds pinging harmlessly off the skulls of supple-leaping bears as they bore down on their doomed prey, I could only too easily sympathise with Dufferin and his crew. Man could not live here, and so did not rule here. It seemed to me only natural that one of the few ways they could assert themselves on their daunting surroundings was by gunning down any animal that crossed their path.

It was a bad day all round. The 90p-a-packet fags had to be set against the £3-a-kilo apples. Then, having cheered myself up at the liquor store with more vodka and Guinness than I had any reasonable need for, I was asked at the check-out to return it all to the shelves. Thanks to some administrative insanity lingering from the days when the mining company ran the town, I needed a locally issued ration card to buy spirits or beer. Partial relief was administered by the news that unlimited quantities of tax-free wine could be purchased.

I'd also climbed up the muddy main drag to the new and comfortable Funkenhotell, where I'd reserved my forthcoming ten days at a reduced rate of 600 kroner (£50) a night. It wasn't the cheapest option – for £20 a night less I could have had a bunk at the youth hostel. But as I'd now realised I'd be spending twenty-three hours a day cowering morosely in my room, I figured that after a life-long career of pulling the boat in, now was the time to push it out.

In a bid to trim at least some of those hours, I'd trudged up the valley to Nybyen (why does a town of 1,000 in Europe's emptiest land need a suburb?) with a view to booking a package of activities from Svalbard Wildlife Services. 'Fossil-plucking on the glacier', 'Over the Isfjord in kayaks' and 'Tour to Mine 3' were the trinity I had selected. There were two difficulties: firstly, all were obscenely dear (36 quid for a walk round a mine?), and secondly, the rather surly staff wouldn't give me a discount, which I suppose represented a reiteration of the first difficulty. SWS is in an enviable position. Yes, there are few tourists, but those who do come find themselves paralysed with polar bear paranoia by any thought of an unguided tour outside Longyearbyen, and paralysed with boredom by one day inside it. I figured I could hold out for maybe forty-eight hours in my hotel watching *Scrappy Doo* in Swedish; then I'd run into the street and wave a thick wad of notes at any passer-by prepared to sing me a traditional mining ballad.

My five hours up, I jogged down to the *Nordstjernen*, lugging my portable wine cellar up the gangplank, past deckhands still hosing last night's puke off the hull, and descended, damp and tired, to 354. Then I opened the door, and found my cabin filled by an enormous bearded Norseman.

'Pål,' he said sadly, but not as it's written or I would have had to disagree. I had completely forgotten Martina's grim shared-cabin curse, and contemplated the obscenities I had left this Pål character to discover. Most related to the previous night's wine inundation:

the wrinkled, crimson paperback, the red splash drops on the bathroom door . . . even, I was appalled to note now, the violent blot that bloodied a pair of underpants on the floor by my bed. 'Pål. Pål, Pål, Pål.' I imagined myself placing a worldly arm upon his shoulder. 'Man is a . . . troubled animal, Pål. We all have our little . . . our little ways, little secrets. You, Pål, you have your beard. Me? I get drunk and mutilate my genitals.'

But even as I faced my own shame I had time to ponder the more selfish hardships of Pål's presence, many featuring a vast bare bottom descending the bunk ladder inches from my face. Thoroughly revolted, I brazenly dumped my wine bags with a great beer-crate clunk and went up to bid au revoir to Longyearbyen.

We were now cruising further up the Isfjord towards Pyramiden, one of the two mining towns run and staffed by Russians, and as we slipped through the broad, waveless channel, the scenery grew perceptibly more awe-inspiring. Here at last were suggestions of the spiky mountains, bare and cold, dirty slivers of snow wedged in their gravelly buttocks, their flanks scored with the strata of millennia, billennia, times when they were vibrant with life. Each peak was a vast fossil, immaculately preserved but creepily inanimate. It was like the Grand Canyon in a minor key.

Of course, all this is precisely what appealed to Dufferin. Spitzbergen is probably the last place on earth where you could still find a mountain to name after yourself. Fred Olsen, the boat bloke, managed to get one. Prince Albert of Monaco bagged a glacier. Most of the mining towns, dead or alive, are named after their entrepreneurial founders – Longyearbyen, Colebukta, Grumantbyen. Dufferin spent just five days here, yet still managed to have himself put down for Kapp Dufferin, a large headland on Spitzbergen's east coast mysteriously distant from anywhere he actually went.

Perhaps now is the time to outline the salient features of Spitzbergen's splendidly bizarre history. After its exciting 3-billion-year continental drift phase, something finally happens in 1194, when Vikings probably discover it. Four hundred years later,

Barents blunders across it; shortly after, Henry Hudson notices the potential of an area where really big and slow marine mammals lie about on beaches. After the walruses are wiped out, the Dutch, Germans, Danes and English start on the whales; so impressive is the scale of slaughter that before the end of the eighteenth century their coastal population has been eradicated, and man's presence on Spitzbergen is reduced to the occasional fur trapper.

Polar adventurers start to arrive. One of the first is Phipps's 1773 expedition, during which the fourteen-year-old Horatio Nelson wrestles with a polar bear. But by the time of Dufferin's visit, with most reasonable folk having accepted the infeasibility of a maritime assault on the Pole, things are quiet again. 'Of late years,' he writes, 'the Spitzbergen seas have remained as lonely as they were before the first adventurer invaded their solitude.'

It is only when the first coal reserves are discovered towards the end of the nineteenth century that the issue of sovereignty becomes an imperative. In 1920, the Treaty of Spitzbergen is signed by forty countries. The archipelago is demilitarised and made a tax-free zone; Norway is given sovereignty, but nationals of signatory states have full residential and commercial rights. (This explains the presence of a Turkish taxi driver in Longyearbyen; also, tantalisingly, it gives me the right to march across the 60,000 square kilometres of unclaimed territory, hammer a sign into the permafrost and thereby claim mineral rights for the next century.)

In the Depression, declining demand for coal closes most mines; some are bought by the canny Soviets, who note the strategic significance of a northern bridge between East and West. This is not lost on the Nazis, who deem Spitzbergen so potentially worrisome that in 1943 they send the mighty *Tirpitz* there to blow the log cabins of Longyearbyen to pieces. They also set fire to a mine which burns until 1966, an impressive feat by any standards.

After the war, Stalin, intrigued by the possibility of a foothold in a NATO country, expands the Soviet mines. By the early Fifties, Grumantbyen, Barentsburg and Pyramiden each have over

1,000 inhabitants, and Soviet citizens outnumber Norwegians in Spitzbergen. The Soviets have their own police but are subject to the Norwegian Governor (Sysselmann); an uneasy co-existence holds.

Norway is expected by its NATO allies to match the Soviets miner-for-miner in a rather silly parallel to the arms race; the Soviets inflate the facilities at their towns to include huge consulates, hotels and sports complexes in the same spirit of puerile gamesmanship. Then comes glasnost, the Soviets become Russians and Ukrainians, and the Cold War rationale which subsidised their presence evaporates. In the early Nineties, all the children in Barentsburg (400 of them) are sent home, and there is talk of abandoning Pyramiden completely.

All this casts a blight on Norway's presence, being as it is little more than a counter to the Soviets. After it is calculated that it would be cheaper for their power station in Longyearbyen to import coal rather than use the stuff mined on its doorstep, all but one of the mines in Longyearbyen are closed. There's suddenly no point being there, and as the region's environmental purity is now of paramount importance, the first voices are heard suggesting man's total withdrawal from Spitzbergen.

That seemed the only sensible option as the *Nordstjernen* turned away from Pyramiden and came face to face with the overwhelming Nordenskiöld glacier. The engines stopped and we lay there in frigid silence, as if trying to stare it out. Huge crevasses in the turquoise quartz threatened to terminate the mismatched stand-off by depositing a bus-sized hunk of calf ice on our foredeck; several such bergs span lazily about beside us. It was hopeless to imagine mankind ever conquering this environment. Just as Dufferin had visited at a time when Spitzbergen had repulsed the whalers, so I was visiting as it girded itself for a final assault on the miners.

It was a billion-watt morning as we turned into Magdalenafjord, Dufferin's landing point, right up near the island's northern-most tip. This was more like it. All Dufferin's lather about the splinteringly bright sun and virgin, frigid atmosphere, the windless stillness, the deadness, the primeval rocks, the eternal ice – everything was laid out before me. Terrific snow-sprinkled spires, definitive spiky mountains, ripped into the blue sky; at the end of the fjord swooped the Waggonway Glacier, cracking off into the sea with a craggy cliff-face of blueish ice.

The *Nordstjernen* wheeled round to face the rocky sand spit which gave the bay the calm anchorage that had made Magdalena a big hit with seventeenth-century Dutch whalers. At last the engines were shut down, and a mighty silence entombed us.

The abandoned marble quarry on our right, the whalers' graves I knew lay carved into the sand spit, the bear-fodder Austrian's corpse: all offered eloquent tribute to the hopeless failure of man's attempts to bring life to Magdalenafjord. And here we were, fly-by-night vultures come to pick about the bones of men and the bones of the whales they came to kill. I felt cheated: on top of the world, but with no creation to look down on.

Such are the thoughts that Spitzbergen inspires. I couldn't recommend it as a holiday destination for anyone seeking to get over a messy divorce or drive-by shooting. Which made the scene which unfolded an hour later, after we'd all been landed ashore in the *Nordstjernen*'s lifeboats for some grisly sightseeing, all the more surprising.

'Look. Some bones.'

I was standing with Pål on a sandy rock heap, trying to look away as he focused on the bleached planks half buried at our feet, and in particular on the browned ribs and femurs that lay amongst them.

'I need to say the reason for my visit. I am not here for tourist.'

He had been talking in this disturbingly portentous fashion ever since we'd left the rest of our colleagues stamping about by the cold shore waiting for the crew to dispense thermoses of gluhwein. I'd been looking forward to the graves, hoping that the open coffin that Dufferin had etched, containing a skeleton identified by a weatherbeaten wooden cross as that of 'JACOB MOOR, OB 2 JUNE 1758, AET 44', might still be there. But now I was just rather afraid of this large bearded man and the boundlessly awful secret he was about to share with me.

'I am a policeman,' he quavered gruffly, his watery gaze fixed on the bones. 'I work in Tromsø. But I am a special policeman.'

Secret policeman? Pretend policeman? Pretty policeman? I was suddenly glad of the presence, however distant, of the two rifle-toting guards who had been placed at either end of the sand spit as polar bear look-outs.

'I look at accidents. Accident investigations. Why they happen . . . and the men who die, their names.'

In a flood of heart-rendingly wayward translations, it all came out. A Russian jet had crashed near Longyearbyen the year before; Pål had been in charge of identifying the 141 burnt and broken bodies shipped back to Tromsø. For a year he had borne his burden; now he had come on a pilgrimage to confront the demons, purge his mind of the awful memories.

His voice trailed off. How much more death could there be in this bloody place? Remorse and melancholy overwhelmed me. But unfortunately, I chose to express this by saying: 'Bad one.'

I watched Pål stumble distractedly back to the shore, where two Italians had commandeered the crew's orange survival suits and were splashing about idiotically. There were dozens of graves and a blubber-boiling station to defile, but my heart wasn't in it any more.

Still, there was one thing I had to do. Outflanking the armed guard and scrambling up the rocks, for once oblivious of the polar bear danger, I turned to survey the vista and was, just as I'd hoped, presented with an exact translation of Wilson's photo that Lola Armstrong had lain out on the Clandeboye billiard table. Yes, Wilson's: though Fitz is billed throughout as the photographer, I had noted that when Wilson spies the Spitzbergen polar bear he is described as 'busily taking photographs'.

So here I was, standing on 6 August 1997 where Wilson had stood on 6 August 1856, photographing a timeless panorama that replicated his shot right down to the position of our respective boats. *Et in Arctis ego*, I thought grandly, borrowing Dufferin's

'ET EGO IN ARCTIS!'

High Latitudes

inscription on his illustration of Jacob Moor's tomb, before the *Nordstjernen* brought me down with a vast fart on its foghorn which ricocheted around the fjord for a good thirty seconds.

North we went, our approach towards the apparently exciting 80th parallel, just beyond Spitzbergen's northern tip, causing a flurry of flag-deck activity amongst the half-dozen owners of handheld GPS plotters. We passed the last abandoned whaling station, the once bustling settlement of Smeerenburg (which I hope sounded better in Dutch than 'Blubber Town' does in English), and then, after an odd length of pancake-flat desert, we were out past Spitzbergen. Right on cue, an enormous flat-topped ice floe, probably the size of the Isle of Man, appeared on the blank horizon.

Then the foghorn sounded, the GPS boys punched the air and a ripple of muted applause moved about the flag deck. We had crossed the 80th parallel, but, with no end-of-the-world wall of ice blocking our way, it was difficult to get excited. So we turned round, and I realised with a tiny anticlimactic sigh that at the same time I had turned for home. It was all south from here.

We cruised into the Woodfjord, past two trapper's huts, horribly uncosy-looking beach shacks dwarfed by pyres of collected driftwood. Why did they do it? Certainly not for the money. I'd been told that the income from reindeer and seal skins rarely exceeded £3,000 a year. But in general, I didn't really care any more. It had long been clear that this place was a theme park for negligent eccentrics who placed a very low price on their own lives.

Anyway, everyone got their polar bears in the end, the captain having got into the what-the-hell spirit of Spitzbergen by nosing the *Nordstjernen* right up to the foot of the Prince Albert glacier through a lethal fleet of car-sized bergs which boomed against our flaking, dented hull with disturbing regularity. The whole fjord was sprinkled with smaller shards floating motionlessly on glassy water, twinkling in the garish 11.45 p.m. sun. It looked like someone had dropped a chandelier out of an airship.

'We have one . . . two. We have three ice bears at our left! Two adults and one small!'

Martina could not disguise her relief. Though all we saw were three brownish, semi-animate specks rooting about a rocky foreland, a photographic orgy instantly broke out. A hundred little erections sprouted from compact zoom cameras, ejaculated in a flash and detumesced with a satisfied hum. Everyone was happy. They had ticked an important box. It was odd to think that, just twenty years ago, the only tourists here were on kill-a-bear-or-your-money-back Arctic safaris. I wondered what would have happened if I had succumbed to an attack of the Dufferins and picked the family trio off with a pump-action shotgun.

Just after 1 a.m., the *Nordstjernen* slowed, then stopped, and there was a clanking of block and tackle. I was sitting in the forward lounge, still hiding from Pål after the morning's disconcerting revelations, and turned to the window to behold a swaying aluminium kayak with two cavemen standing in it being perilously winched out of the sea.

Martina provided an explanation over the tannoy. 'We have now two more passengers. These are a Swedish husband and wife who we arranged to meet here in their kayak. They have been living for one year here in a cabin they made.'

I caught a glimpse of them half an hour later as they were being shown to their cabin. Sure enough, one was a woman. But it had been an easy mistake to make: both had the grimy back-combed manes and waxy complexions of roadies on Europe's 'Final Countdown' tour.

I half thought that after a whole year's isolation they might have regressed to a pair of Greystokes, flinching at the sight of humans and communicating in polar-bear fashion as described on the posters: blowing violently like angry bulls and gnashing their teeth with a smacking sound. But they seemed incredibly unfazed, bored even, at this less than gentle reacclimatisation.

'Welcome back,' I said, and they nodded politely but, I thought, rather sadly. I suppose I felt that we had rescued them from an awful exile, forgetting that they'd actively volunteered for it. 'Could I talk to you? I'm very interested in what you've done.'

'Maybe tomorrow,' smiled the husband quietly, easing their cabin door closed.

I'd just returned from my brush with the Greystokes and was happily seated on the lavatory when Pål stumbled noisily into our cabin. This was a disappointment. I have long been in awe of people who can defecate in busy public lavatories with carefree exuberance, and am convinced that the ability to do so is an important indicator of high self-esteem and leadership potential. I do not possess this ability. Please go away, I silently urged.

He didn't.

Oh dear, I fretted. Please don't knock on the door.

He knocked on the door.

'Sorry for this. Please. Sorry also for today, at Magdalena-fjord.'

I was suddenly very unhappy. But I had to say something.

'Don't be sorry,' I said, trying not to squeak about on the seat. 'You have had . . . a sad time. Very . . . sad.'

'Yes,' he said, thickly. 'Sad. And I have more sad work.'

'Oh,' I said, in a flat voice which I vainly hoped would discourage any expansion on this theme.

'People do bad things . . . a boy kill his mother with hammer. I photograph the body, collect the blood . . . so much blood.'

No, no, no no nononono. No!

'And one more boy kill his father with axe.'

I made some vague sort of despairing, understanding tut. It was a ridiculous sound, the kind of placatory whimper with which a hostage might hope to appease an armed and unstable captor. Then there was silence, and within two minutes, the sound of a big man snoring rumbled under the loo door. Estimating that the probability of me being sacrificed to atone for man's inhumanity to man had diminished to an acceptable level, I crept out of the bathroom and into my bunk.

★

Two evenings later, after brief stopovers at the world's most northerly (and least interesting) town, Ny Ålesund, and Barentsburg, a stupendously grim Russian mining settlement, we cruised back down the Isfjord. As we neared Longyearbyen, the Greystokes set up camp in the blue saloon and held a question-and-answer session. I still couldn't believe their willingness to put themselves through this undignified jostle so soon after returning from twelve months of isolation in a home-made teepee.

The only symptom of their trappist, trapping exile seemed to be the robotic humourlessness of their replies. 'To build the palisade for our winter tent we needed 200 driftwood stocks. Its statistics were 14 metre and 6 metre and 4 and one half metre height. We used 40 cubic metre of driftwood for fuel in winter. The first snow was on August 20, and the coldest day was -34°.'

Well, anyway, all we really wanted to know was how often they washed and how many polar bears they'd seen, and the answers to these were once a week and quite a lot but their two dogs always chased them away. This established, there was an embarrassing, almost hostile silence. They had rejected society, so now, in revenge, society rejected them. When at length someone asked how they had coped with illness, and they replied that in extremis they could have radioed for a helicopter, there was even a muted boo. Cheats.

11

My bedroom at the Funken looked out on to a heap of muddy geological rubble and dumped snow-scooters ugly even by the high standards set by Longyearbyen. A thermometer helpfully placed outside the window told me it was 3°C. In August. The ten days I would spend here stretched out before me like a long, sharp shock. '"Well, Wilson, you see we've made Spitzbergen after all!" But Wilson was not a man to be driven from his convictions by facts; he only smiled grimly, with a look which meant "Would we were safe back again!" Poor Wilson!'

Poor me. What was there to do? While fortifying myself in the deserted breakfast room, I pondered the options. From my table I could see an old mine perched about 500 feet up the other side of the valley, a crude timber cabin that looked like a decapitated version of the wooden rabbit from *Monty Python and the Holy Grail*. Was it . . . could I . . . ? No. It wasn't, and I couldn't. Far better to do the . . . museum, or the . . . the . . . liquor store?

Petrified at how close I'd come to an all-day, tax-free solitary wine festival, an hour later I was at the museum.

'Please – your shoes.'

The teenage curator shyly barred my entrance, pointing at my filthy footwear and then at a rack where it was to be exchanged for a pair of cardboard slippers. Had I known that this would be the first of perhaps a hundred occasions on which I was required to 'please – my shoes' over the following week, I would not have smiled as I complied.

After pondering over a case containing a polar bear's penis bone (only about four inches long, since you ask), I came to the keynote exhibit: a display of photographs and mementos commemorating the centenary of perhaps the most tragic and ill-advised polar expedition of all (and be assured the competition is stiff), that of the Swede Carl Andrée.

In 1897, Andrée and two companions set off from Danskøya, an island we'd passed right up on Spitzbergen's northwestern tip, in a bid to reach the North Pole by balloon. If there had been an East Pole they might have made it: after a few hours they crashlanded on an ice floe which eventually beached 250 miles away on a frozen headland at Kvitøya, an island so hostile and remote that it still hasn't been explored in any detail. They made a tent out of the balloon and bedded down for the winter, knowing of course there was no chance of being rescued, and not being disappointed in this assumption.

How do we know all this? Well, thirty-three years later another expedition chanced upon their remains, as ever EWP (eerily well preserved), as well as novelty memorabilia such as Andrée's glasses and scores of undeveloped photographs. When these ghostly images were processed, they revealed a smiling – *smiling* – Andrée posing before the balloon-tent. A journal described how they'd lived for three months on their provisions, surviving an appalling winter. Ironically, what seems to have done for them was eating infected bear meat. The crew of the *Foam* had been right to chuck their polar platter overboard.

What was it about Spitzbergen that lured ordinary people to commit crimes against rationality? Very possibly the first human to set foot on the 3-billion-year-old archipelago, the Dutch owner of Willem Barents's ship, immediately set off up a peak on Prins Karl's Forland and promptly broke his neck. Dufferin himself writes of a peculiar urge to tackle obviously lethal mountains.

But it was only when I emerged from the museum and found myself first gazing up at, then hypnotically walking towards, the foot of the steep scree slope on which 'my' mine was perched that realisation dawned. Spitzbergen exuded such a powerful sense of man-eating hostility that even whimpering twerps like me felt compelled to rise to the challenge, to climb an unclimbed peak, to plant a flag, to claim the place for themselves and for mankind.

It was all right at first, as I suppose is often the way with mountains. I could have done without the rain this place is apparently famous for not having, and the mining-disaster graveyard I had to traverse just up from the road, but the terrain was carpeted in a pleasantly yielding carpet of moss which made progress comfortable and easy.

The moss petered out; the gradient increased. After ten minutes or so I found myself dropping to all fours, sometimes slipping slightly. Then, while putting my hood up to minimise the rain's penetration, I looked skywards and noticed that the mine appeared to be both further away than it had been at the start and vertically above me. More than vertically: it was as if I had to ascend a giant oblique overhang. Vertigo, I realised, had kicked in.

Having scrabbled and scratched my way to a ledge for an essential rest, I carefully turned and sat down, correctly anticipating that the sight of Longyearbyen laid out at my trembling purple cycling shoes would convulse me with dizzy panic. A tourist bus had stopped on the road directly below me; I could just make out a row of faces angled up in my direction. 'Every year we warn them,' I imagined their guide sighing over the tannoy.

Resuming my ascent, I noticed a pile of fresh droppings on the ledge, a humble sighting which seemed unlikely to open up a new and impressive vista of terror. But a few two-slides-forward, one-slide-back slithers up nature's own slag heap later, I found myself thinking: rabbits? No. No rabbits here. Arctic fox, then? No. Turds too big. Ah! Reindeer! Not, you know, polar bear. Not that. Too small. Even for a small bear. Like the one they saw near the airport just on the other side of this mountain. One of those little leapers, you know, the supple ones with . . . *What in the name of fuck was that?*

I tore my hood off and with whimpering little giggles looked crazily around for any sign of movement. The mine building now loomed, vast yet rickety, a teetering wooden scaffold. Anything could be behind it. Or inside it.

By the time I made it there, after maybe twenty-five minutes, I was reasonably certain that I would find a bear waiting. If I made a run for it, I'd end up cartwheeling neatly into the distant graveyard. And if that happened, or if I didn't make a getaway and was eaten, I would end up on a Tromsø slab as Pål's next case. I was suddenly sorry I hadn't been able to find him to say goodbye when I left the *Nordstjernen*. He would be angry. He might defile my corpse, or take photos of my severed head with a fag stuck in its mouth. In one brief glance I scanned the mine's unremarkable timbers, and turned.

Going down was worse than going up, and somehow required me to bellow out a detailed live commentary of the movements of my limbs. By the time I staggered back on to the road I was drenched with rain and sweat and walking like the infant Bambi.

But now at least I had a mission. In the blackest, bleakest moment of my climb (which looked more feebly benign than ever now that I looked back up at it), I had made a pact with the miners' ghosts that if I ever got out of this, I'd go to the highest authority in the land, plant an angry fist on their desk and in a voice wracked with every emotion known to man, croak 'Why?'

So it was that ten minutes later I was struggling off my shoes (the third time that day, and it was only lunch) and replacing them with a pair of the Sysselmann's own flip-flops.

If this demeaning footwear arrangement was a device to undermine visiting protestors' morale and determination, it succeeded handsomely. Every echoing slap and flap reduced my 'pay-back time' zeal as I approached the reception of her (there's been a Sysselwomann since 1996) extensive new seafront headquarters. The stuffed bear snarling amongst the yuccas didn't help; nor did the noisy wedding party waiting for the Sysselmann's signature.

'She is very busy woman. You can see other persons.' I nodded again, not thinking until later that at least in terms of people under her jurisdiction she was less important than the Mayor of Chipping Norton. There probably isn't even a mayor of Chipping Norton.

But the woman I did see, the Russian settlement co-ordinator, was friendly and helpful. It was she who told me about Kapp Dufferin, and that Pyramiden was probably about to be evacuated. 'It is terrible. More lonely than Barentsburg,' she said, and I shuddered.

She also said, which I couldn't quite believe, that the Russians were genuinely only there for the coal.

'They need this special coal for their power stations. There is no coal in north Russia.'

'Wouldn't it be easier to get coal from the south of Russia or Poland or somewhere?'

She smiled inscrutably, in a way that implied I had a lot to learn about the political and economic realities of the place, and about what she was and was not allowed to say, and that whatever happened I would never learn any of it.

'I am a little busy now. Please take this information leaflets.'

Rather browbeaten and still jelly-limbed, I desperately needed to cheer myself up. Composing a torrent of mindless abuse on a postcard and sending it to Teletext helped, but it wasn't until I was in my room at the Funken, hurling the miniatures from the minibar and replacing them with perishable supermarket snacks, that I felt at peace. At least until I went into the bathroom and noticed the huge Adam Ant stripe of pale slime that had presumably been decorating my nose and cheekbones for the best part of a day.

I read the leaflets over breakfast next morning. There were now a half dozen guests, all like me sliding about the buffet in socks. This shoeless business was so demeaning. The one comfort for me was that the nameless porridgy herring-mess smeared on my plate was an effective distraction from the worse one on my feet.

The third leaflet was entitled 'Take the polar bear seriously!', and managed the unlikely feat of making the supermarket warning posters appear pussy-footingly flaccid. 'Use trip-wires with flares around the camp. Sit facing different directions so you have a good view. Be correctly armed at all times. Big game hunting rifles of calibre 7.62, 30.6 or .308 are the minimum. If you find yourself in a very dangerous situation where you must protect your own and other people's lives, you are to shoot to kill the polar bear. Aim at the chest and shoot several times, not at the head which is easy to miss. Then approach the polar bear from behind and fire again until you are sure it is dead.'

'Do not worry so much,' said a waitress who had obviously connected the leaflet with my hopeless countenance. 'We have not seen ice bears in Longyearbyen this year.'

'What about the campsite?'

'Oh, well. That is West Longyearbyen. They have some few bears there.'

'But no . . . no, um, attacks.'

'No, no!'

'Well . . . that's good.'

'No – I mean not this year,' she continued brightly. 'Last year a young girl was killed on a hill by an ice bear. Very sad!'

'Which hill?'

'You see that wood house up there, part of the old mine?'

I warily followed her finger to the hill I had climbed the morning before, porridge and herring fighting it out in my stomach. The incident was too recent to have been included in the Accidents (Fatal) booklet, but the waitress had all the details and recounted them with breathless relish.

'Two girls are there and see an animal and believe it is a reindeer, but then it is an ice bear and it is too late. One girl stays, the other runs and the bear runs after the running girl. The other girl jumps down the mountain, and falls a long way, but there is still snow so only she breaks these bones [here the waitress indicated her wrists], but she has much blood on her face when she come into town. Then men with guns go up the hill and the bear runs at them, and they shoot it until dead, and it is only a small bear, 80 kilo.'

There was a satisfied pause, which I hoped might signify the end of the conversation. Wrongly. 'So! They find the girl, but she is dead. In fact . . .' here the waitress looked about like a primary schoolgirl preparing to say 'bumhole' '. . . her head is gone. It's sad, but why the girls do not take guns? Every year we tell them . . .'

Now a broken man, I stumbled cravenly back to my room to stare at the filth and drizzle. Buttocks to it all. I'd done what little there was to do in town, and even the nearest geological suburb was now a no-go area. I couldn't even go and watch the glacier move. My one great hour-eating hope – playing pool on the Funken's table – had flopped miserably upon the discovery that the table had no pockets. I was beginning to feel like you do when you've been reading in the bath too long and realise that the water's gone cold. Except that there was no more hot water, and I couldn't get out of the bath for another week. Everything had gone bear-shaped.

This, I supposed miserably, was the last sorry stage of the Dufferin–Moore Chutzpah Challenge. There had been moves to declare it a no-contest after the embarrassments of Jan Mayen; my endless seasickness had caused a steady haemorrhage of credibility points. And now, here was the final and starkest parallel: he saw a man-eating carnivore and ate it; I heard a scary story about one and hid.

For a week *Helen's Tower* had lain amid the glutinous fluff that collects in the bottom of rucksacks, but now, like the defeated coward who tries to tarnish his conqueror's achievement by digging up some dirt, I retrieved it, wiped it down and ploughed on to Dufferin's sad end.

It all started to go wrong after India. His two years as Ambassador in Rome passed without incident, but when sent to Paris in 1892, at the age of sixty-six, he found himself at the centre of a diplomatic storm. The French press decided he had been sent to undermine a burgeoning Franco–Russian alliance. *Le Figaro* called him 'that dangerous man', and he felt compelled to denounce formally a rumour that he had arrived with 3 million francs to bribe journalists and politicians into helping ruin the accord with Russia. After three years he called it a day.

You wouldn't expect someone like Dufferin to widdle away their retirement collecting Franklin Mint 1/42nd scale pewter motorcycles and shambling around Kwiksave with a fistful of expired coupons. Back at Clandeboye, he painted watercolours, landscaped the gardens, sailed his yacht and put his architectural energies to bear upon developing 'an uncontrolled passion for glass roofing' (as old men's uncontrolled passions go, it could have been a lot worse). Dementia was put at bay with a series of demanding intellectual endeavours: 'During this year,' he writes in 1896, now seventy, 'I have learned by heart 786 columns of a Persian dictionary, comprising about 24,000 words.' Beats *The Puzzler*.

But the restlessness of a man who 'loathed being idle' brought him one unfortunate retirement pastime: the chairmanship of the London & Globe Finance Corporation.

When in 1897 the fifty-two-year-old American financier Whitaker Wright started canvassing for an unimpeachably honest and venerable peer to chair his burgeoning mining conglomerate, Dufferin quickly accepted. One can assume news of the mysterious collapse of the Gunnison Iron and Coke Company of Philadelphia, prop W. Wright, six years earlier, had not made its way to Clandeboye.

Within weeks of Lord Dufferin appearing on the London & Globe letterhead, its £1 shares were changing hands for £2; Whitaker Wright ('WW' to his associates) saw his own holdings soar beyond the £1 million mark, a fantastic sum in Victorian Britain.

For three years the L&G boomed, then, in November 1900, rumours began circulating that its stake in the under-construction Baker Street & Waterloo Railway (that's right, the Bakerloo line), was unwisely large. That was all it took. The shares went into freefall, and on 28 December the London & Globe announced its insolvency.

Thousands of investors were ruined; Dufferin himself had a huge stake and lost the lot. A year earlier he had realised how little he understood of the L&G's operations and the Stock Exchange in general. He had repeatedly tried to resign, only to be talked round by Wright's protestations that to do so would undo all confidence in the company.

How could Dufferin, the consummate negotiator, who had forestalled wars in the Lebanon and India through charm and cunning, have fallen for such a smarmy bullshitter? Maybe it was just age. It's like those cowboy builders who latch on to old dears and fleece them of their life savings with lies about rotten eaves and the mystical healing powers of uPVC windows.

Dufferin of course insisted on facing the music, and on 9 January 1901, aged seventy-five, he addressed 2,000 angry investors in London. Even more typically, he somehow managed to get a laugh out of his audience (by saying he didn't have a clue about business, a statement which in the circumstances would surely have earned less captivating personalities a fatal beating). After explaining that his own misfortunes were greater than anyone's, in scale at least, he finished, 'Yet I should regret this less – indeed I should not regret it at all – if my heavy losses of private fortune were to convince you of my bona fides.' He was cheered off. It was the final triumph of a superlative diplomat.

(Three years later, Whitaker Wright was tried for fraud after investigators discovered he'd been cooking the L&G's books from day one. After being sentenced to seven years' penal servitude, he lit a cigar and popped what at his inquest was revealed as a capsule of potassium cyanide.)

Undone by the Bakerloo line. I let out a snort of idiotic laughter. *The Bakerloo line.* Struggling to find a more appropriate emotion, I proposed a toast to the fallen lord.

Half an hour and half a bottle later, in a spirit of high melodrama, I wondered if a disgraced stockbroker could do away with himself by drinking the entire contents of a minibar, stopping just short of a practical experiment when I worked out the cost in this instance as £228.

'Having a party?'

I was in the wine aisle at the supermarket, and before me stood Hilde, a Bergener I'd met on the *Nordstjernen*, here to visit her botany student sister. I looked down at my handbasket and its trio of raffia Chianti bottles, and decided no explanation would suffice.

'So . . . how's your sister?' I blurted.

'Well,' she said uncertainly, 'we're meeting at her hostel later, then there's a disco at the social club. That's if you can stand up after that wine.'

Still, it was good news. I had reclaimed a place in society. As I sludged up the moraine-slopped road back to the Funken, Longyearbyen and its bald surroundings seemed marginally less awful.

As in Iceland, Norwegian weekend socialising involves assembling at a friend's house and not going out on the town until midnight. By then, of course, everyone's bollocksed, and while they set off to paint the town red, it more usually ends up yellow with orange lumps. This policy is a consequence of the price of alcohol: expensive enough for domestic consumption, it's almost prohibitively overpriced in bars and clubs.

This is even more marked in Spitzbergen, where half a bottle of vodka in the liquor store costs as much as one beer in a bar (£2.50). So, by the time I got to the hostel, Hilde and Co. (sister Marte, friend Eline, sister's botany student boyfriend Christian) had already polished off most of a month's ration (two litres of spirits, a litre of liqueur and a case of beer) and in a grotesque parody of a civilised evening had moved on to coffee and chocolates.

Huset, originally the miner's canteen, is a garish pink building stuck half a mile out of town up the side of the valley. We puffed up there at five to midnight, the sun catching our exhalations in its cold glare. There was a slight scrum outside. 'You have to pay to get in after 12,' explained Hilde. *After* 12? You odd nation, you. But sure enough, the queue was still growing at 2.30 a.m.

Inside it was dark and busy. Europop and the B52s were played slightly too loudly to allow meaningful conversation; the clientele were largely students (Christian, Marte and about a hundred others were enrolled in year-long courses at UNIS, the Arctic College) and the few local youths who hadn't gone back to the mainland for the summer. The three middle-aged men at the bar were drinking in a no-nonsense fashion that suggested they were miners.

Everyone seemed drunk in the rather overbearing way that I was getting used to in Scandinavia. An old newspaper clipping proudly framed outside my hotel room revealed that Svalbard had the world's highest per capita alcohol consumption, and here was a literal hands-on demonstration. Blokes were manhandling the barmaids to get their order prioritised, girls were shrieking uproariously at punchlines they couldn't possibly have heard. Everyone was being pushed and elbowed, but only I seemed to mind. It was simply too late for me to enjoy myself, at my age, in this place. The Chianti was evolving into a slight headache, and I lacked the gumption to stave it off by wading into the Darwinian scrum at the bar.

As everyone else flailed about to late-era Cure, I had a flash of insight into what was wrong with Longyearbyen. The students who only came for a year, the miners building up a tax-free nest-egg to take back to Norway, the in-and-out scientists and adventurers: the whole town was a fly-by-night grouping of whoever happened to be there that week, a place lacking a soul and able only to come together to get drunk with the aimless, transient debauchery of a campus. Even the miners were like token mature students real-aleing at the bar.

Passing this arrogant judgement, I felt my features sagging with fatigue and insobriety into perhaps mankind's least appealing expression – the Thomas the Tank Engine Opium-Eating face. It is a loathsome thing, a supercilious half-smile larded over with sickly dissipation, half pornographer's leer, half bully's sneer. You will only ever see it disgrace Thomas's usually sunny countenance once, when he is having his boiler fired up on a cold morning. His eyes still half-closed, a knowing smirk wobbles across his pasty, ravaged face as the familiar narcotic effect takes hold. It is truly repulsive to behold.

Recognising that I would shortly receive a deserved beating for appearing in public wearing such a face, I left them to it at 3.30, returning to the Funken in a jarringly gay sun that had nothing to do with the milky dawn light demanded by reason. It was full-on the-sun-has-got-his-hat-on squint-level sun, though he'd have to do a lot better than 2°C if he was expecting anyone to come out and play with him.

★

I got out of bed at 10.29, and got back into it at 10.33. Within what fine tolerances our lives are led. If that had been a 75-centilitre bottle of Chianti I'd have been downstairs stuffing free bacon into my face; but it had been a litre, and my brain was now far too large for my skull. I dropped a pair of paracetamol, wondering dully why anyone would ever take only one, and fell into standby mode until roused by my phone at 2 p.m. It was Hilde, inviting me on 'a small mountain hike'.

A free walk in the company of decent humans was preferable to a £50 fossil-plucking yomp with the sour conmen of Svalbard Wildlife Services. I heard myself accepting.

Wearing almost my entire wardrobe – two pairs of gloves, erm, corduroy jeans, a couple of Fred Perrys – I walked out of the Funken and was caught full in the bone marrow by a gale blowing off the glacier. It clearly wasn't enough. Even re-equipped with a pair of Christian's windproof over-trousers and fluffy headgear, I was still chattering as we stamped about outside the Nybyen hostel. This process intensified as I watched Christian nonchalantly load a large rifle with five bear-piercing rounds.

Students, cheap alcohol and casually available big-game firearms didn't seem a great combination, but at least they seemed to know what they were doing. 'We all take a day practising with the rifle,' said Christian, slinging it breezily over his shoulder. 'I am more worried by your shoes than some ice bears. Don't you have any shoes to keep waters out?'

We headed out across the broken-paving-slab rubble, and almost immediately had to traverse a sizeable glacial torrent. Christian, exhibiting an ibex-like fleetness of foot, cleared it in two dainty bounds between stepping stones. I strode upstream to find a narrower crossing point, watching as the girls made it hesitantly but safely across.

'Come on!'

I took a huge run-up and to everybody's amazement cleared the icy brown stream in a single glorious leap. 'There. Not bad for an old man!' I shouted with a goal-celebrating salute.

'No, not bad,' yelled Marte. 'But up there you have another river.'

My triumphant smirk first atrophied, then imploded into a little, lost sigh as I noticed the fork in the stream. A minute later, the toes of my right foot now fused together with wet and cold, I hobbled up the valley floor, catching the students as they stopped to gawp at some tiny, browbeaten botanical specimen huddled among the splintered slates.

The pattern was set for the next hour of our slow ascent. They would congregate around a microscopic Arctic daisy, I would poke at EWP Sixties drink cans with dollybirds carrying beachballs, or throw stones at mining wagons outside timbered mine entrances in the teetering slag above us. Occasionally we'd come across a reindeer skeleton and our fields of interest briefly combined, their Dufferinian quest for scientific understanding melding with my Wilsonian morbidity.

'We may shoot reindeers on condition of cutting off his feet and taking them to a government office for registration,' beamed Christian. 'And if you stay for two weeks more, it is the time to kill puffins.' Sweet of you to offer.

We were now working our way towards the dirty brown crust at the glacier's edge. The wind shrieked and roared; it was difficult to hear anything above the buffeting blast. Consequently, when Eline cupped one hand by my ear and bellowed something seemingly related to the blizzard-swirled Matterhorn she was pointing up at with the other, I assumed I had misheard.

'Up there?' I yelled incredulously. She nodded. As we looked, the ice-sheathed granite spire disappeared in a wraith of cloud and snow. It was surely a Duff too far.

'In . . . these shoes?' I shouted in desperation. There was a huddled conference. Finally Hilde yelled, 'You are right. It will be too difficult in those shoes.'

'Bloody shoes!' I tutted to my guides after we'd trekked back down into a protected glen.

'It's a shame,' agreed Marte. 'But at least we can go out here to see the view of Longyearbyen. It's very special.'

I soon saw what 'special' might mean in this context. One minute we were on a broad plateau littered with old prospecting gear; the next we were in single file atop a five-foot wide Grand Canyon promontory with sides that were sheer for a couple of hundred feet before easing into the ridiculous mess of Longyearbyen, almost 2,000 feet below.

By the time we reached the jumble of shattered slate that marked the end of the ridge's walkable flatness, I was bent double by vertigo. 'Well, that is quite a special view,' I said reasonably firmly as we stopped by the teetering stacks of rubble that snaked crazily out before us.

'Yes, but that is not the view we came for,' said someone, I didn't care who. 'We go to the end of this ridge.'

It was too much for me. 'No! No. Sorry. You can't go there. There's nothing to stand on or hold on to – it's all crumbling bits of shit. Look at it! I mean, you're scientists – this is a basic example of erosion in action! It is the job of all those big towers of slate stuff up here to fall off and join their mates down there! See?'

'We're going.'

'Why? Look: there's Longyearbyen! See? Down there? This view is exactly the bloody same!'

'We're going.'

Well, whatever. Go, then. Four die as student prank turns sour. Just don't involve me. 'Okay! Please: go! Go on! I'll see you back here in half an hour.'

'Sure,' said Christian. 'In this case you will need the rifle.'

He unslung it and held the butt towards me.

'Here is the safety handle, here you pull to reload. Only one warning shot, and . . .'

Oh, cock it. Buttocking sod-bollocks.

'Fine! Right! Come on! Let's all go and fucking die, and if anyone should happen to make it I'd like them to tell my wife and children exactly what went on here.'

I would not wish anyone to suffer what I did in the following forty-five minutes, except obviously a chain gang of naked and blindfolded senior Teletext staff. The only other occasion on which I have contemplated the looming certainty of death over such a similarly drawn-out period was when Birna and I went rowing off an island near Helsinki and 'got into difficulties' after drifting into the Baltic.

But this was worse. Then it had been a mere moment's work to shove past Birna and make a swim for it. Now, trapped between Norwegians and clinging to cracked, rocking stacks of debris, there was no turning back. Every few steps I would place a trembling foot on a slate which would see-saw and dislodge a small rockfall into the abyss. It was like trying to walk across the coin overhang of a well-stocked Penny Falls.

Christian was still gaily leaping about, refusing to use his hands for support, but the girls had become markedly quieter. As we picked our way towards the ridge's end they were no longer laughing at my outbursts of crude vocal panic.

I even managed to gain on Eline, who was ahead of me. But this wasn't a good thing to have done. 'We must stay some metres apart,' Marte had said, and now I was to see why.

There was a little CD-sized saucer of slate on a rock I planned to stand on. I flicked at it with a wet shoe, a purple shoe, a stupid shoe. It tumbled off, towards the ledge 5 feet below where Eline was pondering her next move. What happened next was what ought to happen on the Penny Falls machines, but somehow never does. Lightly striking the rock by Eline's feet, my stone dislodged a huge shelf of basalt encyclopedias. A good 3 feet of her 4-foot ledge smashed impressively down towards Longyearbyen, building into a gathering avalanche of scree. She looked up at me with bewildered terror.

'Why did you do this?' she squeaked reedily.

'Er, sorry,' I said inadequately. 'I didn't . . . I . . . sorry.'

We inched our way in silence to the ridge end. Awful, awful vertiginous views of Longyearbyen tolled out below us as we huddled in a 3-foot square scoop presiding over a 340-degree sweep of free-fall. Christian dangled his feet over the precipice, nibbling ruminatively on a McVitie's Digestive, a packet of which they'd touchingly bought especially for me. I buried my face in a crevasse, convinced that if I raised any part of my body the icy gale would heave me over the edge.

'You're maybe not so . . . extreme,' he shouted kindly, brushing from his beatnik beard crumbs which were blown over my head to infinity. Pronounced as if without the final 'e', I was to hear this adjective a lot over coming days, usually introduced with a 'not' and applied to my clothing, physique and character. Loosely meaning 'rugged', or perhaps 'reckless', to be deemed 'extreme' seemed to be the ultimate accolade for a Spitzbergen student.

The walk down the glacier was more the sort of thing I'd had in mind. Hysterically grateful to be alive, I skipped through the mud, pausing to examine the amazing profusion of fossils. Almost every one of the umpteen billion pebbles and rocks about us bore the black imprint of a 50-million-year-old fern frond or leaf, every vein perfectly etched.

'Here we see how deep the glacier is,' said Christian, stopping by an ear-canal vortex that corkscrewed into black ice. 'All students go down a cave like this in winter.' He and I took a large flat rock each and heaved it in. 'Don't slip,' said Hilde. The helter skelter orifice was easily large enough to accommodate an idiot.

The stones swirled round the first curve like bobsleighs, then swooshed out of sight. Swish . . . scrape . . . swish . . . silence. I shrugged and turned. Ten seconds later two low booms thundered out of the hole.

'Jesus. You go down *there*?'

'It is safe in winter. But now, this is why we must be careful of crevasses,' said Christian.

It didn't really matter. It was now clear that whenever it looked as if I might be about to enjoy myself in this stupid place, some mortal threat would present itself. Brittle with weary terror, I rounded off the trip by slipping over in the same stream I'd fallen in on the way out.

I thanked my guides, which was especially polite of me, and stumbled back to the Funken in a battle-weary stupor. Waiting was some good news – a message that I could interview the Sysselmann herself the next day – and some deeply tragic news

– the discovery that I had been missing out on a 'complimentary light evening meal' every night. But in my frazzled despair I treated these two imposters just the same, which was with the tiniest of give-a-shit shrugs.

Only when I drew back the curtains in my room was I briefly roused. The ridge we had climbed, Sarkofagen, filled the end of the valley, looking from this angle monstrously inaccessible. I could see its impossible crags and cliffs and cracks even as I lay down on my bed, and drifted off pledging never, ever to go for a walk with Norwegians again.

There was no milk at breakfast the next day, not at the Funken, not anywhere. Like everything else it's flown in, and the flight had been cancelled. The thin veneer of Spitzbergen's contrived civilisation was once again exposed. A couple of weeks of sustained bad weather and everyone here would be grunting, lawless hunter-gatherers.

In an unsuitably chastened state of mind I eased my ruined body down to the Sysselmann's, hurriedly psyching myself up for the unaccustomed challenge of interviewing someone while wearing borrowed flip-flops.

Minutes from a meeting between Anne-Kristin Olsen, Sysselmann of Svalbard, and Timothy Moore, buffoon, Longyearbyen, Spitzbergen, 11 August 1997, 12.04 p.m.

Mr Moore began by asking how many miners there were in Longyearbyen. Ms Olsen replied that there were 210 miners in Longyearbyen. Mr Moore then ruffled for some time through some papers he was carrying. Ms Olsen began rubbing her nose and looked out of the window. Mr Moore began as if to speak, then stopped, and consulted his papers once more, then after a further pause asked if it was true that Spitzbergen had the world's highest per capita alcohol consumption. Ms Olsen looked directly at Mr Moore and asked if he meant Svalbard. He apologised and said that he did. Ms Olsen replied that this was certainly not the case. The monthly quota, she said, was only one litre of hard liquor. Mr Moore said he had been told it was two litres. Ms Olsen replied that it was not. What about the beer, asked Mr Moore. Ms Olsen waved a hand and conceded that some beer may also be involved. And the wine, said Mr Moore. At this point Ms Olsen smiled, and directed her gaze down to Mr Moore's flip-flops, raising her eyebrows slightly as she did so. Mr Moore swallowed and moistened his lips. He then asked if tourism was replacing mining as Spitzbergen's main source of income. Ms Olsen asked if he meant Svalbard's. He replied that he did. She advised him to refer to the guidelines laid down in the recent management policy document. Mr Moore asked if the concept of wilderness package tours was not a contradiction in terms. Ms Olsen advised him to refer to the guidelines laid down in the recent management policy document. Mr Moore then asked if the polar bear threat was not exaggerated to discourage freelance travel. Ms Olsen advised him to refer to the many families bereaved by polar bear attacks.

Mr Moore said something indistinct. Ms Olsen asked him to raise his voice and repeat it. Mr Moore said that he had been told the position of Sysselmann was in effect that of dictator. Ms Olsen placed her hands on her desk and leaned forward. She looked at Mr Moore for some time, then sat back again and returned her gaze to the window. She could not understand the attitude of some of the locals, she said. The main element of her position was to maintain and uphold Norwegian sovereignty over Svalbard, she said. It was enshrined in the 1920 treaty. The reason anyone was here was purely because the government wanted them to be. The government owned the mining company and employed people on fixed-term contracts, she said. And now that the mining was coming to an end, the government had decided that its employees on Svalbard would work towards making Svalbard a profitable wilderness. But not just any wilderness. This was to be the best-run wilderness in the world, she said. Access would be strictly controlled. But some of the locals could not understand this. Control the tourists, they said, but not us, she said. The loud ones, she said, the ones who wanted more power for themselves, who forgot that they owed everything to the government, who paid 400 million kroner a year to keep them there. But they were not satisfied. Some people never were, she said. They sat there in their little civic meetings demanding more local authority, but did they not realise that they were employees? Not citizens, employees, she said. I even offered to let them control the licensing hours of the local hotels, she said, but that wasn't enough. Not for them. Never enough for them, she said. They talk, but they do not think, she said. How could a little Norwegian council control a town full of Russian citizens? I am the head of police, she said, I am the upholder of sovereignty. They are not taking my powers.

After a pause, Ms Olsen looked back at Mr Moore. After a pro-longed cough, he asked why no one had demolished the old cable car supports that traversed the town. Ms Olsen breathed out loudly, then replied that all artefacts predating 1946 were protected as part of the industrial and cultural heritage of Spitzbergen. Svalbard, said Mr Moore. Ms Olsen smiled, then stood up, moved towards her door, and opened it. Mr Moore thanked her for her time and left, stopping to retrieve a flip-flop which dislodged itself as he did so.

Laboriously rebooted, I went out into a head-on gale so fierce that I could almost see my ribs through four layers of clothing. Well, I thought, I can't really blame her. If I'd been a senior civil servant in cosy Oslo who'd suddenly been posted here I'd take everything personally, too. But it was a shame that my attempt to schmooze the local bigwigs, to Duff them up, had been so humiliatingly inept. Forget the deep potations. I didn't even get a bloody coffee.

Eyes slitted and leaning into the blast I fought my way up to the supermarket, vainly searched for souvenirs amid the dried-reindeer-meat snack-packs and floating-polar-bear toothbrushes, then struggled back to the Funken. I noticed in my bathroom mirror that the wind had blown a neat stream of tears from the corner of each eye to the top of each ear, and that these streams and the collateral dampness in my eye sockets had provided an adhesive surface for whipped up bits of coal dust and powdered swamp fossil, so that it looked like someone had drawn a pair of comedy glasses on my face. Great joke, great place, I thought, as I settled down to watch hours and hours of bad television.

I was beginning to settle into a routine. Ingest unsightly breakfast binge, put on shoes, walk to supermarket, purchase unsightly luncheon foodstuffs to cover up bottle of wine in basket but forget to purchase souvenirs, take off shoes, enter government building in attempt to find interesting pamphlets but be told everyone is on holiday, put on shoes, walk back to Funken, take off shoes, remember souvenirs, put on shoes, walk down to supermarket, despairingly purchase floating-polar-bear toothbrushes and reindeer snack-packs, up to Funken, shoes off, light evening meal, shoes on, student hostel, shoes, wine, shoes, hotel, shoes, bed.

But the routine never succeeded in masking Longyearbyen's astonishing capacity for ugliness and soul-destruction. I noticed one morning that the streets were numbered rather than named. You live in a building that looks like a dole office on stilts with enchanting views of the ancient aftermath of the War of the Worlds, and then your address is No. 17, Road 12.

No wonder everyone buggers off for the summer, I thought as I unshod myself in the abandoned foyer of yet another civic facility, this time in search of the Norwegian Polar Institute's map shop. Amazingly, it was open. Slightly less amazingly, it was run by Christian.

He wasn't surprised by my rather disturbing encounter with the Sysselmann. 'She isn't so popular. Some think she is . . . with her nose in the air.' I could imagine that. With her strictly corralled silver hair and Valkyrian stature she exuded no-nonsense imperiousness like a Xena – Warrior Queen Mother. 'But I feel sympathy with her. People back in Norway – especially newspapers – are saying it is too expensive to run Svalbard the old way. The Russians are leaving, so why should we stay? But she has to follow the treaty, and manage with some people in Longyearbyen who want more power . . . it's difficult. You must remember how quickly everything has changed.'

I certainly must. Longyearbyen hadn't even had live TV until a satellite relay was put up in 1984. Before that they'd made do with videotapes broadcast fourteen days after they appeared in Norway. *That Was The Week Before Last Week That Was.*

But now it's all gone berserk. Laser tills in the supermarket, cashpoints, the world's most northerly one-hour photoshop. Here more than anywhere all this technology seemed a desperate attempt by man to prove his superiority over the Mother of all Natures.

I browsed the shelves and found an improbably large book on Jan Mayen, which included an arresting photograph of seven bearded technicians running nude into the Arctic breakers, doubtless in pursuit of a disappearing Hercules full of wives and girlfriends. There was also a chronological list of landings, which confirmed that Dufferin was the only man to set foot on the island between 1818 and 1861.

Still pondering this as I flicked through the map carousel, I was suddenly presented with a large and familiar spoon-shaped island. It was the first proper map I'd seen of Jan Mayen, and as I scanned its coastline, a familiar name leapt out on the northeast shore. *Clandeboye bukta.* I was amazed. And jealous. Dufferin certainly had clout. All it takes is a throwaway comment: 'We collected some geographical specimens, and having duly christened the little cove "Clandeboye Creek", we walked back to the gig.' Then somehow it is seen to that generations of cartographers etch that legend beside the place you paddled about for half an hour.

Silently awestruck, I bought two copies of the map – one for Clandeboye, one for me – and a copy of the polar-bear-warning poster, a volume of sales which excited Christian so much that he wrote out separate invoices in triplicate and invited me to his and Marte's hostel for a slide show.

It's bad when someone who wasn't even born when Marc Bolan died turns out to be a lot better than you. As well as being taller and fitter, with a six-pack stomach to my six-pinter, he consistently outshone me in all fields of human endeavour.

Each of Christian's photos, even the 25 per cent that depicted silly little plants, surpassed in content, composition and absence of gloved digits any I have taken. Photographic prowess could now be added to his growing list of skills: a natural ease with large-bore firearms; dainty and fearless mountaineering poise; the ability to simultaneously remove two beer-bottle tops by hooking the rims under each other and pulling. It had all been downhill for me since I scored 8,200,000 on Missile Command. In 1986. When he was eight.

What was also clear from his slides was that, as I'd suspected, Spitzbergen in winter – or at least spring – was a very different proposition in terms of not looking like a quarry abandoned after a slump in the world price of crap. When the sun had returned in March, Christian and a few friends set off on a snow-scooter expedition across the frozen fjords, and his photographic record showed a landscape utterly transformed. Gone was the geological squalor, covered in a thick coating of religiously pure whiteness. Spitzbergen's yellow-toothed, gloating sneer had metamorphosised into a dazzling film-star smile.

It must be one of the few places where it is easier to get about in winter than it is in summer. The snow-scooter speed record here is 212 kilometres per hour, and the slides showed Christian's snow-scooter gang shooting up mountains substantially more daunting than the ridge we'd climbed the day before (now referred to by the students, with leaden irony, as Timtoppen), stopping occasionally to pose by abandoned trappers' cabins that had been laid waste to by delinquent polar bears, the doors and walls scarred with claw slashes.

'A bear was on the roof of one cabin we stayed in. We hear it moving, and we are scared a little, because a bear can run through a cabin as if it was some paper and stick-matches. So I go out and explode some flares and it leaves.'

There were also slides from a trek Christian and Marte had made after the snows had gone, down the Isfjord and over a few hefty peaks to Grumantbyen, a mining town abandoned by the Soviets in 1962.

The images depicted were those from the sightseeing tour of my Wilsonian dreams. Racks of keys hung in cabinets labelled in Cyrillic. Chairs were neatly arranged round tables in vast, sun-filled dormitories lined with lockers. There were shoes under beds. It was all there. The ghosts of political and economic defeat, the ideological graveyard, the Cold War theme park kept on ice in the permafrost.

'Let's go,' I blurted.

'Across the mountains?'

'No . . . I was thinking more *around* the mountains.'

'Not possible. There are cliffs up to the sea.'

'Between the mountains?'

'To go between mountains, you must first go over,' said Christian, sounding like Grasshopper's mentor in the *Kung Fu* title sequence.

The projector clicked up a new image on to the sheet hung across their Björk posters. A windswept Marte was dangling from the blade of a 15-foot hammer and sickle built from scaffold poles and left to rust on the Grumantbyen beach handle-deep in minecar axles. I issued a pathetic frustrated-toddler whine.

'Well. Have you been in a fast, small boat?' asked Marte in an oddly accusing way, like a desperate showtrial prosecutor. 'The Polar Institute has a Zodiac and some survival suits. Maybe we can go the day after tomorrow.'

That would be my last day. I agreed with what almost amounted to eagerness.

'So tomorrow,' she continued, 'we can climb one more mountain.'

There was no water the next morning. No hot, no cold, no nothing. 'It happens maybe one time in a month,' said the receptionist brightly. It came back at 10, but was a little more beige than I would have liked. Someone had told me that the overground sewer ran alongside the overground water main. 'No, really,' laughed the receptionist when I phoned again. 'It is absolutely good now. Just some small pebbles.'

During the next few minutes the pebbles trebled. They stopped rolling and gathered moss. Regrettably, I spent these minutes under the shower. By the time I managed to turn it off, I was being viciously flayed by a water cannon cum sand blaster that would have been the envy of any public order enthusiast.

I grabbed blindly for the towel, and having rubbed myself down stood back to survey the damage. The shower tray was completely blocked with black grit. The same substance clung evenly to my body, which I suddenly realised was beneath rasped puce from the unbidden gravel massage. My eyes stung. The towel looked like it had been used to wipe down a locomotive. And all I had to rinse myself off was orange juice.

I wasn't alone. The breakfast room was full of grit-flecked guests, the whites of their eyes unnaturally bright, looking like the survivors of a mining disaster. Every time someone sat down they winced. And I had to climb up a mountain.

In recognition of my undignified loss of bottle on the previous ascent, the students selected a less taxing peak near the fjord. We still had a rifle, we still clambered up towering heaps of crazy-paving slabs littered with evidence of recent femur-shattering rockfalls, but there were no crevasses or soul-swallowing vertical drops. Copious sweat soon sluiced my body gravel into the less discomforting sock area, and, after an hour, we topped a gently rounded summit, perhaps 700 feet above Longyearbyen. The sun came out and, for the first and only time, I looked at the panorama with some fondness.

It had snowed on the mountains the night before, leaving a hint of the majestic beauty bestowed upon this place in spring. Peaks lined up on the horizon with the sun picking out every ripple on their ancient flanks. Yet, said Marte, they were over 100 kilometres away. The glaciers shone like they'd been Ronsealed.

Around us on the plateau were tin openers and old sardine cans alongside bits of cable and iron wheels. I again wondered how many English, Dutch and Norwegian miners had sat here, looking down at their lonely adopted homeland. 'You know, Lars, on a day like this I can almost imagine not having to get drunk every night and wondering what in the name of Christ I've done to deserve being here.' And Lars would mumble, '*Tre man i en båt.*'

I looked back at the distant peaks. With the sun on them, they were a curious deep pink, purplish almost. Mauve? No, paler. Then I saw, quite clearly, that they were unquestionably lilac, and gulped slightly as I recalled the final pages of *Helen's Tower* which I'd read the night before.

January 1901 wasn't a great month for Dufferin. Two weeks after facing the London & Globe's bankrupted shareholders, his Queen died; having attended the funeral, he wrote to his wife of 'the poor dear Lady who had been so kind a friend to me for fifty years'. Finally, at the end of January, he learned by telegram that his eldest son, the Earl of Ava, had been killed in the Boer War.

He returned to Clandeboye exhausted, almost blind, and suffering from 'gastric inflammation'. On 18 January 1902, the doctors threw in the towel and Dufferin's remaining children were summoned to Clandeboye; they spent their days cutting back trees to give him a view of Helen's Tower. He died on 12 February, in the early morning. He was seventy-six.

But three days earlier, he had dictated a letter to the Prime Minister, Lord Salisbury. Having read it, I recognised that despite all the overbearing indefatigability, all the hypocritical Wilson-baiting, all the Latin orations, I would never be able to hate Dufferin.

Being, as the doctors seem to say, on my death-bed, I desire, while I still have my wits about me, to place in your hands my resignation of the Chancellorship of the Royal University of Ireland, as well as the Lieutenancy of the County. I suppose that under the circumstances, ill-health will be regarded as a valid excuse.

Feeling a lump in my throat the size of a knee I looked at the industrial Edwardiana rusting around me and silently proposed a toast to Frederick Temple Hamilton Temple Blackwood, Baron

Dufferin, Baron Dufferin and Clandeboye, Earl of Dufferin and Viscount Clandeboye, Marquis of Dufferin and Ava, Earl of Ava, PC, KP, GCB, GCSI, GCMG, GCIE, DCL, LLD, FRS, Governor-General of Canada, Ambassador to the Courts of Russia, Turkey and Italy, Ambassador to France, Viceroy of India, Lord Warden of the Cinque Ports, Vice-Admiral of Ulster, Lord-Lieutenant and Custos Rotulorum for the County of Down, Justice of the Peace.

It was almost too awful to think of this wise and decent old man suffering so much indignity, sacrificed on the altar of commercialism, an eminent Victorian who had no place in a new era, a new century. He'd lost his fortune to the new aristocracy, the money men whose filthy factories he'd gone to the Arctic and to India to flee. But they'd got him in the end, lured him into their world, bamboozled him, bled him dry. He was wooed to disaster in the same way as the miners who'd been shipped up here, I thought – from opposite ends of the social scale, but both swindled by smooth-talking new money.

And he'd lost his own son to the Empire he'd helped build, but which now, overstretched and overwrought, was at the start of a humiliating, hundred-year retreat. His empire, the Dufferin dynasty, would slowly wither in sympathy. None of his four sons survived beyond 1930, carried off by war and disease; Clandeboye decayed to a musty mausoleum with buckets catching drips in every room. Lindy, my Dufferin's great-granddaughter-in-law, had resurrected the house and its finances, but when her husband died without producing an heir, the Dufferin name died with him.

We turned down a steep valley, the others waiting for me every few minutes while I picked my way gingerly behind them.

'Are British people not extreme?' asked Marte after a particularly long wait. As I smiled helplessly, I realised that Wilson had won. The bold grandeur of Britain's Dufferins died with the Empire; now all we ruled was Tristan da Cunha and Rockall, and the only appropriate national characteristics were off-stage grumblings and defeatist cynicisms. Wilson: the choice of a new generation. It was a comfort of sorts.

The valley came out near the Funken, and the students heigh-hoed and fol-dur-eed back up to Nybyen in ever brightening sun. There we barbecued, an activity which exposed the shallowness of the summery facade. It was so cold that the raffianti placed 2 feet away from the roaring fire to warm up quickly glistened with icy condensation. As soon as the sun dipped below the glacier the valley seemed to sink a thousand feet, the mountains once more loomingly ominous.

Just after midnight, a lone student gunman emerged out of an adjacent hostel and started off towards the foot of the glacier. 'He's going up to the peak,' said Christian.

'*The* peak? The Matterhorn one?' He nodded. 'On his own? At midnight?' He shrugged blandly. I had been about to ask what sort of student would volunteer to spend a year here, but now there seemed no point. *That* sort. *Your* sort. Or chainsmoking albinos with hayfever.

So instead I got told Swedish jokes and was forced to reciprocate by saying 'Hurtigrute' until the valley rang with Nordic mirth. More wind-chilled wine was consumed, and at length I decided the time was right to give the 'frost on my moustache' joke another airing. So it was that the evening ended in distress and confusion, and I slunk back to the Funken down a newly tarmaced footpath which was already being reclaimed by the glacial sludge.

'Yes . . . it's been a remarkable honeymoon,' oiled the Ian Ogilvy-style ageing smoothie to the receptionist. 'Yes. Hasn't it,' said his rather too young new wife evenly.

'Very *different*.' Very different from a nice honeymoon, said her tone. 'We shall hope to see you again,' chirped the receptionist, but neither could bring themselves to do more than smile bravely with the slightest of polite nods.

Jesus. I hadn't even known that there were any other English guests, which I suppose was my fault for always having breakfast eleven seconds before the final deadline. By the time I was stirring up my herring porridge these two were probably out . . . what? What could they have been thinking of? Please, everyone, please don't go to Spitzbergen for your honeymoon. Especially not in the summer. You'd have a more romantic time dredging a container port.

I checked out after they ran eagerly to their waiting taxi, wondering what kind words the receptionist would have for me. But before she had a chance to say, 'Hey, everyone, Mr Filth-socks who eats tins of crap in his room and thinks we haven't noticed all the empty wine bottles in the wardrobe is pissing off at last!', I surprised myself by blurting out all the doubts and queries that had been building up for nearly two weeks. 'Do you live here? Why do you live here? Why does anyone live here? Can anyone ever think of this place as home?'

But I didn't get much nearer the truth. The answers she gave were, respectively: 'No, I'm only working here in the summer'; 'I don't'; 'You should ask some people who live here'; and 'How are you choosing to pay your bill, Mr Moon?'

Norway was so plainly nice; Spitzbergen was so plainly horrid. Moreover, nothing that Spitzbergen offered − snow, mountains, marooned isolation, northern lights, fjords − could not be found somewhere along the mainland's endless coastline. 'Spitzbergen − Realm of the Polar Bear and the Cheap Fag' would be the only honest encapsulation of the archipelago's unique attractions, and it was hard to see that striking up much interest among potential emigrants.

I'd asked the students. They'd said you had to be there in March to understand. Having seen Christian's slides I could begin to believe it. Still, the endless months of slush and darkness seemed a high price for the few brief weeks when this epic snowscape was illuminated. No nearer to resolving this issue, I left my bags in reception and wandered for the last time up the gravelly mire towards Nybyen, between the forlorn tenements of Roads 4–9.

Christian met us at the hostel in a Suzuki estate he'd borrowed from the Polar Institute. 'The news is bad,' he said as I shamelessly grazed from the fridge. It was terrible how quickly I had become a student, or at least an English student. Eating other people's food from communal fridges now seemed not just natural but obligatory. 'Mmthhmmpluth?' I spat fluffily through an oral mire of cocktail sausage and gherkin.

'The wind is strong now. We maybe can't go out in the Zodiac.'

It was gone 4, and the *Nordstjernen* was setting off at midnight. Suddenly the idea of not going to Grumantbyen in a small boat on a stormy sea seemed an eminently sound one.

'Well, there isn't time, anyway,' I said, wiping my mouth on a tea-towel.

'No. There is time, certainly,' said Christian, and I realised too late that I had thrown down a gauntlet.

An hour later I was mummified in a day-glo survival suit with 'Norsk Polarinstitutt' on the back, rooted to a cinder-dust beach by a scrapyard-cum-coal jetty that looked like a setting from *Get Carter*. A survival suit, I decided, was so called after the legal proceedings brought by wearers who somehow managed to escape strangulation. In his suit, Christian looked like Action Man; in mine, I was Michelin Man. A rubberised cowl pressed chokingly around my throat, like a polo neck made from a Wellington, and my frame sagged under the whole ensemble's ridiculous bulk and weight. Pulling the thing on, my trousers had become snagged on the inside rim of the suit's integral waders, and were as a result now rucked up around my loins like a corduroy nappy. I could not bend or turn, and to walk was to perform a grotesque caricature of the Frankenstein's monster gait forced upon me when burdened by my twin rucksacks.

Of the others, only Eline looked at all uneasy as we waddled the bright red 10-foot inflatable towards the gentle fjord, creaking and squeaking as we went. Striding briskly into the Arctic, Christian ran through our usual excursion inventory – Digestive biscuits, spare socks, big game rifle – and stowed the lot under a rubber sheet covering the bow.

'We're going to make friends in here,' I bellowed woollenly through the scarf tied bandit-style round my face. 'Again please?' 'There isn't much space to sit inside.' Three pairs of eyes looked at me above scarves. I recognised the look only too well. It was a look which said, 'Christ, will your capacity for cluelessness never be exhausted, you stupid old foreigner?'

Soon enough I saw. Having rolled artlessly into the boat with a ridiculous rubbery flump, I heaved my non-articulating limbs into place and realised there was of course no question of sitting in the boat. No, no, no. The best type of boat for going out across the Arctic is quite clearly a tiny rubber one where you have to perch on the side with only a little rope loop to grip. Of course. It seemed so obvious now that I thought about it.

Christian and Marte sat at – or more accurately on – the stern to man the outboard; Eline took up position opposite me.

'If you fall in, you will float,' shouted Christian. 'But don't fall in this way' – he mimed someone diving in headfirst – 'or you will not float. The air in the suit will go up to your feet and your head will sink.' With most of his face covered in rubber and wool I could not tell if he was jesting. I didn't want my head to sink. Then he yanked the starter rope and we were shooting in a smooth arc round into the Isfjord. 'Faster!' yelled Eline eagerly, and I realised I was now alone with my fear.

The wind had been skulking about behind the first row of mountains, and as soon as we cleared them it screamed rudely into our faces. What had been a flat, rusty sea billowed up first into khaki hillocks, then froth-crested peaks that sent the whole boat airborne, bows to the heavens. There would be a sudden silence as we left the water, an accelerating whine as the propeller enjoyed its brief liberation; then, horribly, an enormous, jowl-wobbling slap as we smacked back into the sea.

The windproof Goretex mittens I'd been forced to wear struggled for a purchase on the rope. I stole a sideways glance at Eline, and noticed her tear-blown eyes slitted in strain as she grasped her loop. I should have been gratified that I wasn't the only one, but this sight instead confirmed my worst fears. If I relaxed my hold, I was in.

As we passed the quivering tethered aerials by the airport control tower, dull steel against an iron sky, the wind picked up a notch. The waves were now a good 10 feet, and the only way to tackle them safely was head-on. Mucus flowed freely from nostril to scarf, and the latter was soon sloughed in an impenetrable web of thick gossamer. Eline stared at me, and the visible parts of her face contracted in disgust. Fair enough. It was her scarf.

Marte slapped Christian's arm – even yelled conversation had long since been impossible – and he slowed down. I have never felt so isolated. We were miles from what passed for humanity in one of the world's loneliest places, on a sea so cold that even in a survival suit you'd only last an hour. And a broadside hit from any one of these waves would pitch us all in. I'd be found in a month, floating feet up, my face nibbled away by seals, my torso the plaything of libidinous walruses.

Marte and Christian held a brief but vivid gesture-and-eyebrow debate on the advisability of continuing. He wanted to; she didn't. Instantly, the one thing which I had held on to – complete trust in their cast-iron commonsense – whistled away down the fjord. They weren't sure. They didn't know. They wouldn't be the first who'd taken on Spitzbergen once too often, not the first to forget that this place doesn't give you a second chance. But Christian won. He shrugged, twisted the throttle and sent us smack into a half-breaking wave which flayed Eline and I with chilled brine.

We clung to the coast, which had now reared up into the cliffs Martina had pointed out on our first approach. Somewhere on their guano-flecked flanks were dinosaur footprints, but I couldn't look. My tear-smeared gaze was fixed ahead, letting my brittle, rigid body prepare itself for the next soar and crash. If someone had tapped me firmly on the head, I would have shattered.

After half an hour I'd passed through the cramp barrier, and there was still no sign of Grumantbyen. I hadn't moved, yet I was utterly exhausted. We were now flying off the crests of waves that would certainly have sent us turning for home if we'd come across them sooner.

Gradually I felt my grip helplessly weaken, and for the first time I became aware of a huge pain where my signet ring had gouged into a spasmed palm. But soon even this sensation was shunted away down a back alley in my brain. After an hour I was gone, completely gone, resigned to whatever, being tossed about limply like a crash-test dummy.

It's taken this long, I remember thinking, but here I finally am – Dufferining. If not in spirit – he'd have been standing with one foot on the bow, chin jutting, hands on hips – then at least in deed. This was just the sort of pointlessly lethal excursion he'd have embarked upon on a stupid whim. The thought raised my spirits with a dim, last-stand colonial defiance which regrettably drained my body of its last reserves. Then, as my eyelids drooped, I felt us turning landward, and there on a ravaged beach was a 15-foot tall hammer and sickle.

Grumantbyen was an astounding place, so astounding that within minutes my all-encompassing physical distress had shrunk to a simple feeling that I'd recently been flicked repeatedly about the face with a salty towel. Having shakily removed my suit as the others hauled the Zodiac on to the machinery-strewn shingle, I set off through the rusty cables towards the forlorn trio of buildings that were the remains of Spitzbergen's largest town.

I went first to the largest block, a three-storey concrete barn whose royal blue paint bore evidence of a plucky but one-sided battle against thirty-five years of Arctic wind. Staring out at 500 miles of cruel sea, Grumantbyen was utterly exposed; with loading huge coalers a patent impossibility, the Russians had blasted a tunnel through a mile of mountain to ferry the coal to the protected jetty at Colesbukta. It was suddenly obvious why Grumantbyen had been abandoned – with no harbour it had zero strategic importance in the Cold War sub-plot that governed Spitzbergen from the war until Yeltsin.

The armed students joined me, and Christian, Eline and I climbed in through a wind-smoothed, glassless window. Marte stayed outside with the rifle. They'd seen a bear near here when they came in March.

It was difficult to equate the design antiquity of the Soviet accommodation block (about 1895) with either its true year of construction (1962) or the apparent one based on its generally unweathered appearance (1990). Upstairs were windows, most still glazed. Endless banks of grey tin lockers lined the wall, some face down on the floor like soldiers who'd fainted on parade. 'I'm not sure how the Russians were thinking when they went,' said Christian as we walked through a Birkenau-scale shower room, traces of rinsed-off coal dust still clinging to the rims of the vitreous enamel trays. 'They broke some things – like these water pipes – so it would be difficult to live here. But why they didn't just explode these buildings? I think they wanted to keep a possibility of coming back.'

I could believe it. We walked into a panelled office, obviously a senior official's. Coloured fabric-covered wires zinged out of a staved-in telephone exchange. His windows looked straight out at the sea, and through them, high on a cliff to the left, I could see a brick tower that could only be a look-out post. That was the real importance of Grumantbyen, surely. It can't have been worth the Soviets' while to blast tunnels through lonely mountains half a step from the North Pole for the sake of a few boatloads of coal. I could imagine some pissed-off 'naval attaché' in a ridiculously high-peaked cap huddled up by the cast-iron radiator, scanning the horizon for Imperialist running dogs.

We filed thoughtfully down the stairs and out towards the next building, past mossy mountains of bottles and blackened boots. It was like the scene of some recently discovered Holocaust out-rage. The sad, damp atmosphere shivered with the state-decreed suffering of the many at the hands of an only-taking-orders elite. Someone had put a pair of rubber goggles on a reindeer skull, which seemed about the right level of humour.

The second building was where Christian and Marte had spent a night in March, propping a glass-panelled door against the entrance as a polar bear alarm. There were Parisian footprint bogs, wardrobes whose brass handles still gleamed from the manipulations of a generation of communists and, most poignantly of all, a cell for any naughty or ideologically suspect miners amongst the 1,000-odd who'd lived and worked here. Inside, a pair of curled-up shoes were placed neatly under a cast-iron bedframe. An inmate had carved 'Dimitri' on the windowsill.

We went out and found Marte, sitting on a weird, moss-padded promenade complete with benches and the cut-off stumps of streetlights, as if the view was of a balmy sunset at a teeming Black Sea resort or a cityscape dotted with onion domes and wedding-cake Palaces of Culture. No one spoke. It was at least reasonably interesting, I thought, that Dufferin had taken the *Foam* to the Crimea and been bombarded by the Russians, and that now here I was, as close to the front of the most recent Anglo-Russian conflict as I'd ever be.

We filed down the dunes to the sea through a huge mess of twisted girders, mine trucks and telegraph poles. Then, poking above a cavernous fuel storage tank, there it was – the 15-foot hammer and sickle, staring out to sea with rusty, doomed defiance.

For a structure that had withstood thirty-five winters of scarcely imaginable hostility it had weathered well, but there was still something heart-rendingly pathetic about this scaffold-pole edifice. They'd clearly left it as an up-yours to the West in general, but now presiding before the windswept ghost town, this Helldorado, it was clear the gesture had completely backfired. Here, in one compact scenario, was the history of an ideology already in decline in 1962 and now utterly redundant, as stone cold dead as Grumantbyen itself.

We had the wind behind us on the way back, so things weren't nearly as desperate. The students shouted folk songs as we surfed over the waves, and I endeavoured to pull my snotty-wool-sheathed features into a smile. Within an hour we were sweeping across the fjord with *Baywatch* abandon, then Christian killed the engine and we coasted up to the shore. I could see the *Nordstjernen*'s funnel above the buildings around the cruise jetty. All at once my heart, shaken empty of most normal emotions by the extremity of my recent experiences, was filled with a heavy sense of loss and sadness. I knew my ship was there, but in some ridiculous way it had only just occurred to me that I would be leaving on it. I was going. Soon.

Of course, in many important ways I was deliriously happy to be leaving this monstrous place, to be turning for home and my family and whatever it was I liked about London. I hadn't seen the sodding moon in two months, for Christ's sake.

I confronted my melancholy, and found two root causes. The first was a vast gratitude to the total strangers who had re-organised their cosy holiday around me and my manifold feeblenesses. I could have been anyone. Probably I *was* anyone, but they had shut up about it and entertained me. As on the *Fridtjofen*, I still couldn't quite believe that people who weren't evangelical Christians or scheming serial killers would willingly adopt anyone in this way, particularly a hopeless case like me. I certainly wouldn't, just as Dufferin certainly would, which is one reason why I felt as bad as I did. My general response to many of their generosities had been to shower them with foul oaths and their scarves with snot.

And the second was the realisation that my hope of leaving Spitzbergen with a sense of slotting a final piece into the jigsaw of Dufferin: Traveller and Man was a forlorn one. All I'd done was lay out random pieces in a line – country by country, town by town, fjord by fjord – and even then there were gaps. Jan Mayen had been a royal balls-up, and my own protracted incompetence had accounted for plans to duplicate his Norwegian stopovers. I still wasn't certain why he'd come here, or to Jan Mayen, or to Iceland. After returning to Britain and embarking on his diplomatic career, he never returned to the Arctic. Of the two postings where he made his name, Canada perhaps exhibited vague associations with remote Scandinavia, but India emphatically did not. He clearly hadn't been driven here by a hungry obsession for the place and its people, or if he had it was a hunger sated in two months.

Every time I looked at his inscrutable face in the *Helen's Tower* frontispiece I seemed to understand him less. His diplomatic charm, so effective a mask if a mask it were, had proved difficult to penetrate. I had started out with a loose concept of a lost breed of dashing, erudite adventurer whose kind heart and self-directed comedy set him apart from the blustering bullies traditionally associated with the genre. Inspired into emulating his deeds, or at least one of them, I made the stupid mistake of trying to imitate the spirit in which they were undertaken; having quickly failed in this bid, my predictable collapse into whimpering defeatism and bitterness probably explained more than anything why I began to transfer my affections to the apparently awful Wilson, who was less likely to show me up. Wilson blossomed into my talisman and the voyage's stoic mascot; Dufferin became a pompous little mummy's boy with a nasty streak.

But amidst Spitzbergen's almost biblical sense of pathos and suffering, the sadness of Dufferin's final years had proven irresistible. He was a good man who took his downfall with honour, and who by showing a small but crucial lack of judgement had displayed at last a real weakness that made it more difficult to resent him. I might never play up, play up and play his game – the rules had changed too much over the years, and I'd been sin-binned for profane dissent – but at least I'd stood on the same pitch.

Nursing this mixture of melancholy and disappointment, I sat in silence as we drove back into town. 'Okay?' asked Marte. 'Just . . . tired,' I said. That was probably all it was. In the previous eight weeks (was that really all?) I'd endured more wearying, worrying and puke-inducing activities than in all my cloistered adult years combined. I might not be broken, not quite, but I was shattered.

'Hey!' said Eline with a red-cheeked yelp of enthusiasm. 'You must see the reindeers before you leave!'

'Must I?' I said.

'Of course!' There was a small pause as she pondered how to sell the excursion. 'They have short legs and white bottoms!'

We drove through town and out the other side, past Europe's only 'Beware of Polar Bears' roadsign, and out across a savannah-like plain towards Mine 7. 'There are some!' There were some. I stumbled out and pretended to photograph them as they ran away displaying both of the aforementioned physical peculiarities. 'Can we go now?' I just wanted to be off. I'd had enough. My brain was full.

I was ferried up to the Funken to retrieve my belongings, now supplemented by a sack of fossils I would eventually dump into Oslo harbour and two 3-foot tubes of maps and posters, one of which is somewhere outside a dried fish museum in the Lofoten Islands.

There wasn't time to buy my guides and counsellors a thank-you gift, so I rather shabbily gave them 100 kroner for petrol and snot-emulsifying detergents as we parted by the jetty. The *Nordstjernen*'s new intake seemed identical to the previous lot. Passengers in far too many clothes were milling about, comparing sealskin picture frames and 80th parallel certificates; after a week in a Pepsi Max ad, it wasn't going to be easy to readjust to tourist-cruise banality. I was feeling the same sense of done-it-all omnipotence that Dilli and I had succumbed to in the aftermath of our cycling endeavour. These were cossetted tourists, little people, idiots, scum. I, and I alone, was the Explorer.

I heaved my luggage up the gangplank, and was greeted, or anyway met, by Martina. She fixed me with her Englisher pig-dog look. 'You can have 277, or you can share.' I thought of a man with a beard unburdening his soul through a bathroom door. '277,' I said, even though my knowledge of the boat, and in particular its more compact cabins, meant I knew even as I opened its door that an honest precis of 277's attractions would not include the words 'natural light' or 'cat-swingers welcome'.

I sought solace on the deck. We weren't leaving for fifteen minutes, and I spent that time staring. Staring at the purposeless peculiarity of this concrete and cinders Arctic outpost, and how its thwarted, shanty-town impermanence was made all the more stark by the timeless might and bulk of the mountains that shouted it down from across the fjord. Staring at the fragile ridge of Timtoppen, still impressively impregnable even at this distance.

Then, more vacantly, staring at the place as an out-of-focus whole, I wondered how Dufferin must have felt when he sailed out of the deafening silence of Magdalena Bay. He'd left another *Blue Peter* time capsule-style box on the foreshore, dragged aboard (or got Wilson to) the driftwood log we'd seen suspended over

THE GIRLS AT HOME HAVE GOT HOLD OF THE TOW ROPE.

High Latitudes

a stairwell at Clandeboye, then gone. In a couple of days a huge wind caught the *Foam* up, and they careered down the coast of Norway. 'The girls at home have got hold of the tow-rope,' said Mr Wyse. In a fortnight he was in Portsmouth, having sailed 6,000 miles in just over twelve weeks. It was a joyous return. The Gifford denouement was still five years off; ahead lay almost half a century of uninterrupted diplomatic glory before he'd meet his Bakerloo.

He was glad to go, and I couldn't blame him. The Spitzbergen I was leaving comprised at least in some tiny way a community, where people lived and worked and drank themselves to sleep every night. He was sailing out of a frigid, abandoned wasteland of black spikes and rivers of ice, ruled by dangerous, almost mythical beasts like polar bears and walruses, a place as far removed from a game of consequences at Windsor Castle as it is possible to imagine without being silly. 'We bade an eternal adieu to the silent hills around us; and weighing anchor, stood out to sea,' he briskly records. *Eternal* adieu? And a couple of pages before, he'd talked of 'quitting for ever the Spitzbergen shores'. He couldn't wait. And suddenly, thinking of the girls at home getting hold of my tow-rope, nor could I.

EPILOGUE

Two weeks after I returned home, my numb fingers, still fizzy at the tips from the forgotten rigours of the Icelandic interior, fumbled up a letter from the doormat. From Lola Armstrong at Clandeboye, it contained a sheaf of photocopies topped with a note that read simply: 'Welcome back. Found this in the third library.'

It was Dufferin's own introduction to the Canadian edition of *High Latitudes*, published in 1873 when he was the adored Governor-General. I read it.

'I confess to a kindred feeling of embarrassment in being suddenly confronted, after so many years, with the alien self that reappears in the following pages ... Once, through the "enterprise" of a transatlantic editor, a mutilated issue of these Letters obtained an ephemeral publicity in a provincial serial, my spirited impresario having prefaced his piracy with the assertion that "he had commissioned a British Lord at a handsome salary to discover the North Pole".'

I thought about the deep potations, and realised such gloating coverage of youthful debauchery must have been uncomfortable to a pillar of the Empire approaching his fiftieth birthday. Still, the unauthorised reprints and the fact that seventeen years on it was still in demand showed the enduring appeal of his book. But there was more.

'Here I should end my brief apology for this Edition, were it not that I am tempted to seize the opportunity of answering a question that has been frequently put to me: "What has become of Wilson?"'

What? This was a double-taker. Wilson!

'During the 18 months cruise to Syria . . . in the congenial atmosphere of the graveyards of Egypt he displayed indeed a transient sprightliness, which the occasional exhumation of a mummy and such traffic with the dead afforded him, stimulated into spasms of hilarity . . .' That's my boy. It was good to see him on prime form. 'My image of Wilson from that excursion is of him astride a donkey, wearing yellow turban and striped Arab mantle and carrying a skull, his chosen souvenirs, under each arm . . .' Go on. Laugh it out. The old Wilson-looks-a-twat-on-a-horse routine.

'In the Lebanon, we chanced upon a traveller at a hotel, stricken with Syrian fever, a disease which seldom pardons . . . Wilson stole upon his victim, and gliding to the bed-head, whispered: "Well, sir! You do look bad! Syrian fever, I understand, sir? Ah! They say people don't recover from Syrian fever . . . I am Wilson, sir . . . *the* Wilson!", with which ghostlike revelation of his identity he concluded his dismal Avatar, the particulars of which the sick man happily survived to relate.'

The Wilson? He'd become a global celebrity. His restless quest for a meaning to his life had been resolved at last. He'd found happiness, known from Belfast to Beirut as the world's most famous miserable shit.

'It would be more difficult to give an adequate idea of Wilson's kindness and affectionate serviceableness, his resolution in danger, his versatility of resource . . .' Dufferin praising Wilson's noble virtues? This didn't sound too good. 'If every now and then I have endeavoured to enliven my story with glimpses of the share my poor servant took in our daily life, the reader will feel that a loving hand has guided the pencil. To this day I never prepare for a journey without a sigh of regret for my lost travelling companion. Some time after our return to England, Wilson's health became affected by an obscure disease which subsequently developed very distressing symptoms, and after much suffering, borne with great patience, he died in the Hospital for Incurables at Wimbledon.'

Oh, Wilson. Why did I find this so sad? In some ways, dying

in Wimbledon was a suitably suburban final chapter for the gardener's son from Chiswick. Maybe it was the Hospital for Incurables bit – 'Well, Mr Wilson, the bad news is that we're sending you to the Hospital for Incurables in Wimbledon.' 'I see, doctor. And the good news?' 'One of the nurses there has agreed to buy your return ticket.' It was also the implication that Wilson picked up his 'obscure disease' in Syria, no doubt while lugging a load of infected mummies down a hill for his lordship's collection. Mainly, though, I just couldn't accept the notion of Wilson, my Wilson, bearing anything, especially 'very distressing symptoms', with great patience. Not him. No, no, no. He would have gone, like me, moaning at the world to his dying breath. Whinge, whinge against the dying of the light.